SOCIAL POLICY REVIEW 26

Analysis and debate in social policy, 2014

Edited by Kevin Farnsworth, Zoë Irving and Menno Fenger

First published in Great Britain in 2014 by

Policy Press
University of Bristol
6th Floor
Howard House
Queen's Avenue
Clifton
Bristol BS8 1SD
UK
Tel +44 (0)117 331 5020
Fax +44 (0)117 331 5367
e-mail pp-info@bristol.ac.uk
www.policypress.co.uk

North American office:
Policy Press
c/o The University of Chicago Press
1427 East 60th Street
Chicago, IL 60637, USA
t: +1 773 702 7700
f: +1 773-702-9756
e:sales@press.uchicago.edu
www.press.uchicago.edu

© Policy Press/Social Policy Association 2014

British Library Cataloguing in Publication Data
A catalogue record for this book is available from the British Library.

Library of Congress Cataloging-in-Publication Data
A catalog record for this book has been requested.

ISBN 978 1 44731 556 8 hardback
ISBN 978 1 44731 557 5 paperback SPA members' edition (not on general release)

The right of Kevin Farnsworth, Zoë Irving and Menno Fenger to be identified as editors of this work has been asserted by them in accordance with the Copyright, Designs and Patents Act 1988.

Cover design by Policy Press
Front cover: photograph kindly supplied by www.alamy.com
Printed and bound in Great Britain by Short Run Press, Exeter
Policy Press uses environmentally responsible print partners

FSC
MIX
Paper from
responsible sources
FSC® C014540

Contents

Part Three: Towards integrated services? The integration of social policies and other policy domains

List of figures and tables

Figures

Tables

Notes on contributors

Olof Bäckman is an Associate Professor of Sociology at the Swedish Institute for Social Research (SOFI), Stockholm University. His research has mainly concerned poverty, unemployment and social exclusion in a life-course perspective. How structural factors such as social policy, educational policy and the economic cycle intervene in processes of cumulative disadvantage is an important theme in his research. Bäckman has also been involved in several research projects dealing with the dynamics of means-tested social assistance benefit receipt.

Duco Bannink works as an Associate Professor in Governance Studies at Vrije Universiteit Amsterdam. He is currently involved in a multi-year research project on new governance relations in the field of social activation called 'Governance of Activation' (www.fsw.vu.nl/govact). He published articles on the reform, management and implementation of social policies in a changing social context.

Giuliano Bonoli is Professor of Social Policy at the Swiss Graduate School of Public Administration (IDHEAP) at the University of Lausanne. He received his PhD from the University of Kent at Canterbury for a study on pension reform in Europe. He has published some 40 articles and chapters in edited books, as well as a few books. His most recent book, *The origins of active social policy: Labour market and childcare policies in a comparative perspective*, was published by Oxford University Press in 2013.

David Byrne is Professor of Applied Social Sciences at Durham University, UK. His research interests are in complexity theory and its application to the social sciences, in the social impacts of deindustrialisation and in inequality in all its aspects.

Cyrielle Champion completed her PhD at the Swiss Graduate School of Public Administration (IDHEAP, University of Lausanne) in 2013. Her research interests are focused on comparative unemployment and labour market policy as well as on the governance of European welfare states. As a research fellow at IDHEAP, she is now working for the EU INSPIRES research programme on resilience, innovation and policy learning in employment and labour markets.

Cam Donaldson holds the Yunus Chair in Social Business and Health at Glasgow Caledonian University, UK. He is a leading health economist who has also held chairs at the Universities of Newcastle, Calgary and Aberdeen. He has published over 200 refereed journal articles in economics, medical, health policy and health management journals, and co-authored or edited several books on various aspects of health economics and public service delivery.

Marion Ellison is the Permanent Participant from Scotland for the EU INSPIRES research programme on resilience, innovation and policy learning in employment and labour markets. She is Director of HOPES EU Research Network and lectures in social and public policy at Queen Margaret University Edinburgh. Her research and publications centre on European social and public policy, management and governance and work and employment.

Ross Fergusson is Senior Lecturer in the Department of Social Policy and Criminology at the Open University, UK. His principal research interest is in policy development and the governance of marginalised young people at the interface between social policy and youth justice policies. For publications please see: http://oro.open.ac.uk/view/person/raf3.html.

Liam Foster is a Lecturer in Social Work at the University of Sheffield, UK. His current research interests centre on pensions and pension systems, funeral provision and theories of ageing. His research has tended to focus on inequality, poverty and social exclusion, especially in relation to gender and age.

Bent Greve is Professor in Welfare State Analysis in the Department of Welfare and Globalisation at Roskilde University, Denmark. Besides being actively involved in several research projects on the welfare state, he has published widely on different elements of the welfare state including free choice, happiness and vouchers.

Michael Hill is Emeritus Professor of Social Policy of the University of Newcastle and a Visiting Professor at the University of Brighton, UK. He has written on the policy process and social policy, and is author of *The public policy process: Implementing public policy* (with Peter Hupe), *Understanding social policy* (with Zoë Irving) and editor of *Studying* *public policy* (2014). In 2009 he was given the Social Policy Association's lifetime award.

Les Huckfield is a Visiting Senior Fellow at the Yunus Centre for Social Business and Health and a Director of SENSCOT (Social Entrepreneurs Network Scotland). His expertise includes 30 years' experience in workers' cooperatives and community development trusts. He was Member of the European Parliament for Merseyside East, Member Parliament for Nuneaton and Bedworth, and Under Secretary of State in the Department of Industry.

Steve Iafrati is a Senior Lecturer in Social Policy at the University of Wolverhampton, UK. Having worked as a neighbourhood manager in areas of multiple deprivation, Steve maintains an interest in poverty and its geographical impact on neighbourhoods. Recent research has included examining changes in deprivation after New Deal for Communities as well as the economic impact of working with people with substance abuse problems. Steve's current interest is with the combination of changes to Council Tax benefits and 'bedroom tax'.

Vibeke Jakobsen is a senior researcher at the Danish National Centre for Social Research in Copenhagen, Denmark. She received her PhD in economics from Aarhus School of Business in 2004. Her main areas of interest are labour economics (e.g. utilisation of immigrants' qualifications and transition from school to work), family economics (e.g. mate selection and fertility among immigrants) and income inequality.

Timo Kauppinen is Senior Researcher at the Minimum Income Unit of the National Institute for Health and Welfare in Finland. His research interests include, for example, social assistance receipt and educational outcomes among young people, and urban and housing research.

Robyn Keast is a professor in the Southern Cross University Business School, Australia, and is Chair of the Collaborative Research Network for Policy and Planning in Regional Sustainability. Her research is focused on integrated service models, networked arrangements and collaborative practices within and across sectors. Her recent book publications include *Network theory in the public sector* (2014) with Mandell and Agranoff; *Negotiating the business environment: Theory and practice for all governance style* (2011) with Waterhouse and Brown; and *Social procurement and new public governance*, with Barraket and Furneaux (2015).

Madeleine Knight is the Senior Policy Analyst for the British Medical Association working in its Health Policy and Economic Research Unit. Focused on health systems policy, her interests include: integration of health and social care, quality and performance measurement, and system reform and funding. Before joining the BMA, Madeleine worked in health services research relating to organisational governance and Public and Patient Involvement (PPI) at King's College London, and in the policy team at Cancer Research UK, leading on cancer services. Previously, Madeleine worked as a consultant with Technopolis Ltd, a specialist science and innovation consultancy for public sector clients across Europe.

Tomas Korpi is a professor at the Swedish Institute for Social Research at Stockholm University, Sweden. His research deals with social inequality and social policy in relation to the labour market, such as industrial restructuring and education and activation programmes.

Thomas Lorentzen is an associate professor in the Department of Sociology at the University of Bergen, Norway. He works with longitudinal analyses of register data focusing on labour market outcomes and welfare receipt. He also teaches quantitative methods for the social sciences. Lorentzen is currently involved in several comparative register-data-based analyses of the Nordic welfare states.

Neil McHugh is a researcher and PhD candidate based in the Yunus Centre for Social Business and Health at Glasgow Caledonian University, UK. His PhD examines the theoretical and conceptual bases for microcredit for enterprise and evaluates its implementation in the UK. His other research interests include health inequalities, third sector innovations, distributive justice, valuation issues with respect to health service provision and the application of Q methodology.

Renate Minas is an associate professor in the Department of Social Work at Stockholm University, Sweden. Her fields of interest are welfare state reforms in Sweden and Europe with a special focus on social assistance schemes and activation policies from a governance perspective. Minas has participated in several comparative research projects on a European level.

Michael Roy is Lecturer in Social Business at the Yunus Centre for Social Business and Health and Glasgow School for Business and Society, UK. His primary research focus is on the interface between social enterprise and health. He is also interested in various aspects of policy development related to the social economy. He is a board member of the EMES International Research Network.

Sally Ruane teaches health policy in the School of Applied Social Sciences at De Montfort University, UK, and is a co-founder of the Centre for Health and the Public Interest. Alongside taxation, her research interests include the private finance initiative and political aspects of the policy process.

Stephen Sinclair is Reader in Social Policy at Glasgow Caledonian University, UK and a researcher in the Yunus Centre for Social Business and Health. His research focuses on child poverty, financial exclusion and social policy and devolution in Scotland.

Tracey Warren is Professor of Sociology in the School of Sociology and Social Policy at the University of Nottingham, UK. Her broad area of research is the sociology of social inequalities in work and employment. More specifically, she researches on work time, work–life balance/reconciliation and economic inequalities.

Emilie Whitaker is a final-year doctoral researcher at the Institute of Applied Social Studies, University of Birmingham, UK. Currently, Emilie's ethnographic work centres on social work and how paradigmatic and practice knowledge is constructed, enacted and challenged in everyday front-line encounters between professionals, families and institutional actors. She is also interested in virtue ethics and its role in reorienting conceptualisations of praxis in UK health and social care.

Introduction

Part One: The British welfare state

Kevin Farnsworth

This first part of *Social Policy Review* traditionally examines annual transformation in British social policy, usually focused on the 'five giants'. This year the approach is slightly different. Each of the chapters presented in this part focuses on broader themes, many of which tend to be neglected in social policy analysis.

In Chapter One, Tracey Warren focuses on the changing nature of the work–life balance in the light of the economic crisis. While much of the focus of social policy analysis in the past has been on the impact on family life of ever-longer working hours (for those in work), Warren argues that we need to consider also the impact of the post-2008 economic crisis on work-time underemployment and on economic security. Most importantly, she offers insights into the class dimensions of the work–life balance debate, arguing that there is a clear difference between how the middle and working classes experience and manage the work life in the UK.

Liam Foster, in Chapter Two, examines the changing nature of pensions policy in the UK with a particular focus on the gendered dimensions of retirement incomes. Here the focus is on the implications of the Coalition government's policies on pensioners, and especially on women, with a particular focus on changes to private as well as public pensions, and both in the short and longer terms. Foster considers whether, set against rising life expectancies, retirement futures are likely to be more or less stable, equitable and well funded. On each of these questions, the Coalition government's policies are found wanting.

In Chapter Three, Ross Fergusson takes a critical look at the impact of government policy on young people – namely, school leavers. Fergusson's chapter is an engaging and enlightening examination of this relatively under-researched area in social policy. He presents the issues of school leaving age and training for young people in an interesting historical and political economy framework which allows us to see the key links between the economy, social instability and social control and the school leaving age. As he also makes clear, the politics of the school leaving age are also complex and surprising.

David Byrne and Sally Ruane switch the focus towards paying for welfare in Chapter Four, on UK taxation. They argue that it is increasingly important, against the backdrop of economic crisis, rising inequality and austerity, to focus on how we pay for welfare services, and what impact that has on citizens. They map out the different forms of taxation in the UK and their different effects on different groups, most notably the redistribution of the tax burden away from the most wealthy and private corporations towards lower-income groups. What is needed, they argue, is comprehensive reform of the tax system. This, they illustrate, is as important to welfare outcomes as are the services to which much social policy analysis is directed.

Bent Greve's Chapter Five shifts the focus again in a non-conventional way, this time to consider occupational and fiscal welfare. The post-crisis period may, he argues, signify a reconfiguration of welfare state effort, especially if we look beyond the traditional state services. The chapter seeks to promote a greater understanding of the role of fiscal and occupational welfare within welfare states, before looking at the patterns of provision in recent years. Despite problems with the data, Greve offers some interesting insights into what the crisis may mean for the distribution of state and employer provision in future.

Taken together, this collection of chapters points to the need to continue to ask new questions about social policy, in its many guises, its different forms of delivery, its funding and its impact, if we are to make sense of the British welfare state during these times of austerity.

Part Two: The Social Policy Association conference 2013

Zoë Irving

The conference theme for the 2013 Social Policy Association annual conference was 'Social Policy in Challenging Times'. This theme reflects the post-2008 context in which, despite advances made in the social investment agenda, austerity politics compel an academic and political 'defence' of welfare. The contributions in this section consider policy developments linked to some of the key problematics that have both a place in the recent history of trends in welfare reform, and also renewed significance. With little regard to the systemic failings exposed by the economic crises, the financialisation of social policy continues apace, both as a strategic dimension of policy development and as an adjunct to the withdrawal from the solidaristic welfare settlements of the past.

The section begins with Chapter Six, developed by Michael Hill from his plenary paper, which opened the 2013 conference. The chapter is an important contribution to this volume, not just because it provides a significant and critical link from the present to the past, nor because it effectively combines the personal and the political in an incisive and informed analysis of various dimensions of policy implementation, but also because within it are contained many of the persistent quandaries of social policy that are examined in the subsequent chapters. The chapter's key theme is the reconciliation of 'caring' and 'counting', incorporating the enduring questions of the place of rules and discretion in securing just resource allocation; the view of efficiency as a means or an end; the outcomes of 'rough justice'; and the disconnection between the direction of policy concerning social security (in its sense as a 'condition') and the reality of the labour market. These issues are taken up in various ways in the other contributions to Part Two.

In the context of the financialisation of everyday life, a focus on efficiency of administration and the mixing of morals and mathematics is addressed by Stephen Sinclair, Neil McHugh, Leslie Huckfield, Michael Roy, and Cam Donaldson in Chapter Seven, on the development and scope of Social Impact Bonds (SIBs), a policy instrument designed to extend the role of private finance in welfare provision and delivery, following in the wake of previous efforts to outsource public services and expand the mechanisms for 'payment by results'. As the authors demonstrate, in the UK, SIBs represent more than just an expansion of existing privatisation measures; they are part of the financialisation of service provision and delivery, bringing venture capital and the risk calculations and hedging of welfare outcomes to the financial market in an effort to shake up the assumed public sector inertia. As the authors discuss, the assumptions of risk, cost-saving attributes and the measurability of outcomes are all problematic in the financialised framework. The combination of the manipulability of numbers and the metricification of welfare, heedless of its human dimensions, would seem an exercise doomed to fail. What profit motives mean for welfare relationships and the philosophical questions of markets and morals (Sandel, 2011) appears to be lost.

Morals and markets is a theme repeated in Steve Iafrati's Chapter Eight, which examines the rise of payday loans as a means to satisfy financial needs outside the realms of statutory provision. In the context of the geographically uneven incidence of poverty and the multiple economic disadvantages faced by deindustrialised locales in the UK, this chapter focuses attention on the essential problems of household strategies to deal with poverty, but in particularly challenging times, given the combination of cost-of-living increases, frozen benefit levels and reduced eligibility for housing support. While payday loans have been the subject of much recent policy and media attention, the case study of Wolverhampton presented in this chapter illustrates the inadequacy of supply-led regulation in the face of increasing demand, and a lack of willingness on the part of policy makers to recognise the structural causes of this demand. The final discussion further reflects on the alternative possibilities for policy within the limits of 'responsible capitalism'.

Considering the consequences of economic disadvantage from a different perspective, Marion Ellison's Chapter Nine concerns the challenging times within which young people's employment trajectories are currently set. This chapter provides an examination of youth labour markets, drawing on developments in a range of European countries distinguished by their variety of capitalism. Proponents often frame austerity measures as being in the best long-term interests of young people, freeing them from the debt burden accumulated by their profligate and state-dependent forbears. However, the evidence presented in this chapter amply demonstrates that already disadvantaged young people are paying a heavy social cost now for a future where their security is likely to have suffered lasting and cumulative damage in terms of employment prospects and social mobility. The chapter concludes with some discussion of the differentiated effects of social investment strategies in youth employment, depending on their location within an austerity framework or within the recognition of both public and corporate responsibility for securing societal risk.

The final chapter in this section, Chapter Ten, by Emilie Whitaker, is developed from the paper that gained the Best Postgraduate Conference Paper award in 2013, and it returns readers to a central concern expressed by Michael Hill – how street-level processes can be reconciled to best meet differentiated need in the context within which it arises. With a focus on human services, and social work in particular, the discussion uses the policy shift to 'personalisation' to illustrate the conflicts and contests that arise when principles of rationalist bureaucratic practice and new public management strategies are applied to professions that deal with human relationships. In using the Aristotelian division of knowledge forms to explore the value of professional judgement, the chapter makes the case for the recognition of circumstance and experience that are at odds with attempts to 'manage out complexity'. The discussion suggests that within the context of the health and social services' own rule-bound and technicised arenas of operation, and the reported demise of compassion, criticised in recent times, welfare practice continues to adapt its strategies for 'caring', in spite of an imposed preoccupation with 'counting'.

Part Three: Towards integrated services? The integration of social policies and other policy domains

Menno Fenger

Throughout Europe, initiatives can be observed to bridge the gap between social policies and other domains of the welfare state. This year's Part Three explores the backgrounds of these initiatives and analyses practical examples from various countries including Australia, the Netherlands, the UK, Sweden and Switzerland. Although the issue of integrated social services has been around for quite some time, three current developments may be identified that make account for the current renewed wave of attention.

First, theoretically and empirically, the boundaries of the ideas of the new public management (NPM) approach are experienced. NPM promoted the application of private sector techniques in the public sector. NPM led to the introduction of competition, agencification and contract management in almost all domains of the public sector, including social services. In the ideas of NPM, efficient service delivery was guaranteed by cutting up large, inefficient public services into smaller units whose outputs could be closely monitored and benchmarked. In response to NPM, a new stream of ideas has developed since the mid-2000s under the label of new public governance (NPG; see Dunleavy et al, 2005; Osborne, 2010). NPG scholars argue that the ideas of NPM lead to fragmented, uncoordinated and ineffective services. 'Pasting' instead of 'cutting' is the formula of the NPG for the delivery of high-quality, effective services. This implies the introduction of new forms of collaboration between agencies, the introduction of new, integrated and inclusive laws for various types of benefit recipients and new modes of governance.

Second, the financial and economic crisis that still holds Europe in its grip has triggered intensive austerity measures in almost all European countries. Social policies have not been spared from this. On the contrary, in many European countries the crisis has led to large-scale reforms in the area of social policies (see Fenger et al, 2013). These reforms often involve the shift of authorities from one organisation to another, claiming that the efficiency benefits that are involved in this safeguard enable the continued delivery of high-quality social services while simultaneously realising savings on the implementation costs.

Third, a European trend may be observed in the perspective on the welfare state: a shift from the traditional welfare state to the social investment state (see Taylor-Gooby, 2008; Abrahamson, 2010; Morel et al, 2011). In the social investment state, social policy is no longer about the compensation of social risks once they have occurred, but about creating the conditions and affecting individuals' behaviour to prevent the occurrence of social risks. This involves a shift in responsibility for social risks, from the system to the individual (see for instance Ellison and Fenger, 2013). From this perspective, lifestyle choices, education, housing, healthcare, youth care and many other policy domains directly impact on the individual's behaviour. From an activating welfare perspective, all these policy domains should be directed towards one final goal: the inclusion of individuals in society and – if possible – the labour market.

The integration of social policies and other policy domains is a complicated policy issue that involves challenges on three levels of the policy process: the macro, the meso and the micro levels. On the macro level, it deals with the formulation of policies on the national level. Here, the challenge is to overcome the (sometimes artificial) construction of different client groups or activities on the base of different policy regimes. Increasingly, integrated laws and regulations can be formulated that are aimed at integration. From the contributions in Part Three, two important trends may be observed here. On the one hand, we see the integration of vocational training, reintegration measures and other activities aimed at the labour-market inclusion of people who receive a benefit, with benefit regulations. 'Rights' and 'obligations' go together, seems to be the dominant policy discourse. This is reflected in legal reforms. On the other hand, a trend may be observed towards including separated target groups into larger regulations. For instance in the Netherlands, separate regulations aimed at the disabled unemployed, unemployed young people (under 25) and regular unemployed are integrated into one large Participation Act. Duco Bannink's Chapter Twelve extensively discusses this example.

On the meso level, responsibility for the implementation of social services – even if they are based on different regulatory frameworks – may be integrated into a single organisation. This becomes most obvious in the area of training and reintegration measures. In several European countries, responsibilities of the public employment service and benefit agencies are united in integrated front offices or even in single organisations. Several contributions in this part focus on the possibilities, and also the limits, of this meso-level integration, including the contributions of Champion and Bonoli (Chapter Eleven), Minas et al (Chapter Thirteen) and Knight (Chapter Fifteen).

Finally, on the micro level of the street-level bureaucrats who are actually delivering the services, important developments in integrating services can be observed. Different methods of integration can be distinguished at this level. A popular method is the construction of multidisciplinary intervention teams, in which social care workers, youth workers and social assistance benefit workers collectively visit clients in deprived neighbourhoods. In this case, the integration is shaped through the street-level interactions of these specialists. But also, street-level workers may be required to implement different regulations for different agents; for instance, a qualitative assessment for the public employment service as well as a legal assessment on behalf of the benefit agency. Specifically, in Chapter Fourteen Robyn Keast focuses on this micro-level mode of integration and also discusses the meso level.

References

Abrahamson, P. (2010) 'European welfare states beyond neoliberalism: toward the social investment state', *Development and Society*, 39(1): 61–95.

Dunleavy, P., Margetts, H., Bastow, S. and Tinkler, J. (2005) 'New public management is dead – long live digital-era governance', *Journal of Public Administration Research and Theory*, 16: 467–94.

Ellison, M. and Fenger, H.J.M. (2013) 'Social investment, protection and inequality within the new economy and politics of welfare in Europe', *Social Policy and Society*, 12(4): 611–24.

Fenger, M., Van der Steen, M. and Van der Torre, L. (2013) *The responsiveness of social policies in Europe: The Netherlands in comparative perspective*, Bristol: Policy Press.

Morel, N., Palier, B. and Palme, J. (eds) (2011) *Towards a social investment welfare state?*, Bristol: Policy Press.

Osborne, S. (ed) (2010) *The new public governance? Emerging perspectives on the theory and practice of public governance*, New York: Routledge.

Taylor-Gooby, P. (2008) 'The new welfare state settlement in Europe', *European Societies*, 10(1): 3–24.

Part One

The British welfare state

ONE

Economic crisis, work–life balance and class

Tracey Warren[1]

Introduction

Labour market evidence suggests that the 2008–09 recession and subsequent on-going economic crisis in the UK have led to a reduction in the proportion of workers reporting over-long working hours and an expansion in work-time underemployment (Bell and Blanchflower, 2013, 2011). The study of 'work–life' balance has a long-standing interest in the impact of work-time and work-time preferences on work–life imbalance. This interest has largely concentrated on work-time intensification, with a common conclusion that spending 'too many' hours in the labour market can impact negatively on work–life balance. If there are indeed fewer workers working 'too many' hours, albeit with more working 'too few', then this development raises vital questions about the potential impact of economic crisis on work–life balance in Britain. There are concerns too about work–life balance and class during this crisis because working too many and too few hours are both related to workers' class positions. What have been the class ramifications so far of this crisis, heralded originally as 'the first middle class' UK recession: have recessionary work-time developments in the UK impacted on class differences in work–life imbalance?

This chapter offers a consideration of work–life balance and class in the context of economic crisis. To do this, it incorporates an economic root of work–life imbalance rather than a focus only on work time. The chapter is influenced by the author's argument (Warren, forthcoming) that we need a more holistic understanding of work–life balance if we are to give recognition to the types of work–life imbalance that are experienced more by the working class. It proposes that the analysis of economic-based work–life imbalance is overdue, and is particularly apt in this time of economic crisis. Data from the *British Household*

Panel Survey (BHPS) and its follow-on *Understanding Society* (US) are analysed to explore class variations over time. The chapter concludes that the persistence of class inequalities in self-reported economic security raises serious questions about the work–life balancing of the working class in the UK.

The economic crisis and work-time developments

Economic crises can have inconsistent impacts on the number of hours committed to the labour market. Table 1.1 groups these impacts into categories and summaries the types of labour market based work-time changes that can occur as an outcome of recession. First, a rise in unemployment serves to dampen overall hours in the labour market as jobs, and their work time, are lost. Second, any replacement of full-time jobs with reduced and/or part-time hours contracts for incoming workers brings further work-time reductions, as do, third, cuts to the work time of those already in employment. Fourth, and in contrast, hours worked can increase for some workers. Work-time expansion can result for some workers when a downsized organisation requires remaining staff to increase their workload and/or when workers increase their hours to demonstrate commitment to a firm. Fifth, workers may seek longer work time to compensate for lost income within their household and/or when living costs are rising.

There is evidence to support the reality of all these potential work-time scenarios in Britain since 2008–09. Overall, however, hours have fallen. Grimshaw and Rafferty (2012 p 13) calculated a drop in average hours for men 2008–09 from 36.9 to 36.2 hours (a fall from 589 to 556 million total weekly hours) and for women from 26.6 to 26.2 hours (from 354 to 353 million total weekly hours). Further, Bell and Blanchflower (2011, p 215, r25), analysing *Labour Force Survey* (LFS) data, found that the proportion of workers saying that they would 'prefer longer hours' of work increased by 20% between the start of recession and 2010, while the numbers of workers saying that they would 'prefer fewer hours' fell by 2.3 million over the same time period (see also ONS, 2012). Being underemployed, in effect not having enough paid work, has been interpreted in various ways but it is the notion of work-time underemployment that is its most prevalent usage (ILO, 1998; Strangleman and Warren, 2008).

Work time and work-time preferences are strongly classed in the UK. It is argued next that developments in work time – in hours and

Table 1.1: The economic crisis and work-time developments in the UK

	Labour market work-time developments in an economic crisis	Work-time impact
1	**Unemployment** The rise in the level of unemployment that follows a recession brings about substantial reductions in the paid work time of those who have lost their jobs.	Reduction
2	**Involuntary part time** Organisational work-time responses to economic crisis have meant that jobs that would previously have been available full time to applicants have instead been offered in only a part-time capacity.	Reduction
3	**Labour adjustment** Companies that opted for a process of labour adjustment saw work time fall: usual over-time hours were commonly the first hours to be shed, followed by cuts in contractual hours.	Reduction
4	**Work intensification** Companies' attempts to improve competitiveness and/ or to deploy staff to cover the work of those who had been 'let go' saw hours rise for some. Workers' informal attempts to preserve their own jobs in a time of job uncertainty can also lead to more (potentially unpaid) hours.	Increase for some workers
5	**Income-related work intensification** Paid hours may rise if workers need to boost their take-home pay because of a reduction in household income and/or when living costs are rising.	Increase for some workers

Sources: Gregg and Wadsworth, 2010; Hogarth et al, 2010; Lyonette and Baldauf, 2010; Parek et al, 2010; Bell and Blanchflower, 2011; Hijzen and Venn, 2011; Levell and Oldfield, 2011; Muriel and Oldfield, 2011; Campos et al, 2012; European Foundation, 2012; Grimshaw and Rafferty, 2012.

preferences – raise fundamental questions for researchers interested in issues of work–life balance in this time of crisis.

Work–life imbalance, work time and class

The above changes to work time have prompted interest in the potential of economic crisis for work–life balance. Work time has long been identified as a key variable in the achievement of the smooth reconciliation of demands from 'work' and 'life' (White et al, 2003; Bond, 2004; Warren, 2004; Dex and Bond, 2005; Gershuny, 2005; Crompton and Lyonette, 2006, 2008; van der Lippe et al, 2006; Eikhof et al, 2007; Scherer and Steiber, 2007; Fagan et al, 2008, 2012; Gregory and Milner, 2009, 2011; Hennig et al, 2012; Lyness et al, 2012). This chapter was stimulated by the prioritisation of the problems that arise from long and, in particular, 'too many' hours (Veblen, 1963; Linder, 1970; Schor, 1991; Riedmann et al, 2006). In the UK, we know that long hours' working is concentrated among workers, mostly men, at the top *and* bottom of the occupational hierarchy (Fagan and Norman, 2012). Yet the workers who are most likely to express preferences for hours' reductions are those in higher-level occupations, and it is this select group of long hours' workers who dominate the work–life imbalance literature.

There has been far less attention paid to workers who report that they work 'too few hours' and would prefer more, but such work-time underemployment can surely also impact on work–life balance. A small number of studies that look across the topics of class, hours' preferences and work–life have also shown that even when working hours are long, *economic-based fears* of having 'too few' hours emerge as a common concern for working-class employees, men in particular (Lautsch and Scully, 2007; Warren et al, 2009).

It would seem then that there are two broad typologies of work–life imbalance: one that has roots in the temporal and one that emerges from the economic. These typologies predominate for different social groups. Temporal work–life imbalance is more prevalent among middle-class workers, in the UK and elsewhere: the lives of many have been depicted as time poor, time squeezed, time rushed and harried. Economic-based work–life imbalance seems far more pertinent for the analysis of working-class workers, but this economic cause of imbalance has been rather overshadowed in work–life debates. Accordingly, we urge more consideration of questions of class inequalities in work–life imbalance at this time of economic crisis. Before moving on to the chapter's findings on class inequalities, the next section outlines its methodological approach.

Researching work–life imbalance and class

People's experiences of work–life balance or imbalance have been subject to detailed methodological attention. Work–life research has been particularly innovative for building upon the 'quality of life' agenda, a key tenet of which is to explore qualitative data. This is apparent even within large-scale survey-based research, which is the approach adopted in this chapter, where subjective variables are analysed (in which respondents self-report on their lives). A common approach is also to focus upon a specific life 'domain' that is key in the achievement of a balanced work life. Many domains have been specified in the quality-of-life literature, including jobs and job conditions; leisure time; friendships; health; and people's evaluations of their overall lives, to cite only a few examples (Cummins, 1996; Hsieh, 2003; Massam, 2002).

Drawing upon this research tradition, this chapter looks specifically at the economic domain, and at class diversity here. The economic context of people's working lives provides a crucial backdrop for any analysis of the reconciliation of the demands of 'work' and 'life', but the chapter argues that the economic has been somewhat overlooked in work–life debates. This is despite the fact that the economic is a fundamental domain in the quality-of-life literature. It has been shown to interrelate closely with other life domains and has critical ramifications for all other aspects of well-being (Schrecker, 1997; Gudmundsdottir, 2013).

The chapter draws upon secondary analysis of large cross-sectional data from the BHPS, and its follow-on US. Between them, the two surveys have collected nationally representative data that span two decades (Taylor, 2011). The most recent full wave of US data that was available at the time of analysis was collected over a two-year period (2010–11). It holds data on 100,000 individuals in 40,000 British households (US 2011). For our concerns in this chapter with work–life imbalance and class, we focus upon variation by occupational class (as measured by 'standard occupational classification') among working-age employees. We look to class variation in work time and in self-reported financial situations.

Work–life imbalance and class

Comparing BHPS data from before the crisis hit (2005–06) with US Wave B (2010–11), one of the most striking work-time developments among working-age employees has been the growth in part-time working (1–29 hours a week) for men in certain manual occupations (Figure 1.1). This is amid an overall increase in male part-time employment (up from 3% to 8%). Very long-hours working (49 or more hours per week) dropped a little for men (from 25% to 22%), but it remained concentrated at the top of the occupational hierarchy. Fully a third of men in management/administration worked very long hours in both years, for example, as did 27% of male professionals. Among manual workers, large minorities (27–29%) of men in plant/machine work also worked very long weeks in both years, but the figures fell for men in elementary/other, sales and personal/protective.

Figure 1.1: Weekly working hours* of male employees (aged 18–64), sorted by part-time hours

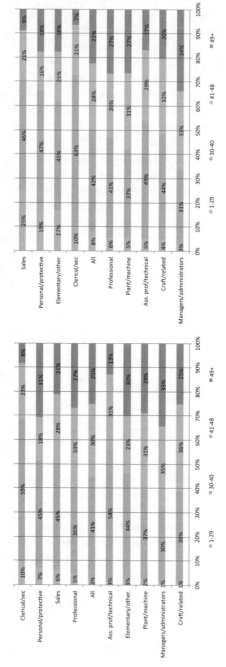

Note: * Paid and unpaid job hours

Source: Author's analysis of 2005–06 (BHPS Wave O) and 2010–11 (US Wave B) data.

The lesser proportions of women working very long hours changed little in the same time period but, similar to the picture for men, certain manual occupations saw substantial growths in workers with part-time hours (elementary/other, craft/related, plant/machine) (Figure 1.2).

Looking at hours' preferences in the most recent wave of BHPS data available (the US does not ask about hours' preferences), we can see how workers in higher-level occupations in 2008–09 reported more work-time dissatisfaction (Figure 1.3). The group of men who were most likely to express a preference for working fewer hours were managers/ administrators (fully 45% would have liked to reduce their hours). For women, it was professionals (47%) and then managers (39%). Only small percentages of employees overall reported that they were working 'too few' hours. But work-time underemployment was highest for workers in manual occupations: elementary/other and sales for women and men; plus plant/machine and personal/protective for women and clerical/ secretarial for men. Lautsch and Scully (2007) even argue that such data tend to underreport working-class employees' preferences for reducing their hours because these preferences are overwhelmed by a concentration on managing financially.

One of the most substantial sections of the work-time underemployed in the UK labour market features involuntary part-time workers: those working part-time hours but preferring full-time. The bulk of *new* part-timers since 2008–9 have cited their inability to find full-time work as the main reason for these hours, and new male part-timers are more likely than female to express a wish for full-time hours (Grimshaw and Rafferty, 2012). In 2010, the proportion of part-timers in the UK saying that they wanted full-time hours had hit 1.1 million, compared with 700,000 in 2008 (Parek et al, 2010, p 40), and figures have grown since (Bell and Blanchflower, 2013). In our BHPS data, we can see the link between hours worked and hours' preferences. Part-timers are the group of employees most likely to express preferences for more hours, especially men, and particularly male part-timers in manual occupations (Figure 1.4).

Unfortunately, BHPS respondents who expressed a preference for a different number of hours were not asked why they might prefer these (or indeed what obstacles were preventing the enactment of these expressed preferences, Fagan et al, 2012), but there is evidence of economic forces at play. LFS data show that wanting to work more hours is associated with being in a low-level occupation (ONS, 2012), and the BHPS data here affirm that the work-time underemployed –

Figure 1.2: Weekly working hours of female employees (aged 18–64), sorted by part-time hours

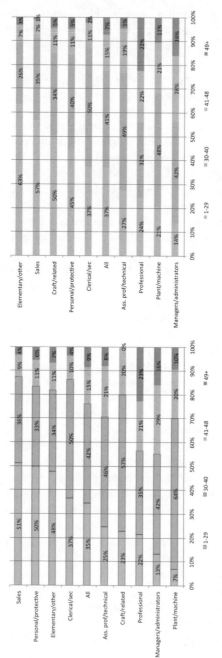

Note: * Paid and unpaid job hours`

Source: Author's analysis of 2005–06 (BHPS Wave O) and 2010–11 (US Wave B) data.

Figure 1.3: Hours' preferences by occupation, employees (aged 18–64)

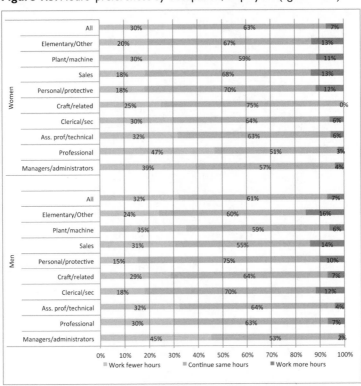

Source: Author's analysis of 2008¬09 (BHPS Wave R) data.

especially men – were the group most likely to report being in financial difficulties (Figure 1.5).

This section supports the work–life theory that, if we derive 'imbalance' as spending long, and in particular 'too many', hours in the labour market, work–life imbalance is classed and to the detriment of the higher-level workers. Indeed, by 2010–11, we saw some manual males fall out of the group of occupations marked by a high concentration of employees with very long working weeks, potentially suggesting a deepening of this middle-class disadvantage. However, when we operationalise temporal work–life imbalance as working 'too few' hours, a different picture of class work–life inequality emerges, with manual workers more likely to fare poorly. The proportion of workers impacted on by work-time underemployment was low in the BHPS, but LFS data show that this proportion has been growing over the years of the crisis and that the

Figure 1.4: Proportion of employees (aged 18–64) who want to work more hours, by occupation and work time

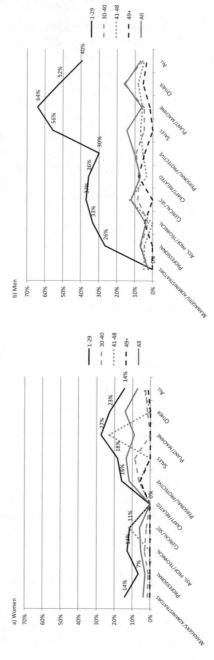

Source: Author's analysis of 2008–09 (BHPS Wave R) data.

lowest-waged occupations have been most affected. The ramifications of work-time underemployment warrant far more investigation.

Figure 1.5: Proportion of employees (aged 18–64) in financial difficulties by hours preferences

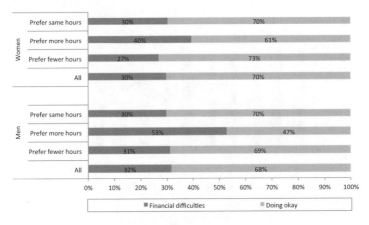

Source: Author's analysis of 2008–09 (BHPS Wave R) data.

Finally, to support the assumption that underpins this chapter – that the working class feel more financially disadvantaged than the middle class – we looked to respondents' subjective reports of financial difficulty in the crisis. Is there indeed substantial class variation in responses to the overarching question 'How well would you say you are managing financially these days?'. Figure 1.6 presents the proportion of employees in financial difficulties: it merges those who reported that they were 'just about getting by' with those 'facing difficulties'. Manual workers stand out with the greatest proportions of reported difficulties. Moreover, although the overall proportions of women and men reporting financial problems have increased since the onset of the crisis, the increases are especially noticeable for workers in low-level manual occupations (elementary/other and plant/machine). For example, by 2010–11, fully one half of elementary/other workers reported 'being in financial difficulties/just about getting by'.

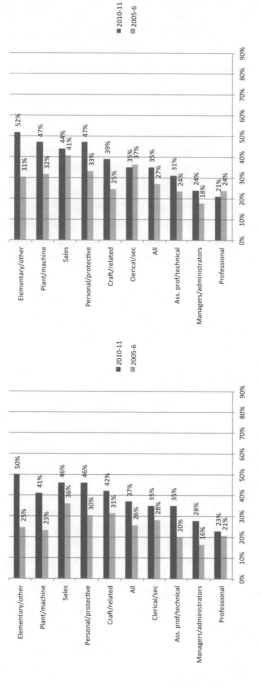

Figure 1.6: Female and male employees (aged 18–64) of working age reporting 'financial difficulties/just about getting by'*, sorted by most difficulties to least, in 2010–11

Note: * How well would you say you yourself are managing financially these days?

Source: Author's analysis of 2005–06 (BHPS Wave O) and 2010–11 (US Wave B) data.

Discussion and conclusions

The economic crisis in the UK is altering the number of hours spent in the labour market. There is evidence that, since 2008, there has been a drop in the number of workers reporting very long working weeks and a growth in short-time working.

The hours that we spend in the labour market, and our evaluations of our work time, have long been fundamental to work–life debates. The chapter has argued, however, that the critical problems that can result from working long and, in particular, 'too many' hours have drowned out the difficulties that can arise from working 'too few' hours. Yet work-time underemployment has serious ramifications for workers. Though we have not addressed 'zero-hours contracts' (ZHC) in this chapter, recent media interest in those workers in the UK who have no guaranteed hours of work at all has placed work-time underemployment more firmly onto the policy agenda. In summer 2013, the Department for Business, Innovation and Skills committed to an informal review of ZHCs. Estimates from diverse sources of the extent of ZHCs vary widely, and so in late 2013 the ONS began a review of how best to collect data so that debate and policy on ZHCs can be better informed (ONS, 2013). In terms of work-time underemployment, we do not know yet the extent to which workers on these contracts would prefer more hours, and any variety across different occupations (Brinkley, 2013).

It has been argued in this chapter that the dominance of the temporal in the conceptualisation of work–life balance has left the economic domain comparatively under-researched by work-life analysts. The social preferences of some workers to spend more time out of work have attracted far more attention than other workers' economic preferences for longer hours. This neglect of the economic has ramifications for how we understand class inequalities in work–life imbalance, with the experiences of workers in high-level occupations dictating 'work life discourses', according to Lewis et al (2007). In the context of the current economic crisis, this chapter has looked towards economic (in) security, arguing that the economic should also be core to work-life studies. It has proposed that post-recessionary growth in work-time underemployment and the economic ramifications of working too few hours raise questions about the work life of workers in lower-level occupations. Before the crisis, manual workers were more likely than non-manual to report dissatisfaction with their financial security. These problems have deepened since the onset of the crisis.

The emphasis on the economic for work–life balancing here is not arguing that the working classes do not experience work-time problems. Working-class temporal work–life imbalance is in evidence, but it is less likely to be rooted in working 'too many' hours. Although we have not explored other measures of working time here, working-class temporal work–life imbalance has been related to a lack of 'time sovereignty' and poorly 'time-synchronised' lives. Working-class employees are over-concentrated in jobs that are marked by shift working, unsocial schedules, and work-time tightly monitored by employers (Fagan et al, 2008).

The impact of the current economic crisis on working conditions is likely to be prolonged. We are seeing a growth in involuntary short-time working that may persist for some time, even after recovery. Alternatively, work-time underemployment may dissipate with the resumption of economic growth. Bell and Blanchflower (2011) have argued that when recovery comes employers are more likely to increase the hours of their underemployed workers than take on new staff, reducing work-time underemployment but dampening any positive impact of recovery on job gains. The final wave of data explored for this chapter was collected in 2010–11, before the double dip of 2012 and before the Coalition government's programme of cutbacks. Clearly, then, further research, including on new waves of US data as they are released, is essential to facilitate an on-going examination of the classed experiences of work-time, economic hardship and work–life balance.

Note

[1] The research on which this chapter draws was funded by a British Academy Research Development Award (BR100093). *British Household Panel Survey* and *Understanding Society* data were made available through the UK Data Archive and were collected by the Institute for Social and Economic Research (University of Essex) and the National Centre for Social Research. Neither the original collectors of the data nor the Archive bear any responsibility for the analyses or interpretations presented here. The author would like to thank the editors and reviewers of the *Social Policy Review*, and the organisers and participants of the symposium on 'Work and family in austerity: Britain and beyond' at the Social Policy Association conference 2013 for valuable feedback.

References

Bell, D.N.F and Blanchflower, D.G. (2011) 'Underemployment in the UK in the great recession', *National Institute Economic Review*, 215: R23–R33.

Bell, D.N.F and Blanchflower, D.G. (2013) 'Underemployment in the UK revisited', *National Institute Economic Review*, 224: F8–F22.

Bond, S. (2004) 'Organisational culture and work life conflict in the UK', *International Journal of Sociology and Social Policy*, 24(12): 1–24.

Brinkley, I. (2013) *Flexibility or insecurity? Exploring the rise in zero hours contracts*, London: The Work Foundation, August.

Campos, C., Dent, A., Fry, R. and Reid, A. (2011) 'Impact of the recession', *Regional Trends* 43(10/11), London: Office for National Statistics.

Crompton, R. and Lyonette, C. (2006) 'Work life "balance" in Europe', *Acta Sociologica*, 49(4): 379–93.

Crompton, R. and Lyonette, C. (2008) 'mothers' employment, work life conflict, careers and class', in J. Scott, S. Dex and H. Joshi (eds) *Women and employment. Changing lives and new challenges*, Cheltenham: Edward Elgar.

Cummins, R.A. (1996) 'The domains of life satisfaction: an attempt to order chaos', *Social Indicators Research*, 38: 303–32.

Dex, S. and Bond, S. (2005) 'Measuring work–life balance and its covariates', *Work, Employment and Society*, 19(3): 627–37.

Eikhof, D.R., Warhurst, C. and Haunschild, A. (2007) 'Introduction: what work? What life? What balance? Critical reflections on the work life balance debate', *Employee Relations*, 29(4): 325–33.

European Foundation for the Improvement of Living and Working Conditions (2012) *2011 Yearbook – living and working in Europe*, Luxembourg: Publications Office of the European Union.

Fagan, C. and Norman, H. (2012) 'Trends and social divisions in maternal employment patterns following maternity leave in the UK', *International Journal of Sociology and Social Policy*, 32 (9–10): 544–60.

Fagan, C., Lyonette, C., Smith, M. and Saldaña-Tejeda, A. (2012) *The influence of working time arrangements on work life integration or 'balance': A review of the international evidence*, Geneva: International Labour Organization.

Fagan, C., McDowell, L., Perrons, D., Ray, K and Ward, K. (2008) 'Class differences in mothers' work schedules and assessments of their "work life balance" in dual-earner couples in Britain', in J. Scott, S. Dex and H. Joshi (eds). *Women and Employment. Changing lives and new challenges*, Cheltenham: Edward Elgar.

Gershuny, J. (2005) 'Busyness as the badge of honor for the new superordinate working class', *Social Research: An International Quarterly of Social Sciences*, 72(2): 287–314.

Gregg, P. and Wadsworth, J. (2010) 'Employment in the 2008–2009 recession', *Economic and Labour Market Review*, 4(8): 37–43.

Gregory, A. and Milner, S. (2009) 'Work–life balance: a matter of choice?' *Gender, Work and Organization*, 16(1): 1–13.

Gregory, A. and Milner, S. (2011) 'Fathers and work life balance in France and the UK', *International Journal of Sociology and Social Policy*, 31 (1–2): 34–52.

Grimshaw, D. and Rafferty, A. (2012) 'Social impact of the crisis in the UK: a focus on gender and age inequalities', in D. Vaughan-Whitehead (ed) *Work inequalities in the crisis: Evidence from Europe*, London: Edward Elgar.

Gudmundsdottir, D.G. (2013) 'The impact of economic crisis on happiness', *Social Indicators Research*, 110(3): 1083–101.

Hennig, M., Stuth, S., Ebach, M., Hägglund, A.E. (2012) 'How do employed women perceive the reconciliation of work and family life? A seven-country comparison of the impact of family policies on women's employment', *International Journal of Sociology and Social Policy*, 32 (9–10): 513–29.

Hijzen, A. and Venn, D. (2011) *The role of short-time work schemes during the 2008–09 recession*, OECD Social, Employment and Migration Working Papers, No 115, OECD Publishing, http://dx.doi.org/10.1787/5kgkd0bbwvxp-en.

Hogarth, T., Owen, D., Gambin, L., Hasluck, C., Lyonette, C. and Casey, B. (2010) *The equality impacts of the current recession*, Equality and Human Rights Commission Research Report 47, Manchester: EHRC.

Hsieh, C.-M. (2003) 'Counting importance: the case of life satisfaction and relative domain importance', *Social Indicators Research*, 61: 227–40.

ILO (International Labour Organization) (1998) *Resolution concerning the measurement of underemployment and inadequate employment situations*, ILO: Geneva, www.ilo.org/global/statistics-and-databases/standards-and-guidelines/resolutions-adopted-by-international-conferences-of-labour-statisticians/WCMS_087487/lang--en/index.htm (accessed 28 November 2012).

Lautsch, B.A. and Scully, M.A. (2007) 'Restructuring time: implications of work-hours reductions for the working class', *Human Relations*, 60(5): 719–43.

Levell, P. and Oldfield, Z. (2011) 'The spending patterns and the inflation experience of low-income households over the past decade', *IFS Commentaries* C119, London: Institute For Fiscal Studies.

Lewis, S., Gambles, R. and Rapoport, R. (2007) 'The constraints of a "work life balance" approach: an international perspective', *International Journal of Human Resource Management*, 18(3): 360–73.

Linder, S. (1970) *The harried leisure class*, New York: Columbia University.

Lyness, K.S., Gornick, J.C., Stone, P. and Grottoa, A.R. (2012) 'It's all about control: worker control over schedule and hours in cross-national context', *American Sociological Review*, 77(6): 1023–49.

Lyonette, C. and Baldauf, B. (2010) *Quality part-time work: Responses to the recession*, London: Government Equalities Office.

Massam, B.H. (2002) 'Quality of life', *Progress in Planning*, 58(3): 141–227.

Muriel, A. and Oldfield, Z. (2011) 'Financial circumstances and consumption', in J. Banks et al (eds) *Financial circumstances, health and well-being of the older population in England*, London: Institute For Fiscal Studies.

ONS (Office of National Statistics) (2012) 'Underemployed workers in the UK, 2012', 28 November, http://www.ons.gov.uk/ons/rel/lmac/underemployed-workers-in-the-uk/2012/index.html (accessed 28 November 2012).

ONS (2013) 'Zero hours consultation', http://www.ons.gov.uk/ons/about-ons/get-involved/consultations/consultations/zero-hours-consultation/index.html (accessed 5 January 2014).

Parek, A., MacInnes, T. and Kenway, P. (2010) *Monitoring poverty and social exclusion 2010*, York: Joseph Rowntree Foundation.

Riedmann, A., Bielenski, H., Szczurowska, T. and Wagner, A. (2006) *Working time and work life balance in European companies*, Luxembourg: Office for Official Publications of the European Communities.

Schor, J. (1991) *The overworked American: The unexpected decline of leisure*, New York: Basic Books.

Scherer, S. and Steiber, N. (2007) 'Work and family conflict? The impact of work demands on family life', in D. Gallie (ed), *Employment Regimes and the Quality of Working Life*, Oxford: Oxford University Press.

Schrecker, T. (1997) 'Money matters: a reality check, with help from Virginia Woolf', *Social Indicators Research*, 40: 99–123.

Strangleman, T. and Warren, T. (2008) *Work and society: Sociological approaches, themes and methods*, London: Routledge.

Taylor, M.F. (ed) with Brice, J., Buck, N. and Prentice-Lane, E. (2011) *British Household Panel Survey user manual volume A: Introduction, technical report and appendices*, Colchester: University of Essex.

US (Understanding Society) (2011) *Understanding society – UK household longitudinal study:Wave 1, 2009–2010, user manual*, 24 October, http://data.understandingsociety.org.uk/files/data/documentation/wave1/User_manual_Understanding_Society_Wave_1.pdf (accessed 28 November 2012).

van der Lippe, T., Jagger, A. and Kops, Y. (2006) 'Combination pressure: the paid work-family balance of men and women in European countries', *Acta Sociologica*, 49: 303–19.

Veblen, T. (1963) *The theory of the leisure class*, London: New English Library Limited (originally published in 1899).

Warren, T. (2004) 'Working part-time: achieving the ideal work life balance?' *The British Journal of Sociology*, 55(1): 99–121.

Warren, T. (forthcoming) 'The conceptualisation and measurement of work–life balance and imbalance: time, money and the dominance of the middle class'.

Warren, T., Pascall, G. and Fox, E. (2009) 'Innovative social policies for gender equality from Europe: implications for the work life reconciliation of low waged women in England', *Gender, Work and Organization*, 16(1): 126–50.

White, M., Hill, P., McGovern, P., Mills, C. and Smeaton, D. (2003) 'High-performance management practices, working hours and work life balance', *British Journal of Industrial Relations*, 41(2): 175–95.

TWO

Towards a fairer pension system for women? Assessing the impact of recent pension changes on women

Liam Foster

Introduction

The UK pension system has been characterised by an abundance of changes since the Basic State Pension (BSP) scheme was introduced following the Second World War. Successive governments have essentially built upon the Beveridge blueprint in the context of social and economic change. However, a rather piecemeal approach to pension reform has led to the development of an extremely complicated pension system which creates uncertainty regarding the pension people can expect to receive in retirement. This complexity is compounded by a long-term decline in the relative value of the BSP, an increasing reliance on means-tested benefits and a patchwork of add-ons (DWP, 2013a). Changes in relation to private pensions, including forms of tax relief, contracting-out mechanisms and further regulation have added to this complex picture. This complexity has acted as a deterrent to pension saving, making it difficult for people to engage with decisions about their saving (Foster, 2012; Crawford et al, 2013). Ultimately these changes have also failed to eradicate concerns about the future sustainability of pensions systems and their ability to provide sufficient resources to remove the risk of poverty in retirement and also incentivise pension saving. Overall, it has been estimated that in the UK there are approximately 11 million working-age individuals who face inadequate retirement incomes, as compared to the level they expect to receive, with under-saving a common theme (Foster, 2012; DWP, 2013a). Concerns about the adequacy of people's saving are exacerbated by increasing levels of longevity, which have seen male life expectancy at birth rise from 71.7 years in 1985 to 78.5 years in 2010, and female life expectancy at birth from 77.4 years in 1985 to 82.4 years in 2010 (ONS, 2011).

In practice, the Coalition government continues to face similar challenges to its predecessors: ensuring that government pension spending remains stable (this is particularly difficult during periods of high unemployment, lower growth, increasing national debt and financial market volatility) while reducing pensioner poverty, where women are over-represented (Foster, 2011). Gender differences in levels of saving reflect the fact that women are more likely to undertake caring responsibilities which lead to interrupted work histories and to be employed on a part-time basis, in lower-paid jobs (Ginn, 2003; Price, 2007). As a proportion of men's median full-time hourly pay, women full-timers receive 81% and part-timers only 52% (Pike, 2011). Women are more likely to be in receipt of means-tested Pension Credits, allocated to the poorest pensioners, and, on average, receive a smaller pension in retirement than their male counterparts. For instance, in the UK in 2011/12, the average net income for a single male pensioner after housing costs was £256 per week, as compared with £212 for women. The main difference between the genders occurs in occupational pension income, with single men receiving £102 per week on average from this source, compared with £63 per week for single women in 2011/12 (DWP, 2013b). Organisation for Economic Co-operation and Development data found women aged 65 and over were 6% more at risk of poverty than men of the same age, and that this was a persistent trend (Zaidi, 2010).

Since the turn of the century, there has been a greater awareness of female pensioners' inadequate pension entitlements (Ginn, 2003; DWP, 2005; Pensions Commission, 2005; Price, 2007; Foster, 2010; Ginn and MacIntyre, 2013). However, the challenges presented by a pension system that is facing increasing demands and also ensuring that the needs of the poorest pensioners are met, among whom women are over-represented, is a difficult proposition and one that previous governments have largely failed to adequately address. Since its election the Coalition government has announced a number of measures that are transforming the pension landscape and ultimately reducing its complexity. However, it remains to be seen what these changes mean for the pension prospects of women, especially in the long term. This chapter will first briefly outline the recent changes to public and private pensions under the Coalition government. Then it focuses on how these changes are likely to affect women's pension prospects, both in the short and long term. Finally, it considers whether, against a backdrop of record levels of life expectancy for both men and women and people spending longer in retirement, the new regime will provide a more stable and less complex system that will improve the outlook for future generations of female pensioners.

Pensions and the Coalition government

The Coalition government came to power following a period under which New Labour had embarked on a series of changes that were said to 'amount to the most radical overhaul of the pension system since 1948' (Evandrou and Falkingham, 2009, p 157). New Labour largely advocated an increased role for means testing and private pension provision, building on the legacy of its predecessor. However, particularly later in its tenure, there was an acceptance that the UK pension system was increasingly complex and required simplification. There was also a need to 'encourage' more low-income earners, including women, into private pension systems and to promote individual saving (Foster, 2010). Despite initial concerns that 'with the enormous deficit and savage spending cuts on the horizon, [pensions] are likely to receive minimal attention from the incoming Government' (Hawthorne, 2010, p 1), evidence thus far has been rather different. The Coalition government has been busy, largely implementing proposals made by the Pensions Commission (2005) and started by the New Labour government, which obtained cross-party and stakeholder consensus (Price and Livsey, 2013). Under the Coalition government there has also been a recognition that the current system is too complex and does not work in a manner which sufficiently encourages individual saving (DWP, 2013a).

In order to reflect increasing longevity the Coalition government accelerated the speed of equalisation of the State Pension Age between men and women in the 2011 Pensions Act, ensuring that this will now be achieved in November 2018 and that the rise to 66 years will now be complete in October 2020 for men and women. In order to halt the long-term decline in the value of the BSP, reform to the indexation of the state pension has been introduced that will see its value rise through time, relative to average earnings (Mabbett, 2013). This reform is called a 'triple lock' measure, with the BSP rising each year in line with prices, earnings or 2.5%, whichever is the highest. The impact of indexation on pensions should not be underestimated, given that, had the indexation arrangements for the BSP not been changed in the early 1980s, the BSP would now be worth around £145 a week (Crawford et al, 2013), rather than just over £107 a week.

In the 2011 Budget the government stated that the State Pension system would be substantially reformed, with the BSP and state second pension (S2P) (an Additional State Pension (ASP) which replaced the State Earnings-Related Pension Scheme (SERPS) in 2002) replaced by a new Single-tier State Pension (STP) for those below the State Pension Age in 2016. On 14 January 2013 the government published a White Paper, *The single-tier pension: a simple foundation for saving* (DWP, 2013a), and this was followed on 9 May 2013 by the Pensions Bill. The new STP will be set just above the current Guarantee Credit level, at £144 per week (in 2012/13 prices), with 35 years of National Insurance (NI) contributions required to qualify for a full entitlement (although the actual level will be set by the government closer to the implementation date). A minimum of 10 years' contributions will be required for any entitlement and all derived benefits in the state pensions (spousal, survivor and divorcee) will be phased out. It is also envisaged that the triple-lock policy will still operate (Ginn, 2013b). The STP will be easier to operate than the two-tier structure and it is hoped that greater clarity will lead to increasing levels of saving (DWP, 2013a). The new STP is also likely to reduce the need for means-tested Pension Credit (PC) to supplement an inadequate state pension. The PC provides most help to the poorest 20% of pensioners, among whom women are over-represented (Bridgen and Meyer, 2007). Furthermore, although it is in principle redistributive, around a third of those entitled to PC do not claim it, missing out on an average of £34 a week (DWP, 2012a).

The introduction of the STP is not seen as reversing the drive to promote private pensions (Mabbett, 2013). A solid state pension is seen as important to the successful introduction of auto-enrolment (Price and Livsey, 2013). Automatic enrolment of individuals into a low-cost saving scheme encouraging individual responsibility was planned by New Labour and has subsequently been introduced by the Coalition government. The intention of auto-enrolment, introduced in a phased manner from July 2012, is to offer access to a portable occupational pension to millions of people without access to good-quality work-place provision, while allowing existing schemes with benefits or contributions above the National Employment Savings Trust (NEST) (the default option auto-enrolment scheme) minimum to continue (DWP, 2007). Employers can choose the qualifying scheme they utilise, which could include the NEST. NEST was established to underpin automatic enrolment by providing a work-place pension scheme for any employer who wished to use it to meet their automatic enrolment duties (DWP, 2013b). Contributions are currently set at 4% for the employee, 3% for the employer and 1% in tax relief (total 8%). It is estimated that around 11 million people will be eligible, with six to nine million people newly saving or saving more (DWP, 2013c). In the first eight months (October 2012 to May 2013), Britain's largest firms have automatically enrolled around 670,000 workers into pension saving for the first time, while opt-out rates have so far been lower than expected (DWP, 2013c). The logic behind auto-enrolment is that, while structured advice and information can improve understanding, behavioural barriers, including myopia, cynicism and inertia can still inhibit action in relation to pension saving (Wicks and Horack, 2009). Therefore, the principle of auto-enrolment is partly a result of the concern that a population of provident savers is unlikely to be provided by increased financial education and information alone (Ring, 2010). Auto-enrolment represents 'a clear shift in the underlying values of the British system' (Bridgen, 2010, p 82), with an end to the voluntarist principle for employers.

In 2010, the government invited Lord Hutton to undertake a review of public service pension provision, given disparities between public and private sector pension provision and concerns about the system's sustainability (IPSPC, 2011). His Independent Public Service Pensions Commission (IPSPC) set out recommendations for reform in March 2011, which were broadly accepted by the government, and the Public Service Pensions Bill, introduced to Parliament on 13 September 2012, sets out the framework for these schemes (DWP, 2013a). These include ending the link to final salary and increasing schemes' Normal Pension Ages. These are in addition to previous changes to public sector pensions, including reducing their value by changing the indexation method from the Retail Price Index (RPI) to Consumer Prices Index (CPI). The Public Service Pensions Act received royal assent on 25 April 2013.

These pension policy changes have considerable implications for disparities in savings habits, and the subsequent retirement income of men and women in particular. It is to this consideration that the rest of the chapter now turns.

Changes to first-tier pensions and their effects on women

The disparities in private pension income between men and women emphasise the need for inclusiveness within state pensions and to ensure that they are set at an adequate level. Therefore, any reductions in the eligibility for state pensions erode their redistributive function (Curdova, 2010). The fact that women are less likely to accumulate private pensions means that state pension provision tends to be more important for women than men (Foster, 2010). Therefore, it is important to consider what the recent state pension changes mean for women.

State Pension Age

Due to the increase in the speed of changes to the State Pension Age (it will be extended to 66 in October 2020, nearly six years earlier than planned in 2007 under the New Labour government), approximately 4.4 million men and women will have to wait up to a year longer for their state pension (PPI, 2011). These rises are on top of the gradual equalisation of women's State Pension Age. Since April 2010, the State Pension Age for women has increased from 60 to 61½ and it will reach parity with men (at age 65) in 2018 (PPI, 2011). About 500,000 women must wait between a year and eighteen months extra as a result of the increasing speed of pension age equalisation (Cribb et al, 2013). A one-year increase in the state pension age represents £5,587 for a woman who qualifies for a full BSP (£107.45 a week) and no additional pension, rising to £14,008 for a woman who qualifies for a full BSP and a full additional pension entitlement (based on a full BSP and a maximum S2P entitlement of £161.94 a week) (Cribb et al, 2013). These rises in State Pension Age will also affect eligibility for the winter fuel allowance, concessionary travel and other age-related benefits, meaning that many women in their fifties will not receive these benefits when originally expected (Ginn and MacIntyre, 2013). This may be problematic for women (and men) who have already made work, saving and retirement decisions based on having a particular State Pension Age and who may not be able to adjust to receipt of a state pension at a higher age by working or saving longer (PPI, 2012b).

While raising the State Pension Age gradually is justified, given the pressures presented by rising life expectancy, Ginn and MacIntyre (2013, p 100) argue that there is 'no guarantee of individuals' health permitting, continued employment nor of the availability of jobs. Many older workers in the future will be left in limbo, too old, sick or occupied with caring to undertake paid work and too young to receive a state pension'. Given significant differences in employment rates of women and men in older age, particular attention needs to be paid to the gender aspects of longer working lives and active ageing (Foster and Walker, 2013). In 2011 the employment rate for men was 74% for those aged 55 to 59 and 55.2% for those aged 60 to 64. For women aged 55 to 59, who are nearing the State Pension Age, the employment rate was 65.6%. It fell substantially to 34.2% for those in the 60 to 64 age group, which mainly comprised of women who are over State Pension Age (ONS, 2012). While long-term trends have seen older women's employment rates rising for many years, these have been more substantial recently. Cribb et al (2013) suggest that increases in the female State Pension Age explain an estimated 85% of the growth in the employment rate of older women that has occurred since early 2010. However, there is still a considerable shortfall for many between the age at which they retire and pension age (Foster and Walker, 2013).

STP

In principle, the introduction of the STP is a welcome development for many women. Aimed to 'provide clarity and confidence to better support saving for retirement' (DWP, 2013a, p 8), it should provide a stronger foundation than its predecessor for most in the short term (although long-term prospects are less positive). Although the STP will ensure that most women will have a state pension in their own right in retirement, it is apparent that women will be less likely than their male counterparts to receive the full amount. This is as a result of the stipulated 35 years of National Insurance (NI) contributions or credits required for receipt of the full STP, which is less likely to be achieved by women, given their greater likelihood of time out of employment which do not qualify for NI credits (Ginn, 2013a). Furthermore, those who have fewer than 10 years of contributions or credits will not receive a state pension under the STP scheme. Once again, these are more likely to be women than men. While a later State Pension Age may assist some women to achieve the 35 years of NI contributions or credits required (DWP, 2013a), as previously identified, ill-health, caring responsibilities and a lack of suitable employment opportunities may result in an inability to 'catch up' lost years (Vickerstaff, 2006). Given that the STP is to be set just above the PC threshold, eligibility for means testing is likely to continue to be higher for women than for men (although the Savings Credit element of the PC will also be removed).

There are large proportions of women who are already retired or due to retire in the near future who will not be eligible for the STP and will continue to receive the state pension in its current form (PPI, 2013c). If the STP were to include those reaching the State Pension Age prior to 2016, including existing pensioners, by 2025 this would reduce the projected percentage of pensioners living in relative poverty from around 11% of pensioners under current policy to around 7%, rather than 10% when just including those reaching the State Pension Age post-2016 (Carrera et al, 2012). There are approximately 430,000 women born between 6 April 1952 and 16 June 1953 who will miss eligibility for the STP by a period of months. This will result in a £36 per week loss if they have no S2P (Ginn, 2013a). This is the difference between the current BSP of £107.45 and the STP of £144.18 (not taking into account PC eligibility). These women are caught between two pieces of legislation, the 1995 Act regarding gender equalisation of retirement ages and the 2013 Bill. Therefore, they pay NI for several extra years, receiving their state pension later than women for whom the State Pension Age was 60, but they are also likely to receive a lower pension than women whose State Pension Age is a few years later. However, if they have fewer than 35 qualifying years, or have been contracted out of the ASP, not all would have been entitled to a full STP and therefore would necessarily have been better off under the STP system.

It is apparent that women with low lifetime earnings are likely to be the major beneficiaries of the STP (if partnered and thereby ineligible for means-tested PC) (Ginn, 2013b). In effect, the STP will supply more widespread crediting of unpaid activities than was provided by many ASPs in the past, especially for periods of unpaid activity that occurred prior to 2002. This should reduce the number of women (and men) with extremely low state pension entitlements (DWP, 2013a). Crawford et al (2013) predict that women are significantly more likely than men to have an immediate gain as a result of STP, with 44% of women facing an increase in their entitlement as of 2016, as compared with just 6% of men. In the longer term, the STP will be less generous than the current system for most people. This includes those born in 1986 or later, and potentially includes those born as early as 1966. This is as a result of a lower accrual rate than the combined accrual rate of the BSP and S2P, and, also, almost all the same activities create entitlement under the current system as the STP. For instance, since 2002, coverage under the current pension system is nearly as broad as under the STP (activities including unemployment and looking after children aged under 12 are all credited as contributions), and the annual pension from such activities accrual is higher under the current pension system (Ginn, 2013b). Therefore, in the long run, Crawford et al (2013) predict that the reform will not have the effect of increasing pension accrual for part-time workers and women who take time out to care. These groups may end up with a lower pension under the new system than under the current system.

Between 1987 and March 2012, it was possible to contract out of the additional second-tier state pension (SERPS and then S2P) into a Defined Contribution (DC) pension scheme, paying lower NI contributions. Prior to this (and since April 2012), it has been possible to contract out only into a defined benefit (DB) pension scheme. A significant fraction of workers have contracted out for large parts of their working lives. The Pensions Bill 2013–14 presents legislation to abolish contracting out. The implications of this are that those who would have contracted out of the S2P will accrue greater state pension entitlement for each year of activity under the STP than under the current system (Crawford et al, 2013). This means that the Treasury will gain an extra £6bn annually for the NI Fund from the higher NI contributions paid by employers and employees (Ginn, 2013b), but it will lead to further pressure on DB schemes (PPI, 2012b). Given men's greater tendency to contract out, this is likely to affect more men than women. However, it is likely to affect a large number of female public sector workers in particular.

A further component of the STP is the ending of the current system of derived and inherited rights (different rules apply in the case of the married women's stamp). Therefore, for those reaching State Pension Age after 2016, it will no longer be allowed to accrue pension entitlement based on a spouse's contributions. At present, married women can be entitled to a BSP based on their husband's contributions (unless their own pension is higher). Known as Category B pension, it is £64.40 in 2012–13, about 60% of the full pension (PPI, 2012a). Currently a widow or divorcee can also get a full pension on her late or ex-husband's contributions if she has not remarried before pension age. These changes may represent an acknowledgement of the need for more women (and men) to build an adequate pension in their own right. Pension planning which focuses on a partnership can be problematic, given that the number of divorces has risen from 11% of the number of marriages in 1948 to about 50% in 2012 (DWP, 2013a). Therefore it is rather worrying that Scottish Widows (2012) found that over half (54%) of women under the age of 30 are relying on joint savings for a retirement that may well be 40 years ahead. Therefore, more needs to be done to encourage women to save for retirement in their own right (Ginn, 2003; Foster, 2011).

Changes to private pensions and their effect on women

The proposed reforms to the state pension system may ultimately encourage private saving (Mabbett, 2013). It will result in a reduction in the state pension income most younger individuals can expect and provide further clarity about the level they are likely to receive. As such, the response may be to increase their private saving to compensate for this (Crawford et al, 2013). Over recent years, particularly as a result of the economic crisis, the decline in rates of return on investment and the persistently low interest rates have placed pension funds at risk of huge losses, with considerable implications for private pension provision (Natali, 2011). This has meant that moves towards DC schemes from DB ones have sped up. In 2007, 45% of DB schemes were not open to new members, and this figure had reached 58% by 2011 (PPI, 2012a). The move towards DC schemes represents a change from a more buffered system to a more individualized exposure to financial market risks (Ebbinghaus and Wiß, 2011). In DB pensions financial and longevity risks are borne by the scheme sponsor, as benefits to members are usually based on a formula linked to members' wages and employment length. Benefits to members in DC schemes are a function of the amount contributed by the member and sponsor and any subsequent return on that investment. Members have no guarantee concerning the level of their future pensions, since it depends entirely on interest on capital invested (Euzéby, 2010). The Coalition government is also discussing the possibility of alternative Defined Ambition (DA) schemes, which more effectively share risk (DWP, 2012b).

Career breaks, most likely to be experienced by women, generally have a stronger impact on pension benefits in DC than in DB schemes, as the calculation of benefits in DB schemes is not necessarily as closely related to the contribution record as in DC schemes (EC, 2010b). As existing employees are more likely to remain covered by existing DB schemes, it is new entrants, many of whom have many years left until retirement, who are most likely to be affected. Recent falling equity prices and declining annuity rates mean that a larger DC fund is now required to provide a decent retirement income (Foster, 2012). While pension losses may not be permanent, the recent financial crisis has shown the vulnerability of pension levels in DC schemes, notably for individuals who are close to retirement and whose savings' portfolios might not recover during their remaining period of working life. This is more likely to be problematic for women, as a result of their more limited employment opportunities (D'Addio and Whitehouse, 2010). The move towards DC occupational schemes is also likely to have further consequences for women on the death of a spouse, as about 70% of annuity purchases are for single annuities (DWP, 2005). The adverse implications for many women, particularly those with caring commitments, of any shift towards greater individual responsibility and risk in pension saving (with increasing moves towards DC schemes) is particularly problematic and has repercussions for income in older age, creating new challenges and risks (European Commission, 2010a).

Public sector pensions

By law, DB pension schemes have to provide yearly increases to pensions in payment. The government decides which index to use to calculate increases, and has tended to utilise the RPI. However, from April 2011 statutory indexation and revaluation increases have been in line with the CPI rather than the RPI. As the CPI typically rises more slowly than RPI, this is expected to reduce the costs of providing DB pensions, and reduce benefits (PPI, 2013a). For instance, the switch to the CPI from the RPI is likely to reduce the value of public sector pensions by 15% on average (IPSPC, 2011). DB pension coverage has always been higher in the public sector than in the private sector. Around 85% of public sector employees participate in occupational pension schemes, as compared to around 30% in the private sector (IPSPC, 2011). Even those, including women, in low-paid positions in the public sector still have access to DB schemes. Ending the link to final salary and increasing schemes' Normal Pension Ages is also detrimental to the fund accumulated. The PPI (2013c) suggests that the reforms will reduce the average value of the benefit offered across all scheme members by more than a third. However, basing public sector pensions on a career average is less likely to impact as heavily on women as on men, who are disproportionately represented among those promoted to higher salaries at a later stage in their career. However, women's significant representation in the public sector is likely to see many women disadvantaged in the changes which take place (Disney et al, 2009). Furthermore, the large number of public sector redundancies, especially since the economic crisis, has adversely affected women's employment levels in this sector.

Auto-enrolment

The introduction of auto-enrolment will increase the numbers of lower earners saving into pensions. However, even after automatic enrolment has been fully phased in, the distribution of tax relief will benefit higher-rate taxpayers, mainly men, more than basic-rate taxpayers. The level of tax relief paid by the Treasury to subsidise private pension saving (about £45bn in 2012) will increase with auto-enrolment (PPI, 2013b). The NEST, the default auto-enrolment option, incorporates DC-type features of investment choice and individualised risk (Strauss, 2008). As such, extra saving may not be advisable, due to its potential interaction with means testing (Price, 2007). This threat will remain while the state pension is barely above the threshold for means testing (Ginn, 2013b). There is no guarantee that the fund at retirement will exceed the value of contributions paid. The problem applies especially to those who are likely to receive less than the full STP, and those aged over 45 in 2012 (Ginn and MacIntyre, 2013). For women, the risk of a wrong decision is especially high, 'as unpredictable careers and future relationship status are combined with the uncertainties of future investment returns, charges and annuity rates' (Ginn, 2013b). As such, it remains to be seen whether auto-enrolment is a suitable option for all women.

Decisions about whether to contribute to the NEST are not helped by the fact that free advice will be generic, while individual advice is costly. Price and Livsey (2013) note that, since employers may choose the scheme and investment utilised, auto-enrolled workers could find themselves in badly run or fraudulent funds, with substantial annual charges significantly reducing their pension's value. Furthermore, the introduction of the Retail Distribution Review (RDR), aimed at making the investment market more transparent and attractive to consumers, is set to increase the immediate cost of advice further, given that financial advisers will move from commission towards a fee-based model (Price and Livsey, 2013). Unwillingness among lower earners in particular to pay a fee for advice will mean that it will no longer be viable for advisers to service the mass market, potentially leading to an advice gap (Scottish Widows, 2012). Furthermore, there is a concern that many low to middle earners, including a large number of women, will lose out from the levelling down of pension provision to minimum standards, since average contributions by those employers who make them are approximately double those that will be required by auto-enrolment (Van de Ven, 2012).

Women are more likely to be excluded from accessing the NEST, given that those with an income below £9,440 per annum are not auto-enrolled, and even if those earning below £5,668 opt into NESTs they will not attract an employer's contribution (these figures are reviewed annually). Furthermore, 'sustaining a limit gives employers substantial financial incentives to keep the wages of part-time workers low, and restrict their hours of work in order to exclude them from pension scheme membership' (Foster, 2010, p 40). There is also a concern that everyone, including the low-paid who do not join the NEST, will ultimately pay for the employer contribution through lower wages and higher prices (Price and Livsey, 2013). Unlike first-tier state pension provision, but in accordance with other forms of private pension, no credits are provided for periods of family caring, either for children or parents, and, as such, men may be more likely to benefit from auto-enrolment (Foster, 2012). Therefore, an alternative fully portable pay-as-you-go scheme which includes carer credits as in state pensions (through either cross-subsidy or a grant from the Exchequer in lieu of tax relief), thus avoiding the penalty for caring years incurred in private pensions, has been advocated by Townsend and Walker (1995) and, more recently, by Ginn and MacIntyre (2013). Furthermore, a lifetime limit rather than the current annual savings limit of £4,500 (the government is currently exploring possible changes to this) would be more beneficial to women, as it would enable those (where possible) with career breaks to 'catch up' by making extra contributions.

Conclusion

This chapter has explored the extent to which recent pension policy is likely to limit gendered inequalities in pensions. It has shown how a desire to decrease the level of complexity in the British pension system and to encourage individual saving has been central to the Coalition government's pension policy (DWP, 2013a). The impact of these pension policy changes on women has, thus far, proved to be rather mixed. In the short term there are many women who are 'winners' in relation to the new STP, especially those women with low lifetime earnings (Crawford et al, 2013). The STP will provide more widespread crediting of unpaid activities than was provided by many ASPs in the past, reducing the number of women (and men) with extremely low state pension entitlements (DWP, 2013a). In the longer-term, there will be many 'losers' with the new system less generous than the current system for most men and women as a consequence of a lower accrual rate than the combined accrual rate of the BSP and S2P. While Iain Duncan Smith, the Work and Pensions Secretary, claimed that the reform would 'stop this shameful situation where they [women] are let down by the system when it comes to retirement because they have taken time out to care for their family' (Jowit, 2013), it is worth noting that the STP will be set at only about 25% of average wages and, as such, will be well below the internationally accepted poverty level of 60% of median population income. This means that by 2050 over 40% of pensioner households are still expected to be eligible for Housing Benefit and Council Tax Benefit, which are means tested (Carrera et al, 2012). These households are more likely to include female pensioners. Furthermore, caring commitments (which don't accumulate NI credits) may result in women not contributing to the STP for the required number of years to obtain any level of income from this source and, as such, the continuation of means testing. The main purpose of STP for policy makers and private pension providers is to limit, for low to moderate earners, disincentives to extra voluntary saving that may be caused by the interaction with means testing. Yet the STP's low level and the fact that it excludes a proportion of women could result in undermining this aim.

In the long run, on the whole, lower state pension income may ultimately increase the need to save privately. However, the increasing reliance on DC pensions in the private sector presents further risks to women in building up a suitable pension in their own right (Curdova, 2010). There is also an insufficient understanding of the links between pension contributions and assumptions about individual rationality, capacity and (desire for) choice, and comprehension of (and tolerance for) financial risk (Strauss, 2008). The introduction of auto-enrolment and NEST, targeted at low and medium earners, will offer new possibilities for many women who otherwise lacked access to an employer's contribution. However, it does not take caring commitments into account and excludes the lowest earners, including many women. Maternal roles and entrenched assumptions about gender still restrict women's employment and subsequent pension accumulation (Ginn and MacIntyre, 2013). Furthermore, it remains to be seen whether it will ultimately pay to save in this manner. Therefore, Ginn (2013b) argues that, like other forms of private pensions, auto-enrolment in the form of NEST cannot remove the gender gap in income in retirement. It is evident that moves towards individual provision for retirement through private pensions are likely to result in greater income inequality between older women and men, and between those who have had an intermittent or low-paid employment history and those with an advantaged position in the labour market (Foster, 2010). Pension penalties arising from earlier caring roles will continue to be magnified, creating increasing income disparity among women in older age according to their employment, partnership status and care history. These inequalities are exacerbated by tax relief on private pensions. Therefore, while the new pension regime may reduce complexity and encourage retirement saving, it will not do enough to reduce the gender pension gap in older age.

References

Bridgen, P. (2010) 'Towards a social democratic pension system? Assessing the significance of the 2007 and 2008 Pension Acts', in I. Greener, C. Holden and M. Kilkey (eds) *Social Policy Review 22: Analysis and debate in social policy,* Bristol: Policy Press, pp 71–96.

Bridgen, P. and Meyer, T. (2007) 'The British pension system and social inclusion', in T. Meyer, P. Bridgen and B. Riedmuller (eds) *Private pensions versus social inclusion? Non-state provision for citizens at risk in Europe*, Cheltenham: Edward Elgar, pp 223–51.

Carrera, L., Redwood, D. and Adams, J. (2012) *An assessment of the government's options for state pension reform*, London: Pension Policy Institute.

Crawford, R., Keynes, S. and Tetlow, G. (2013) *A single-tier pension: What does it really mean?*, Institute For Fiscal Studies Report R82, www.ifs. org.uk/comms/r82.pdf.

Cribb, J., Emmerson, C. and Tetlow, G. (2013) *Women working in their sixties: Why have employment rates been rising?* IFS Observations, www. ifs.org.uk/publications/6662.

Curdova, A. (2010) *Decent pensions for women*, Doc 12274, Council of Europe, http://assembly.coe.int/Mainf.asp?link=/Documents/ WorkingDocs/Doc10/EDOC12274.htm.

D'Addio, A. and Whitehouse, E. (2010) 'Pension systems and the crisis: weathering the storm', *Pensions*, 10(15): 126–39.

Disney, R., Emmerson, C. and Tetlow, G. (2009) 'What is a public sector pension worth?' *The Economic Journal*, 119: 517–35.

DWP (Department for Work and Pensions) (2005) *Women and pensions – the evidence*, London: The Stationery Office.

DWP (2007) *Personal accounts: A new way to save – summary of responses to the consultation*, London: The Stationery Office.

DWP (2012a) *Income related benefits: Estimates of take-up in 2009–10*, London: The Stationery Office.

DWP (2012b) *Reinvigorating workplace pension*, London: The Stationery Office.

DWP (2013a) *The single-tier pension: A simple foundation for saving*, White Paper, London: The Stationery Office.

DWP (2013b) *The Pensioners' Incomes Series*, London: The Stationery Office.

DWP (2013c) *Supporting automatic enrolment. The government response to the call for evidence on the impact of the annual contribution limit and the transfer restrictions on NEST*, London: The Stationery Office.

Ebbinghaus, B. and Wiß, T. (2011) 'Taming pension fund capitalism in Europe: collective and state regulation in times of crisis', *Transfer: European Review of Labour & Research*, 17(1): 15–28.

EC (European Commission) (2010a) 'Joint report on pensions progress and key challenges in the delivery of adequate and sustainable pensions in Europe', *European Economy Occasional Papers 71*, Brussels: European Commission.

EC (2010b) *Private pension schemes: Their role in adequate and sustainable pensions*, Luxembourg: Publications Office of the European Union.

Euzéby, A. (2010) 'Economic crisis and social protection in the European Union: moving beyond immediate responses', *International Social Security Review*, 63(2): 71–86.

Evandrou, M. and Falkingham, J. (2009) 'Pensions and income security in later life', in J. Hills, T. Sefton and K. Stewart (eds), *Towards a more equal society? Poverty, inequality and policy since 1997*, Bristol: Policy Press, pp 157–77.

Foster, L. (2010) 'Towards a new political economy of pensions? The implications for women', *Critical Social Policy*, 30(1): 27–47.

Foster, L. (2011) 'Privatisation and pensions – what does this mean for women?' *The Journal of Poverty & Social Justice*, 19(2): 103–15.

Foster, L. (2012) '"I might not live that long!" A study of young women's pension planning in the United Kingdom', *Social Policy & Administration*, 46(7): 705–26.

Foster, L. and Walker, A. (2013) 'Gender and active ageing in Europe', *European Journal of Ageing*, 10(1): 3–10.

Ginn, J. (2003) *Gender, pensions and the life course: How pensions need to adapt to changing family forms*, Bristol: Policy Press.

Ginn, J. (2013a) 'Austerity and inequality. Exploring the impact of cuts in the UK by gender and age', *Research on Ageing & Social Policy*, 1(1): 28–53.

Ginn, J. (2013b) Written evidence submitted by Dr Jay Ginn, Session 2012–13 House of Commons Select Committee, www.publications.parliament.uk/pa/cm201213/cmselect/cmworpen/writev/1000/m09.htm.

Ginn, J. and MacIntyre, K. (2013) 'UK pension reforms: is gender still an issue?' *Social Policy & Society*, 13(1): 91–103.

Hawthorne, S. (2010) 'Coalition!', *Pensions World*, June.

IPSPC (2011) *Independent Public Service Pensions Commission: Final report*, London: Independent Public Service Pensions Commission.

Jowit, J. (2013) 'State pension reform unveils future £144 per week flat payment', *Guardian*, 14 January 2013, www.theguardian.com/money/2013/jan/14/state-pension-reform-flat-payment.

Mabbett, D. (2013) 'The second time as tragedy? Welfare reform under Thatcher and the Coalition', *The Political Quarterly*, 84(1): 43–52.

Natali, D. (2011) 'Pensions after the financial and economic crisis: a comparative analysis of recent reforms in Europe', *Working Paper 2011.07*, Brussels: European Trade Union Institute.

ONS (Office for National Statistics) (2011) *2010-based period and cohort life expectancy tables*, www.ons.gov.uk/ons/dcp171780_238828.pdf.

ONS (Office for National Statistics) (2012) *Pension trends*. Available at www.statistics.gov.uk/pensiontrends/

Pensions Commission (2005) *A new pension settlement for the twenty-first century: The second report of the Pensions Commission*, London: The Stationery Office.

Pike, R. (2011) 'Patterns of pay: results of the Annual Survey of Hours and Earnings 1997–2010', *Economic & Labour Market Review*, 3(5): 14–40.

PPI (Pension Policy Institute) (2011) *What are the implications of the government's latest legislation increasing the state pension age?* Briefing Note 60, London: Pension Policy Institute.

PPI (2012a) *The pensions primer: A guide to the UK pensions system*, London: Pension Policy Institute.

PPI (2012b) *The changing landscape of pension schemes in the private sector in the UK*, London: Pension Policy Institute.

PPI (2013a) *The implications of the coalition government's public service pension reforms*, London: Pension Policy Institute.

PPI (2013b) *Tax relief for pension saving in the UK*, London: Pension Policy Institute.

PPI (2013c) *The impact of the government's single-tier state pension reform: Pension briefing*, London: Pension Policy Institute.

Price, D. (2007) 'Closing the gender gap in retirement income: what difference will recent UK pension reforms make?' *Journal of Social Policy*, 36(4): 1–23.

Price, D. and Livsey, L. (2013) 'Financing later life: pensions, care, housing equity and the new politics of old age', in G. Ramia, K. Farnsworth, and Z. Irving (2013) *Social Policy Review 25: Analysis and debate in social policy*, Bristol: Policy Press, pp 67–88.

Ring, P. (2010) 'Governance and governmentality: A discussion in the context of UK private pension provision', *Economy & Society*, 39(4): 534–50.

Scottish Widows (2012) *Women and pensions report: Mind the gap*, www.scottishwidows.co.uk/documents/generic/2012_women_and_pensions_report.pdf.

Strauss, K. (2008) 'Re-engaging with rationality in economic geography: behavioural approaches and the importance of context in decision-making', *Journal of Economic Geography*, 8(2): 137–56.

Townsend, P. and Walker, A. (1995) *The future of pensions: Revitalising national insurance*, London: Fabian Society.

Van de Ven, J. (2012) 'Implications of the national Employment Savings Trust for vulnerable sectors of the UK labour market: a reduced-form statistical evaluation', *National Institute Economic Review*, 219: R77–R89.

Vickerstaff, S. (2006) 'I'd rather keep running to the end and then jump off the cliff: retirement decisions – who decides?' *Journal of Social Policy*, 5(4): 479–83.

Wicks, R. and Horack, S. (2009) *Incentives to save for retirement: Understanding, perceptions and behaviour – a literature review*, Research Report No 562, Leeds: Stationery Office.

Zaidi, A. (2010) *Poverty risks for older people in EU countries – an update*, Policy Brief January (11), Vienna: European Centre for Social Welfare Policy and Research, www.euro.centre.org/data/1264603415_56681.pdf.

THREE

Warehouse, marketise, shelter, juridify: on the political economy and governance of extending school participation in England

Ross Fergusson

Introduction

In November 2011, the UK's Conservative-Liberal Democrat Coalition government drew back from the brink of criminalising 16- and 17-year-olds in England who did not participate in education, training or employment. It amended the legislation of the previous Labour government, whose 2008 Education and Skills Act (E&S Act) made failure to participate the subject of attendance notices and panels, breach of which would have resulted in fines. Failure to pay such fines would have made persistent non-participants eligible for custodial sentences. The Coalition's 2011 Education Act empowers the Secretary of State for Education to keep under review those clauses of the original legislation that require local authorities and employers to monitor and enforce young people's participation. The resultant suspension of what is in effect a law against non-participation is subject to review in 2016, which could yet trigger legislation to restore the original E&S Act's requirements.

Few recent policy reforms have a greater capacity to invoke the bitter education debates of the 1970s and 1980s than that of the E&S Act's apparently innocuous Raising of the Participation Age. Following the 2008 Act, since September 2013 all 16- to 17-year-olds have been required by law to extend their attendance at school or college for a further year, or to undertake specified part-time training alongside full-time employment. In September 2015, this requirement will be extended up to the age of 18. This reform exhumes fundamental questions about the purposes of statutory state education that have been debated in struggles for more than a century and a half. Since the 19th century, profoundly contested claims about whether young people were better placed in school or in the labour market for an additional year have repeatedly exposed the motivations, social priorities and purposes of governments of all hues, and of interested groups. In varying guises, reformists, egalitarians, meritocrats, social conservatives and economic liberals lived out, through these and other related struggles, their ambitions for the kind of society they wished to shape. As we will see, many shades of these positions were in evidence in the parliamentary debates on the E&S Act.

These debates were occasionally heated, but their critical points of contention rarely percolated into public debate. This apparent indifference is historically rare. Comparable legislation was variously defeated, cancelled, obstructed, delayed and repealed. It reputedly won and lost general and municipal elections, bitterly divided minority governments and political parties, and prompted at least one secretary of state to resign (Barker, 1972; Simon, 1991). The purposes of extending compulsory participation in education remain disputed in the current policies. Any appearance of consensus masks deeply conflicted claims about its social and economic benefits. As ever, it is in the study of the exercise of powers within and through the policy process, in the detail of specification and in the latitude of implementation (Hill, 2014) that the inherently ideological character of policy and its often-polyvalent purposes and potentials are at their most tractable.

This chapter focuses on some key points of contestation around important historical legislative moments that secured multiple successive increases in the required age of compulsory schooling, with the intention of highlighting their continuing presence in the 2008 E&S Act and its amendment in 2011. The next section begins this work by exploring the principal political–economic and governance rationales for increasing or maintaining the age of compulsory participation. This framing is then taken forward by a more detailed selective historical review of the ways in which political–economic rationales have shaped competing positions on participation policy that have variously advanced, slowed or attempted to subvert efforts to raise the minimum leaving age. The emerging analysis is then applied to the 2008 E&S Act policy reforms and their dilution in 2011, to identify the central points of contention and their likely effects on post-16 participation in significantly altered political and economic conditions. The analysis finally leads back to reviewing the mooted importance of governance rationales for understanding extended participation, and to some concluding comments on the ways in which the political choice between criminalising legal minors and neglecting the needs of some of the most vulnerable of them has been constructed.

The political economy and governance of extended participation

Rationales and modalities of extended participation

With few exceptions, the histories of debates about raising the age of compulsory participation in education can be broadly understood in relation to three framing rationales, each realised through specific modalities with specific priorities. *Social ideals rationales* are realised in largely competing modalities of social progress that prioritise diverse notions of social advancement/modernisation; of social mobility that prioritise the amelioration or management of inequalities; and of forms of social justice that seek to optimise equal rights and/or outcomes. Dominant *political-economic rationales* manifest themselves in largely complementary modalities of adding value to a skilled, educated workforce; of warehousing fractions of the workforce as a way of managing labour supply; and of marketising labour in ways that maximise wage competition. *Governance rationales* variously promote activity that shelters surplus labour and prioritises the protection *or* containment of prospective non-participants; that tracks prospective non-participants by identifying them or monitoring their activity; and that 'juridifies' those who persistently refuse to participate by enforcing participation or criminalising non-participation by extending the reach of statute law into an ever-increasing range of social realms. Table 3.1 summarises these rationales, the modalities through which they are realised and the priorities associated with them.

Table 3.1: Rationales for extending the age of compulsory participation

Rationale	Modality	Priority
Social ideals	Social progress	Advance/modernise society
	Social mobility	Ameliorate/manage inequalities
	Social justice	Optimise equal rights/outcomes
Political-economic	Add value	Skill/educate workforce
	Warehouse	Manage labour supply
	Marketise	Maximise wage competition
Governance	Shelter	Protect/contain non-participants
	Track	Identify/monitor non-participants
	Juridify	Enforce participation/criminalise non-participants

Narrative histories of the advance of compulsory schooling tend to be heavily imbued with generalised 'social progress' rationales (e.g. Armytage, 1964). The school leaving age has been raised nine times since the emblematic 1870 Elementary Education Act that nominally marked the beginning of the universal state provision of education. But behind this 140-year chronology and its Whiggish and often teleological representation of inexorable progress lies a rarely accounted history which greatly illuminates current policy developments. As a corrective to this 'progressive' view, this chapter gives precedence to accounts framed by political-economic rationales and by the governance of prospective or actual non-participation in education, training or employment. In particular, it is concerned with the ways in which decisions about extended participation are associated with warehousing and marketising the youth labour force, and with their impact on labour markets, within political-economic rationales; and with the capacity of policies on participation in schooling to shelter prospective non-participants, to track them or to subject their non-participation to the force of law (that is, to 'juridify' it) within governance rationales. These are the five modalities highlighted in Table 3.1

Political-economic rationales

Histories of education often highlight correspondences between the development of state education and the needs of the economy, but histories that offer a developed political-economic reading of extended school attendance are rare. Brian Simon's are an exception, one critical thread of which takes account of the relationship between changes in the statutory school leaving age and changes in levels of recorded unemployment (Simon, 1974, 1991). Unsurprisingly, increases in the school leaving age during the 20th century have consistently resulted in reductions in overall unemployment rates, of varying degrees, in the two or three following years. These are clearly visible in relation to the 1918 Fisher Act, the 1944 Butler Act and the later increase in the leaving age to 16. Other less predictable synchronicities that are too detailed to account here emerge from a careful study of correspondences between growing school populations and reduced levels of youth unemployment at several other key junctures, notably in 1936, 1947 and 1973. The subsequent sea-changes in policy that resulted in a 40-year moratorium on raising the leaving age were signalled by the first of a lengthy series of youth training and workfare programmes for 16- to 18-year-olds implemented in 1983, as unemployment rates following the 1980–82 recession exceeded the barometric three million threshold.

No inferences of causality are intended by this highly compressed account of correspondences. Only in the case of the conjunctures of a reduction in the rate of total unemployment immediately after increases in the statutory minimum school leaving age could any such relationships be demonstrated through careful statistical analysis. These observations therefore caution against deterministic economistic readings. It is nevertheless difficult to ignore the synchronicities of policy change and changes in the labour market in any interpretation which seeks to explain the eventuality and timing of successive episodes of raising the school leaving age, when qualitative assessments of the relationship like Simon's indicate strong causal connections. Furthermore, changes in the duration of compulsory schooling both create and respond to dynamic labour market conditions, and this dialectical relationship itself takes many forms, notably including those of the political economic modalities indicated in Table 3.1. Firstly, an extra year in school prospectively 'adds value' to young people's prospects of becoming employed if they gain qualifications or new skills, and to the economy, and, as we will see, this rationale was prominent in the case for the E&S Act. Secondly, by definition, extending the school leaving age also removes an entire age-cohort of prospective young workers from the labour market. But if, as under the E&S Act, the option to remain in school or college is complemented by an option to take employment, it also 'warehouses' a self-selecting part of each cohort as a 'reserve army' that can be called upon if the demand for labour increases. And thirdly, as those who are warehoused opt to enter the labour market early, their lower wage expectations (associated with their lesser experience) provide cheaper labour and/or bring downward pressure on older, more experienced workers to reduce their own reservation wage thresholds.

These three political-economic modalities of the relationship between extended schooling and the labour market (adding value to the young workforce, warehousing it, marketising it) are in play at every juncture at which compulsory schooling is extended. Each has the potential to serve the interests of young people and employers, but in very differing degrees in different contexts. Added-value arguments are readily deployed when the demand for labour is low, but fade when it is high. Warehousing usefully manages labour supply for employers and the economy as a whole, but is detrimental to the interests of young people who would rather work than attend school or college. Marketising the labour power of the least experienced and least qualified youngest workers may give them access to jobs, but their competitive advantage over older workers is entirely contingent on their scope for meeting employers' interests by accepting the lowest pay rates. In practice, an equitable balance between the best interests of young people, employers and the wider economy is rare, and much of the dispute over extending compulsory schooling is, at root, attributable to conflicting projections on the part of differing interests as to which of these modalities will prevail and to what effect. Such conflicting projections have a clear capacity to account for many of the historical conflicts over whether or not to extend the legal requirement to participate in education or training.

Governance rationales

Similar considerations apply to the three modalities of governance in Table 3.1. As the counterpart of warehousing, for the first modality, 'sheltering' young people is ambivalent in its capacities both to protect them from the depredations of depressed labour markets and lost time, and also to 'contain' them. For the second, extending the age of participation keeps potential non-participants who would otherwise lack work and an income 'off the streets' and under the gaze of state-run/regulated institutions. Willingly or not, those who are required by law to attend school or college are thus identified and can be 'tracked' and monitored. In addition, historically, there have always been powers to enforce the laws of attendance, in the shape of Education Welfare Officers for example. And for the third, these powers can be escalated to 'juridify' the refusal to participate in ways that tip it past the enforcement of civil law and into the ambit of criminal law – such that failure to comply with civil orders or pay fines criminalises those who refuse, as the E&S Act proposed.

Once again, conflicted interpretations and projections as to whether young people are willingly protected or unwillingly trapped in school, and benignly tracked or officiously monitored and criminalised, have variously infused the contested debates about the mandatory extension of the age of participation throughout its history – up to and including the E&S Act.

The labour market and extended schooling

Almost every juncture at which the required age of attendance at school has been increased has been ambivalent in its rationales and conflicted and compromised in its effects. Social ideals were frequently and consistently compromised by political-economic and governance considerations. The analytical inseparability of school attendance and the pressures to include children and young people in the formal and informal labour markets of the time, *or to exclude, protect or contain them*, are fundamental to this ambivalence. Conflicted intentions of extending compulsory participation and the uncertainties of its effects in complex social, political and economic conditions have exacerbated contested projections of which interests stood to benefit most.

The dynamic tensions between schooling and work are evident in this history from the outset. The 1870 Elementary Education Act enshrined the long-standing half-time arrangements for school attendance above the age of 10 for almost half a century, allowing children to continue in employment, albeit with subsequent adjustments. It was then the great achievement of the 1918 Fisher Act to break this limitation on educational provision and require full-time attendance up to the age of 14 years, despite powerful opposing interests in maintaining the half-time system. Conflicted cases for adding value, warehousing and marketising more labour were multiple and forceful (Lewis, 1917; Garrett, 1928; Barker, 1972; Simon, 1974, 1991). The effects of the Act were diluted and compromised by the 20-year delay in achieving universal free provision. And in the conditions of the 1920s' recession the Continuation Schools that were legislated to provide day-a-week attendance for those who left school at 14 were largely unimplemented, thus diminishing the added value and maximising the flexibility of warehoused labour (see Simon, 1991, p 31).

Contestation continued in the years between the 1918 Fisher Act and its implementation in the face of the infamous Geddes Report (1922). Throughout the late 1920s and early 1930s, in conditions of continuing high unemployment and depression, the conflicting warehousing and marketising arguments continued (Barker, 1972). Conflicted interests were played out around the issues of cheap labour, the displacement of adult workers and the loss of vital income to impoverished households, alleviating the exploitation of children, and the case for a maintenance allowance (Tawney, 1934, pp 4–5). The unimplemented 1936 Act attempted to maintain employers' access to cheap young workers by making compulsory school attendance up to the age of 15 years a form of residual provision for the unemployable (Simon, 1991, p 28). The 1944 Butler Act refused this compromise and the continuing demands for cheap labour (Simon, 1991, p 99), but, following its implementation in 1947, the succeeding minority Conservative government repeatedly discussed the option of reverting to a leaving age of 14, to fund Cold War rearmament (Simon, 1991, pp 162–8).

The first move to implement the Butler Act's provision to raise the leaving age to 16 was made in 1964, and deferred in 1968 to a 1973/74 start date. The Crowther Report of 1959 had been equivocal on the economic 'added value' case for it, and recognised young people's impatience for greater financial independence.

Such dilemmas, and the fundamentally conflicted social ideals and political-economic rationales they embody, partly explain why 1973 may forever be the last legislated increase in the age of English compulsory school attendance. As the burgeoning youth and adult unemployment in the late 1970s and early 1980s reached crisis proportions in the febrile run-up to three million unemployed in 1983, warehousing- and marketising-driven arguments for and against extended schooling disappeared from the policy discourse. In the critical vocationalising moment of the New Training Initiative in 1981, the newly ascendant Manpower Services Commission (MSC) re-versioned the added-value arguments in the form of work-based part-time training up to the age of 18 for all young people not in full-time education (Department of Employment, 1981, para 1). The successive removal of unemployment and other benefits entitlements for under-18s effectively removed the option of being 'inactive' for many. And for the next three decades, all crises of youth unemployment were addressed by successive generations of MSC-run training schemes, and then replaced by New Labour's New Deal for Young People (NDYP). Extended schooling disappeared from the policy agenda, in large part in favour of a major shift towards *governance* rationales for the extended participation for unemployed young people in (often simulated) work settings with some notional non-accredited training.

Rethinking compulsion: raising the participation age (RPA)

After a 40-year legislative silence on extended compulsory participation in education, the Labour government's 2008 E&S Act surprised many. The E&S Act proposals were ostensibly driven by added-value considerations, brought into sharp focus by the Leitch Report (2006) on future skills needs. But, consistent with the history of increasing the participation age, the E&S Act arose in favourable labour market conditions that informed the proposals, but was implemented in very different conditions. Proposals for the 2008 RPA legislation emerged when it became clear that levels of non-participation in education, employment and training among 16- to 18-year-olds had remained stubbornly close to 10% since the introduction of NDYP, with an underlying upward trend between 2004 and 2008, when the rate twice exceeded 10% (DfE, 2013a). The National Audit Office warned that there needed to be hard-to-manage annual improvements close to 1% over three years for the government to meet its own Public Service Agreement targets by 2010 (NAO, 2008). It was particularly stinging to be warned in the same year that in 2005 the UK's non-participation rate was the fifth-highest of the 29 richest countries, after Turkey, Mexico, Italy and Greece (OECD, 2008). The under-18 labour market had been heavily oversubscribed since the early 1980s and the established tendency of employers to use stratified qualifications as a pre-selection filter had particularly affected this age group (Simmons and Thompson, 2011; Wolf, 2011). After a decade in power the government had anticipated the criticisms by recognising that no policy based on NDYP and a statutory leaving age of 16 would deliver significant improvement.

The 2008 E&S Act reforms

The E&S Act places a duty upon all young people in England to participate in education and training for a minimum of 540 hours per year; or to take an apprenticeship or full-time work or volunteer activity, combined with part-time education or training equivalent to a day a week leading to a qualification. Local authorities were to promote the effective participation of all 16- and 17-year-olds, make arrangements to identify young people who were not participating and issue attendance notices and parenting contracts and orders. Young people were to be fined for persistent contravention, and would in the last instance have been eligible for custodial sentences on default. Employers were to ascertain that under-18s had made arrangements for education or training, and to facilitate and monitor their attendance, or receive penalty and enforcement notices and pay fines.

Several lengthy debates about the Labour government's E&S Bill in both Houses of Parliament were broadly positive, with many approving comments from the opposition benches on the general ambition to raise participation rates and improve skill levels (UK, House of Commons Hansard, 2008; UK, House of Lords Hansard, 2008). Some MPs and peers criticised a government of 12 years' standing that had been unable to lift the UK in the OECD rankings, and objected that this reflected inadequacies with the curriculum and other aspects of provision that were unable to ensure that half of pupils in England gained five grade-C GCSEs that included English and maths (DCSF, 2009); or unable to maintain the interest of more 17- to 18-year-olds. Of greatest concern for all political parties was the persistence of rates of non-participation in education, training or employment among 18-year-olds (16% in 2008; Department for Education, 2013a, Chart 5). Interpretations varied widely on the perceived causes, but there was wide agreement that the E&S Act was right to put forward an approach which, set against decades of workfare-based policy responses, appeared innovative and even radical, in the finest traditions of the much-cited 1918 and 1944 Acts. Supportive appeals to the rationales of social mobility and social justice were plentiful; endorsements using the 'added value' rationale of a better-prepared workforce were prominent.

The sole source of deep disagreement presented itself in the form of almost-philosophical principles. At its most elevated, argument turned on whether social justice or individual liberty has primacy. Government ministers exhibited ostensibly near-missionary zeal in their determination to release the most socially and economically deprived localities and individuals from the poverty and disadvantage associated with low or no qualifications and youth unemployment. Opposition spokespeople and their supporters relentlessly stressed young people's right to choose whether to study, train, work – or, by implication, be unemployed. In protracted debates most Labour MPs argued in favour of measures that extended education or some form of training by statute, as the only way to alleviate the entrenched disadvantage of the least well-educated, trained and qualified 10% of young people. Most Conservative and Liberal Democrat MPs argued that 16-year-olds who are deemed mature enough to be at liberty to marry, parent and serve in the armed forces should also be free to choose not to participate. Second-order issues then became the focus of dispute. By what criteria was adult maturity to be judged – especially when under-18s are also denied a range of independent rights, including the right to vote? How was the legal requirement to attend to be enforced, especially among young people who chose full-time work and part-time training?

The most persistent points of dissent surrounded the proposed enforcement mechanisms of the Bill, and in particular the potential criminalisation of young people and the obligations on employers to make time for training and monitor it, or face civil penalties. These issues remained unresolved when the E&S Act finally passed into law by virtue of the government's majority.

The Education Act 2011

As we have seen, legislative and policy efforts to delay, subvert, reverse, dilute and cancel the extension of the statutory requirement to participate in education and training have a long history. Similarly, the incoming Coalition government of 2010 subverted the contested provision of the E&S Act in three surgically brief clauses of its Education Act 2011. These allowed the Secretary of State to keep under review the appropriateness of commencing the E&S Act enforcement mechanisms, including the criminal offence for failure to comply with an attendance notice, the duties on employers and parents, and the requirement on local authorities to identify young people who do not comply (UK Parliament, 2011, 74/354).

By August 2013, the Secretary of State had deployed his fullest latitude. Local authorities are now relieved of their obligation to enforce participation. Employers need not establish or monitor young employees' part-time participation in training, nor agree suitable hours of work to allow training. At the time of writing, although it appears that parenting contracts and orders, and young people's enforcement notices and panels, will remain statutory requirements, sanctions will not apply for breaches (Department of Education, 2013b, 2013c).

The 2011 amendments to the E&S Act and the changes that followed occurred in dramatically altered conditions from those in which the Act was introduced. During 2011, in the middle of the double-dip recession, UK unemployment among 16- to 24-year-olds exceeded one million for the first time (ONS, 2013). Retrenchment in welfare-related public spending was massive. The 2011 amendments undoubtedly reduced the costs of implementing the E&S Act by removing all processes of monitoring and enforcement. It also seems likely that this will very substantially reduce the costs to the Exchequer of additional provision for large numbers of school and college students, while underlying youth non-participation and unemployment will, at best, return to the internationally shaming levels that triggered the E&S Act in the mid-2000s.

The rationale for the changes made by the Coalition government was transparent in the parliamentary debates. What remains opaque is how far the principled assertions in favour of free choice (or compulsory participation) are now and were always underwritten by other interests, or actively used to mask them. The costs of monitoring and enforcement concerned the Coalition partners. Their liberal principles were also at odds with Labour's zealous drive to legislate a path to a more socially mobile society, and especially with the burdens the E&S Act would have placed on employers. Some of the most tangible effects of the amendments have therefore been to neutralise the economic disadvantages of the E&S Act to employers, while leaving intact the scope for warehousing surplus labour and/or releasing the cheapest labour. It is notable that these changes resemble aspects of the conditions of the half-time systems that operated before the 1918 Fisher Act, and of the subsequent repeated failures to provide guaranteed part-time training for young employees by means of Continuation Schools in 1922 and County Colleges in 1947 – all supported at the time by unashamed arguments in favour of maintaining the supply of cheap labour, and sparing employers the costs and complications of releasing staff for training purposes.

Other policy changes and prospective effects of the amended E&S Act

The suspended enforcement elements of the E&S Act mean that, for the time being at least, young people remain free to decide whether or not to elect to register for full-time education or training, or to take a full-time job – exactly as previously, when 97% of 16-year-olds and 90% of 17-year-olds already participated in education and training (Department for Education, 2011, Table 1). But this does not mean that the *status quo ante* prevails. Two important policy changes alter it. First, the E&S Act was passed when the Education Maintenance Allowance (EMA) was in place for 16- and 17-year-olds who had a demonstrable need for support for costs of travel, basic subsistence and books. The EMA was withdrawn by the Coalition government in 2010 – again recalling successful historical objections to proposals for maintenance allowances as 'bribes' and 'indiscriminate doles' (Barker, 1972, p 61; Dean, 1969, p 290). The second change was a contemporaneous requirement for all young people up to the age of 18 who had not achieved grade C in GCSEs in English and mathematics to continue studying those subjects if they were in full-time education or training (again informed by the Wolf Report) (BBC, 2013).

The removal of the EMA greatly diminishes the possibilities of full-time study for those who come from households that can no longer wholly support them financially – much as the late 19th- and early 20th-century arguments for extended participation were successfully opposed because poor households relied on their children's incomes. By the same token, for low-achievers in general, and for number-phobics and those whose first language is not English in particular, extra years(s) in school and college were substantially less attractive in 2013 than in 2008.

The combined effect of these changes by the Coalition government will almost certainly be to incline substantially more of the non-participant target group towards the 'full-time work with part-time training option'. In the present adverse market conditions, while the offer of cheap labour will secure work for some, poorly qualified 'early leavers' are more likely to return to the nameless, unsupported interstitial space between education, training and work than to the classroom or workshop.

Governing non-participation

There are alternatives. Apprenticeships and volunteering may be valued, but they remain scarce in conditions of financial stringency. Similarly, the Youth Contract (YC) for 16- to 17-year-olds continues as an incongruous fall-back that spares low-achievers from being contained or warehoused in the institutional sites of their underachievement. But the YC has been dramatically unsuccessful, with tiny numbers of placements (barely 4,000 16- to 17-year-olds in England, fewer than 600 in London, whether because of limitations of supply or of demand for places), and no positive outcomes for almost three-quarters of participants (Department of Education, 2013d). The YC therefore serves at once as a spur and as a shelter that contains young people as much as it protects them. Its poor reputation tests the resolve of those who refuse school and college, and reinvigorates the conflicted dynamics of choosing between unpalatable training and unobtainable employment. The YC also offers residual provision, much as post-14 schooling was to have done in the cancelled 1936 Act, by providing legitimising protective cover for the weakest and most vulnerable. But the YC also corrals and contains reluctant, recalcitrant and alienated 'refusers' in one place, where they can be monitored and 'occupied'.

An increasingly prominent and important analysis of modes of administration like those of New Labour's 1997–2010 engagement with all who call on the state's welfare provisions recognises that their underlying responsibilisation strategy is in effect a mode of governance (Rhodes, 1996; Rose, 1999). Provision is made ever more conditional on participation in approved productive activity, or, in its absence, on acceptable conducts and behaviours. Those services of welfare that offer shelter also track their subjects. They identify, profile and monitor, and then analyse and model data in unproven efforts to predict and pre-empt the un-responsibilised behaviours of others (Marston, 2006). The youth justice system in particular is now notorious for commuting the instruments of behaviour management into techniques for identifying – and in some cases criminalising – proscribed conducts (Case, 2007; Haines and Case, 2008). Anti-social behaviour orders (ASBOs) had the capacity to prosecute breach of orders through the criminal courts. Indeed, many of the proposals of the escalating wedge of interventions for non-participation that were proposed in the original E&S Act resemble the sequential stages of ASBOs.

Non-participation in the forms which the E&S Act sought to address is now becoming understood more as a problem for governance under arrangements overseen by the state than as a problem of a dysfunctional, barely regulated market economy. When the labour market of the early 1980s began to implode under the strains of monetarist doctrine as a precursor of neoliberalisation, the high visibility of youth unemployment was addressed by transformative changes in the functioning of the state, which oversaw schemes whose priority was to remove young people from the registers of social security and unemployment counts, and contain them in what were often little more than masquerades of training and work experience. Unemployment thereby began its journey along the long path from being a failure of political economy to being a problem for governance. A problem of structures, values and social and economic organisation began to be reworked as a problem of individuals. Exogenous explanations for unemployment and non-participation became reworked as endogenous accounts of unsuitably skilled, unadaptive or poorly motivated individuals – especially among the young (see Fergusson, 2013). If, as this chapter has argued, the E&S Act is best understood as part of an extension of the history of the political economy of extended schooling in the context of unstable labour markets, it must also be recognised as the latest episode in a different historical lineage of governing problematised populations of young people (Muncie, 2009).

Conclusion

The very short history of the E&S Act has been to achieve what opponents of extended schooling failed to do in 1922, 1936 and 1947: reverse or disrupt it. It is a history that is already marked by troubling resemblances to other aspects of the education reforms of the late 19th and early–mid 20th centuries. It is far from clear whether the 2011 reversal will also ultimately fail, and by what criteria the outcomes of the debilitated E&S Act will be judged in review in 2016.

It is idle to ask whether the Coalition government's step back from enforcing participation is a retreat from an unwelcome breach of basic liberties, marred in particular by criminalising those who refuse to participate; or a historic lost opportunity to open up new prospects for the 10% of young people who have benefited least from 11 years of compulsory school attendance. The Hobson's choice between New Labour's hyper-interventionism of tracking, monitoring and enforcing participation through punitive sanctions, and Coalition's apparent *laissez-faire* neglect of the most vulnerable (and perhaps least governable) of young people in times of rapidly polarising conditions of poverty and wealth is unanswerable (Fergusson, 2014). It is also an entirely context-bound construct of a specific political-economic conjuncture that easily blinds out the alternatives to the two hybridised variants of neoliberalism that underpin the binary choice on offer. And while it remains extremely difficult to explain the absence of public debate, both over the original E&S Act legislation and over its subsequent debilitation, it may be that the collective political construction of an impossible choice between punishment and neglect has met with the public bemusement (or contempt) it deserved.

The principal flaw in the 2008 legislation was not its attempt to compel participation: such requirements were ramped up and uncontroversially enforced roughly every quarter-century since 1870, until extending compulsory attendance was abandoned in favour of schemes concerned more with governing non-participants than educating or training. Rather, the flaw lay in E&S Act's incapacity to find an *enforceable and tenable* developmental alternative for those who would not profit from full-time education or training. All the known variations on the old themes seem to have become exhausted, now that it is clear that youth workfare programmes are discredited currency, that the unregulated formal labour market will never meet the demand for jobs from new entrants and that employers have to prove that they can be relied upon to facilitate and monitor accredited training.

The alternatives, though, are legion, for those with the vision and political conviction to recognise the social and economic costs of whole cohorts of young people who are unable to learn or earn within the frames of existing provisions and structures. It is possible to conceptualise policy alternatives that refuse the dominant terms of the present conjuncture and offer new solutions to a now-transnational problem that is simplistically dubbed 'mass global youth unemployment' and is gaining a sanguine and resigned reputation for being intractable. Rebalancing the gross disparity between the needs of young people without prospects and the cultivated expectations of corporate employers who will countenance few adaptations to any policies that slow the pace of escalating profits might be a sound starting point – one that still has the power to capture the imaginations of those best placed to change policy and act to stay the alarming advancing normalisation of mass non-participation among young people.

References

Armytage, W.H.G. (1964) *Four hundred years of English education*, Cambridge: Cambridge University Press.

Barker, R. (1972) *Education and politics 1900–1951: A study of the Labour Party*, Oxford: Clarendon Press.

BBC (2013) 'Teenagers have to keep studying English and Maths', 2 September, www.bbc.co.uk/news/education-23925033.

Case, S. (2007) 'Questioning the evidence of risk that underpins evidence-led youth justice interventions', *Youth Justice*, 7(2): 91–105.

Crowther, G. (1959) *Fifteen to eighteen: A report of the Central Advisory Council for Education (England)* (The Crowther Report), London: Her Majesty's Stationery Office.

Dean, D.W. (1969) 'The difficulties of a Labour educational policy: the failure of the Trevelyan Bill, 1929–31', *British Journal of Educational Studies*, 17(3): 286–300.

DCSF (Department for Children, Schools and Families) (2009) 'GCSE and equivalent examination results in England 2007/8 (revised)' (SFR 02/2009), http://webarchive.nationalarchives.gov.uk/20130401151655/www.education.gov.uk/researchandstatistics/statistics/allstatistics/a00195931/gcse-and-equivalent-results-in-england (last accessed 30 September 2013).

Department for Education (2011) *DfE Statistical First Release SFR 15/2011: Participation in education, training and employment by 16–18 year olds in England*, London: Department for Education.

Department for Education (2013a) *DfE Statistical First Release SFR 22/2013: Participation in education, training and employment by 16–18 year olds in England*, London: Department for Education.

Department for Education (2013b) *Raising the participation age (RPA) – information for employers*, http://media.education.gov.uk/assets/files/pdf/f/130729%20employers%20factsheet.pdf) (last accessed 30 September 2013).

Department for Education (2013c) *Raising the participation age (RPA) – myth buster for young people*, http://media.education.gov.uk/assets/files/pdf/r/130729%20mythbuster.pdf (last accessed 30 September 2013).

Department for Education (2013d) *Youth contract provision for 16- and 17-year-olds not in education, employment or training*, www.education.gov.uk/childrenandyoungpeople/youngpeople/participation/a00203664/youthcontractprov (last accessed 30 September 2013).

Department of Employment (1981) *The New Training Initiative: A programme for action*, London: HMSO.

Education Act (2011) *Education Act, 2011: Explanatory notes* (S74/para.354) www.legislation.gov.uk/ukpga/2011/21/contents (last accessed 30 September 2013).

Education and Skills Act (2008) www.legislation.gov.uk/ukpga/2011/21/section/74/enacted?view=interweave (last accessed 30 September 2013).

Fergusson, R. (2013) 'Against disengagement: non-participation as an object of governance', *Research in Post Compulsory Education*, 18(1–2): 12–28.

Fergusson, R. (2014) 'Regulate or abandon: two-speed tracks to criminalising precarious youth', *Criminal Justice Matters*, 96(1).

Garrett, J.H. (1928) *Mass education in England: A critical examination of problem and possibility*, London: E.J. Burrows.

Geddes Report (1922) *Labour and national 'economy'*, National Joint Council (Great Britain), Committee on National Expenditure, London: The National Joint Council.

Haines, K. and Case, S. (2008) 'The rhetoric and reality of the "Risk Factor Prevention Paradigm" approach to preventing and reducing youth offending', *Youth Justice*, 8(1): 5–20.

Hill, M. (2014) *The public policy process* (6th edn), Harlow, Pearson Educational.

Leitch, S. (2006) *Prosperity for all in the global economy: World class skills: final report* (The Leitch Review of Skills), London: HMSO.

Lewis, J.H. (1917) *Report of the Departmental Committee on Juvenile Education in relation to employment after the war* (The Lewis Report), reproduced in J.S. Maclure (1965) *Educational documents: England and Wales, 1816 to the present day*, London: Methuen.

Marston, G. (2006) 'Employment services in an age of e-government', *Information, Communication & Society*, 9(1): 83–103.

Muncie, J. (2009) *Youth and crime* (3rd edn), London: Sage.

NAO (National Audit Office) (2008) *Young people not in education, employment or training*, London: National Audit Office.

OECD (2008) *Jobs for youth: United Kingdom*, Brussels: Organisation for Economic Cooperation and Development.

ONS (Office for National Statistics) (2013) *A01: Summary of labour market statistics*, www.ons.gov.uk/ons/taxonomy/search/index.html (last accessed 30 September 2013).

Rhodes, R.A.W. (1996) 'The new governance: governing without government', *Political Studies*, 44: 652–67.

Rose, N. (1999) *Powers of freedom: Reframing political thought*, Cambridge: Cambridge University Press.

Simmons, R. and Thompson, R. (2011) *NEET young people and training for work: Living on the margins*, Stoke-on-Trent: Trentham Books.

Simon, B. (1974) *The politics of educational reform, 1920–1940*, London: Lawrence and Wishart.

Simon, B. (1991) *Education and the social order, 1940–1990* London: Lawrence and Wishart.

Tawney, R.H. (1934) *The school leaving age and juvenile unemployment*, London: Workers' Education Association.

UK Parliament, House of Commons, Hansard (2008) for 14 January, 17 November.

UK Parliament, House of Lords, Hansard (2008) for 10 June, 11 November.

Wolf, A. (2011) *Review of vocational education: The Wolf Report*, London: Department for Education.

FOUR

The political economy of taxation in the 21st-century UK

Sally Ruane and David Byrne

Introduction

Taxation is always on the political agenda but, in a context of a government programme of deficit reduction principally through cuts to the welfare state rather than tax rises, it is notable that 'fair taxation' has become a major political issue. It has been taken up not only by political activists and trade unions but also by the House of Commons Public Accounts Committee in relation both to tax avoidance as an industry and to the abilities of particular transnational corporations to avoid paying corporation tax. While all the main parties endorse austerity, the extent to which paying tax seems to be a voluntary activity, both for very affluent individuals/households and corporations, has become a public scandal and source of genuine popular discontent. The aim of this chapter is to offer a class analysis of taxation and set out some existing proposals that could increase the progressivity and redistributive potential of the UK tax system. After an overview of the main taxes, the chapter will present a selective history of taxation, with a particular emphasis on the role of taxes in mediating the relationship of the propertied and labouring classes. It will then examine the functions of taxation from a political-economy perspective, and some of the means by which the tax system has been modified since the 1980s with the effect of reducing the relative contribution of the affluent and large corporations. Finally, it will outline some proposals that can contribute to addressing the enormous increase in inequality in the UK since the 1970s.

The main UK taxes in 2012

First, we will consider what taxes are currently collected in the UK. Taking the forecasts for 2012/13 as a snapshot (Table 4.1 below), we see that the vast majority of tax revenues are raised through personal rather than corporate taxation. The largest single revenue-raiser is income tax, which is a direct tax on earned and unearned income, accounting for over one quarter of all revenues. It is the tax that has the highest profile both in terms of public recognition and in terms of media reporting. Its annual yield, however, is outweighed by that of indirect taxes, including Value Added Tax (VAT), when taken together. Indirect taxes are 'indirect' because they are collected by an intermediary (such as a retailer) from those bearing the economic cost (typically the consumer); they include excise duties on tobacco, alcohol and hydrocarbon oils and stamp duty on house purchases, and they account for around one third of all revenues. National Insurance Contributions (NICs) which, because they have been largely de-linked from specific benefits, are very similar to income tax albeit levied on earned income only, raise about one sixth of all revenue. Income tax, NICs and indirect taxes including VAT between them account for around three-quarters of all tax revenues. Taxes on businesses, including corporation tax, which is levied on profits, raise a modest amount of revenue, around one eighth of the total. At the local level, business rates and Council Tax raise about the same amount as each other. The contribution of other taxes is very small in comparison with these main taxes.

Table 4.1: UK taxes 2012/13 – forecasts

	Revenue £bn	% of total tax receipts
Income Tax, net of tax credits	150.6	26.5
National Insurance Contributions	105.6	18.6
VAT	102.0	17.9
Other indirect taxes	66.4	11.7
Capital Gains Tax	3.8	0.7
Inheritance Tax	3.0	0.5
Stamp Duty Land Tax	6.4	1.1
Stamp Duty on shares	3.0	0.5
Corporation Tax net of tax credits	43.9	7.7
Petroleum Revenue Tax	1.6	0.3
Business rates	26.2	4.6
Bank levy	2.2	0.4
Council Tax, net of Council Tax Benefit	26.3	4.6
Other taxes and royalties	27.9	4.9
Total	568.8	100.0

Source: Derived from figures given in Browne and Roantree (2012).

Of all the main taxes, only income tax is progressive throughout the income scale (that is, on average the better-off pay a larger proportion of their income in tax than do the less well-off). Indirect taxes are regressive (the better-off on average pay a lower proportion of their income in tax than do the less well-off) and NICs are progressive only until a certain point on the income scale, after which they become regressive (see Table 4.2, column 6, which demonstrates this). This is because National Insurance (NI) is levied (after an allowance) at 12% on income up to an 'upper earnings limit' (£795 in 2013/14), but at only 2% on any income above that. The impact of the tax system, and particularly the distribution of the tax 'burden' in relation to the real units of personal economy, which are not individuals but households, can be seen in Figure 4.1 and Table 4.2. With the exception of the bottom 10% of households, we have something close to a flat tax system (and see Byrne and Ruane, 2008 for a fuller discussion of this).

Figure 4.1: Total tax take as a percentage of gross household income by decile, 1978 and 2011/12

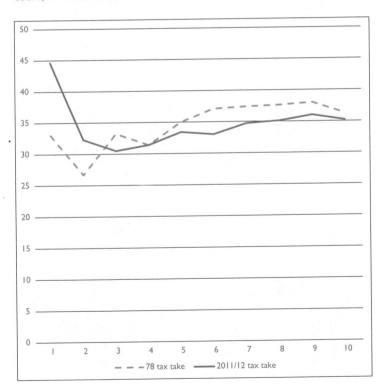

Table 4.2: Gross household income and the tax take, 2011/12

Decile	% gross household income taken in all taxes	All taxes £	Gross Income £	% gross household income taken in Income Tax (net)	% gross household income taken in Employee NICs	% gross household income taken in VAT	% gross household income taken in all indirect taxes	All indirect taxes £	% of all tax paid by decile	% of gross income received by decile
1	44.6	4,693	10,523	3.87	1.05	11.67	30.39	3,198	3.62	2.81
2	32.28	4,989	15,456	3.17	1.49	9.25	23.30	3,602	3.85	4.12
3	30.46	5,741	18,845	3.95	2.34	8.10	20.23	3,812	4.43	5.03
4	31.39	6,805	21,676	5.61	2.47	8.26	19.41	4,207	5.25	5.78
5	33.35	9,158	27,464	8.51	3.73	7.46	18.00	4,943	7.06	7.33
6	32.97	10,815	32,801	8.75	4.29	6.84	16.67	5,469	8.34	8.75
7	34.68	13,443	38,763	10.99	5.15	6.67	15.45	5,987	10.36	10.34
8	35.11	16,793	47,826	13.08	5.82	5.95	14.10	6,743	12.94	12.76
9	36.01	21,671	60,181	14.79	6.27	5.80	12.67	7,624	16.70	16.06
10	35.17	35,627	101,291	18.85	5.05	4.62	9.74	9,863	27.46	27.02

A selective history of taxes and their role in mediating the relationship of the propertied and labouring classes

Elements in the taxation table above have a varied history but all were originally raised for particular purposes. Originally the sovereign was supported from his or her own estates through rents and indirect taxes, including excise duties and, importantly in history, customs duties were levied to support the state in its activities. However, taxes could be levied for exceptional purposes, particularly the conduct of wars. Income tax was originally introduced to pay for the Napoleonic Wars, abolished for a time, and then reintroduced as a relatively small source of general revenue during the 19th century (Sabine, 1980). In graduated form, it assumed great political significance with Lloyd George's 1909/10 radical reforming budget. In this budget for the first time taxation of the wealthy was overtly presented as part of a redistributive programme (Fraser, 1984). It also attempted to tax wealth primarily through taxation on inheritance. Alterations to the rules surrounding Inheritance Tax, especially since the 1980s, have reduced its impact and made its avoidance through estate planning relatively easy. While in 1974 it contributed 2.4% of all tax revenues (Boadway et al, 2011), it now contributes just 0.5%, as seen in Table 4.1.

Property taxes, including business rates, that is, taxes levied on 'real' property (property incorporating land) originate from the poor rates developed in England in the 16th century and codified in 1601 – the Old Poor Law. These property taxes funded poor-relief payments and were a response to social and economic change (Boyer, 1990). Those who benefitted from the change paid a tax to support those who lost out. Elements of the system included settlement, a procedure that linked entitlement to benefits to residence in a specific place. The system was designed to maintain social order and to prevent the kind of mobility of the poor that had been a key feature of *jacquerie* revolts in medieval France and of the peasant rebellions in 16th-century Germany (Wells, 1922). There was an element of communal and moral responsibility underlying the measures but social control was its main purpose (for example, Greif and Iyigun, 2013). The primary object of taxation was agricultural land and the tax was based on a calculation of the potential rental income that the real property (both land and improvements to land, including buildings) could secure in relation to the purpose for which it was used.

Developments in the late 18th century, when labour-hiring farmers dominated decision making about local poor-relief policy, are of particular significance in relation to the current debate. From 1795, the local system of poor relief in Speenhamland, Berkshire provided for a sliding scale of support to top up wages, assuring a minimum income in step with changing bread prices and weighted according to the number of the labourers' dependants. This was a response to high grain prices and the increasing seasonality of agrarian employment, as well as to the rural unrest that accompanied this (Polanyi, 2001). The Speenhamland system, as well as being a humanitarian response to rising unemployment and prices, represented an attempt to resolve the contradiction between the agricultural employers' need for a flexible labour force and their inability to pay sufficiently high wages to support the labourers' families. It also represented a partial transfer of the cost of agricultural wages onto the poor rate system – that is, effectively a subsidy to farmers and the socialisation of part of the costs agricultural production. Similar systems were introduced widely in agrarian areas and other approaches that tailored local poor relief to local labour systems were adopted elsewhere.

Polanyi (2001) noted that, at a particular moment of transition, taxes were used to achieve humanitarian, social control and economic purposes, and that farmers, as well as benefiting from this arrangement, also contributed to its costs. In Boyer's (1990) view, the Speenhamland iteration of the poor law reversed the Elizabethan enforcement of labour and instead provided an income to supplement a reduced labour input by the worker both in terms of hours and in terms of productivity. In this way, it can be seen as part of a process whereby the labourer was able to reduce the extent to which the farmer extracted surplus value from his labour, that is, it reduced expropriation. Significantly, the system supported families, both a necessary source of seasonal labour and the future labour force. In agrarian capitalism there were three classes: farmers as capitalists, labourers as rural proletarians and landowners as *rentiers*. The poor rate was a charge on the land and, as such, had an impact on rents. Both expropriating classes (farmers and landowners) were paying taxes to support proletarian incomes. So the taxes went some way to reducing expropriation of labour power in an era when trade union organisation was criminalised. Contemporary commentators, such as Prime Minister Canning, remarked that the existence of the Poor Law was an important factor in the absence of revolution in England and Wales, in contrast with France (Polanyi, 2001).

Much later, the extension of democracy and emergence of the Labour Party led to modifications and, ultimately, the introduction of a system of NI as part of the pre-First World War Liberal reforms. This was explicitly modelled on Bismarck's social insurance initiative in Germany and, like Bismarck's programme, addressed the political issues and tensions consequent on the development of an industrially and politically organised working class. Then, and until later in the 20th century, it was intended to be a state-administered system for pooling the risks of sickness and unemployment for workers. The original *medical* elements were about getting people who were sick back to work (and thus applied to the insured worker, and not his dependants) so that they would cease to draw benefits (Fraser, 1984). The system extended to cover different groups in different ways and also to cover old-age pensions. The NI system became very complex, but what matters here is that, unlike earlier systems of support, the benefits were in return for payments, and transfers were horizontal among waged workers.

So two components of the UK taxation system – the local rates and NI – have historically been directly associated with benefits, although there is now limited connection between insurance payments and the receipt of associated benefits, particularly for those of working age. Post-war, NI paid old-age pensions to all who had any sort of established pension rights. However, Beveridge, whose war-time report (Beveridge, 1942) substantially shaped the post-war welfare state, had argued that NI should accumulate a fund and not pay full pensions until full rights under the new scheme had been established. Systems of social assistance, beginning with national assistance, developed beyond Beveridge's original conception of their role as an ultimate safety net during the transition period after which insurance-based pensions would become general. Instead they became a permanent feature of the UK benefits system. Social assistance took on a major role in dealing with the inadequate level of basic insurance benefits and it was this that began the process of breaking the link between contributions and benefits. Thus, to some extent, NI has become a tax that is not perceived as a tax, although it imposes a considerable tax burden on average-income working households. (For example, for basic-rate income tax payers, NICs add an additional rate of tax of 12% on top of the 20% income tax, but for the more highly paid a lower additional rate.)

In the third quarter of the twentieth century, the elements of the post-war settlement (that is, a redistributive welfare state and full employment as an objective of macro-economic policy) led to the greatest degree of equality among households ever measured in the UK, with the Gini coefficient[1] (the most widely used summary measure of inequality based on levels of income) at its lowest point in 1978 – around 23 and down from about 26 in 1960 (Berruyer, 2010). Household incomes rose in the post-war period as a function of economic growth, the increasing workforce participation of married women and the strength of trade unions in the context of full employment and the absence of a significant levels of unemployment (just 2.6% in the early 1960s, for instance, in contrast to 10% for much of the 1980s – Nickell et al, 2005).

However, since the early 1970s we have seen a creeping re-emergence of the essence of Speenhamland, the use of tax revenues either to subsidize low wages directly or to achieve the same objective through exempting individuals from certain taxes or charges (for example, exemptions in relation to Council Tax and prescription charges). NI payments were transformed from being flat rate to earnings related, originally as the basis of earnings-related benefits but now essentially as a tax. NI generates £106 billion annually but only £80 billion is paid out as contributory-based benefits, by far the greatest part as old-age pensions.

From the late 1970s onwards, globalisation and increased productivity in manufacturing led to huge deindustrialisation in the UK economy, at an extreme level since the character of macro-economic policy (particularly in relation to exchange rates) and the absence of any coherent industrial policy exacerbated general trends across old industrial nations. The policy of both Conservative and New Labour administrations was premised upon a belief that the UK must become post-industrial and earn its global living through services, and in particular through financial services. Anti-trade union legislation introduced from 1980 onwards and retained by New Labour eroded the ability of organised labour in most sectors to resist expropriation through industrial action.

What taxes do

So, historically, we can see that taxes have served a number of class-related purposes. Today, taxation continues to facilitate capital accumulation but also, particularly within a welfare state, can reduce expropriation through capturing a share of the surplus value for expenditure on the social wage.

Taxation and capitalism

The capitalist system as a whole benefits from the uses to which tax revenues are put. O'Connor (1973) devised a typology of public spending. He identified state expenditure as being in large part about facilitating capital accumulation through either increasing the productivity of labour power (social investment) or reducing the reproduction costs of labour power to capital (social consumption). These two elements constitute social capital. The state also spends for purposes of social expenses – expenditure that does not facilitate the accumulation of capital in any direct way but operates to maintain the integrity of the capitalist system through purchasing surplus capitalist production and enhancing social harmony through legitimating the character of the system as a whole. This is a typology of purposes, not of expenditure headings, and any state programme may perform all of these functions. For example, healthcare expenditures maintain a healthy workforce (social investment), exempt employers from paying for healthcare as part of the remuneration of workers (social consumption), absorb elements produced by capital and make the system politically acceptable (social expenses).

Redistributive taxation as a basis for funding state expenditures forms part of any Keynesian-style programme of maintaining aggregate demand. The US tax theorist (and practitioner as a tax lawyer, and designer of federal tax systems as a New Dealer) Randolph Paul argued in *Taxation for Prosperity* (1947) that a well-planned tax system would avoid regressive taxes on ordinary consumption (such as US sales tax and UK VAT) and focus on a progressive income tax system since the transfer of income from the affluent to the poor would act as a mechanism against high levels of saving and 'absorb the excess that would otherwise wind up devoted to destabilizing speculation'. Redistribution funded by a steeply progressive tax system would maintain aggregate demand both through direct state expenditures and through transfer payments, given the much higher marginal propensity to consume of low-income individuals and households. Redistributive taxation funded the Keynesian mode of accumulation and the relative social stability and equality of that unique period in the history of capitalism.

We have long left that era behind. Nonetheless, vast amounts of public spending are now devoted to advancing the interests of business, although the failure to maintain aggregate demand is dysfunctional for much of business. Taxation is still being used to top up wages and to provide in-work benefits as a subsidy to employers who pay workers too little to survive. Working Tax Credits and Child Tax Credits, benefits paid to waged workers, cost around £29 billion in 2011/12 (HMRC, 2012). This is a direct subsidy to employers of low-paid labour, frequently part-time labour, and to it we have to add the costs of Council Tax and rent discounts received by those in work. These payments are a contemporary equivalent of Speenhamland, facilitating the social reproduction of the low-paid labour force of flexible capitalism. The key difference is that, while the farmers under Speenhamland *contributed* to the cost of in-work benefits as well as benefiting from them, the ability today of corporations and the very affluent to avoid taxation, such that they pay a proportionate, but scarcely more than that, share of the tax burden (see Table 4.2), means that these benefits are now, to a considerable extent, paid for by the rest of us.

Farnsworth (2012) points out that subsidising low wages is only one of numerous ways in which businesses receive benefits and services from the state as a result of tax-funded public expenditure. In myriad ways, for instance through grants and subsidies, through cheap or underwritten loans, investment through the purchasing of shares, through fiscal welfare benefits, through marketing, advice and advocacy services, through businesses' use of physical infrastructure, through socialised services that reduce the cost of labour to employers, as well as through in-work benefits that reduce labour costs to the individual employer, the state provides welfare benefits and services, paid for by taxation, to business. Farnsworth estimates that hundreds of billions of pounds are given to businesses annually through these channels. These subsidies, grants and benefits enhance the profitability of companies by reducing the wage bill, sharing the cost of investment and mitigating risk.

Taxation and expropriation

Taxation can more directly benefit workers by reducing expropriation. Expropriation is delimited by the proportion of gross national income that is expended on workers either individually or collectively, since obtaining a share of the national income is a measure of the extent to which employers are forced to share the value created by workers. At the individual end of the spectrum a worker receives a wage and can invoke individual rights that are commonly shared (such as rights to the minimum wage and holiday time, and to equal treatment with respect to gender, ethnicity, sexual orientation, religion, disability). Collectively, shared terms and conditions of work, including health and safety provision, also serve to limit expropriation. At the most collective end of the spectrum are shared goods and services provided through government departments and local authorities and funded by taxation – such as street lighting, emergency services, defence, education, social security entitlement. These are enjoyed by all, though some are subject to rules of eligibility. This latter is called the social wage, defined by Bryson

(1992, p 32) as the 'sum of collective benefits which are transferred to individuals or families in both cash and kind via the state'.

Expropriation can be resisted or reduced by any means which force employers to share their profits or, more precisely, by means which reduce the amount of surplus value. This can be achieved through the legal and regulatory framework within which businesses operate, governing legal rights such as equality provisions, health and safety and the minimum wage as well as the fiduciary duties of corporations. Expropriation can be reduced during the productive process through worker control or influence over the labour process to hold down intensification of work and to maintain the number of people required to do the job, influence over recruitment to maintain wages, representation on boards, consultation and negotiation, and industrial action to maintain and enhance terms and conditions; and through the use of the privileges vested in professionalism. These are all facilitated by a strong trade union presence. So the rights to organise collectively and to recognition are important in checking expropriation. More widely, the social and cultural expectations of employers can help to resist expropriation where minimum levels of treatment of workers are expected (for example, that lunch breaks are paid; that contracts have specific hours; that wages go up, the longer someone works for a company). Action against companies that are perceived to have breached these expectations – such as lobbying for parliamentary inquiries into the conduct of firms or forms of direct action designed to inflict reputational damage on a firm, thereby harming its market position – can also reduce the effective level of expropriation. All of this can be understood as forms of countervailing power.

The worsening position of labour and the redesign of the tax system since the late 1970s

The situation at present is that most of these means by which expropriation can be resisted are weak: trade unions have a weak legal position and have been reluctant to challenge this; participation in trade unions has declined in its perceived usefulness and desirability. Cultural expectations of employers are relatively weak, with casual work and zero-hour contracts widespread and accepted (CIPD, 2013). Successive governments have pursued deregulatory policies and these have typically reduced protections for workers.

Unsurprisingly, wages have suffered. Reed and Himmelweit (2013) report that between 1977 and 2008 the wage share fell from 59% of national income to 53%, while the share of profits in national income rose from 25% to 29%. According to Reed and Himmelweit, the whole upward trend in the profit share of national income can be attributed to the growth in the financial sector, which accounted for 1% of all profits in the 1950s and 1960s and 15% by 2008–10. Importantly, income from investments is very unequally distributed in comparison with income from wages. If wages had grown at the same pace as the national economy between 1980 and 2010, median annual earnings for full-time workers would today be £7,000 higher. The decline in wages arises to a significant extent from the decline in sectors that paid higher wages and from a growth in sectors that tend to pay lower wages (Reed and Himmelweit, 2013), a shift which, broadly speaking, mirrored a decline in more strongly unionised sectors and growth in weakly unionised sectors.

The *alternative* to persuading employers to share the value created by workers directly with them through better wages, terms and conditions is to enable (or force) them to share it more indirectly through the social wage – that is, through the provision of shared services funded through a tax system that recoups a significant portion of the income and wealth secured by businesses and those who benefit from the weakened position of labour and the financialisation of the economy.

However, a number of measures since the late 1970s have (with the exception of the poorest 10% of households) narrowed the differences between the deciles in the total rate of tax they pay and shifted the distribution of tax liability (see Figure 4.1, based on ONS, 2013. Note that undeclared income lies outside this representation of tax liability.) We mention just a few of these measures here. Cuts were made in the top rate of income tax on earned income so that between 1988 and 2010 the top rate of tax was just 40% (down from 83% in 1979), and even now the top rate is just 45% on income above £150,000. The overall effect has been to reduce the progressive potential of income tax. Second, tax thresholds have been lowered in real terms so that those on lower relative incomes are drawn into higher rates of tax. Indirect taxes have been increased and extended significantly (for example, with VAT rising from 15% in the 1980s to 17.5% in 1991 and 20% in 2011) and these have a dramatic and disproportionately heavy impact on those on lower incomes. Corporation Tax has dropped from 52% in 1979 to a main rate of 21% in 2014. Capital Gains Tax (CGT) was harmonised with income tax under Nigel Lawson as Chancellor of the Exchequer in the 1980s to remove from higher earners the temptation to reclassify income as capital gains. However, following New Labour reforms, CGT stands at 28% in 2013/14 for higher-income individuals, in contrast with higher rates of income tax of 40% and 45% (HMRC, 2013a; IFS, 2013).

Our system of taxation is not simply about rates and thresholds. It is also about tax breaks, legal loopholes, the interpretation of legislation and the strength of enforcement. Despite the enormous benefits enjoyed by businesses through public spending in their interest, the avoidance and even evasion of tax obligations by large, usually transnational corporations has become a prominent feature of the tax landscape. The 'tax gap' for 2011/12 (that is, the difference between theoretical tax liabilities and what is actually paid) amounted to £35 billion, or 7% of tax revenue, according to Her Majesty's Revenue and Customs (HMRC, 2013b), but around £100 billion for avoidance and evasion alone (dwarfing annual benefit fraud at £1.2bn), according to tax expert Richard Murphy (Unite, 2013). The difference between these two figures arises largely from different methodologies, including different interpretations of what Parliament intended (for example see Murphy's (2010) detailed analysis). The tax gap consists of non-payment of tax due, errors by HMRC, avoidance that is technically legal but is not what Parliament intended and illegal evasion.

Tax evasion can occur through: reallocating income to another person (or company) with a lower tax liability; reclassifying transactions (for example counting income as capital gains); altering where a transaction or activity occurs; delaying the recognition of an income so as to defer a tax liability; and obscuring information about a transaction so that what is happening cannot be identified (Unite, 2013). Occasionally, the tax-avoiding activities of affluent individuals find their way into the mainstream press, as in the case in 2012 of comedian Jimmy Carr, who used a Jersey-based scheme avoiding a higher income tax liability. The tax arrangements of Sir Philip Green in recent years demonstrate the close connection between corporate tax avoidance (legal, according to the letter of the law) and the accrual of benefits by wealthy individuals (for example Matthiason, 2005). The reports of the House of Commons Public Accounts Committee (for example PAC, 2013), chaired by Margaret Hodge, MP, have provided a legitimacy to wider criticism. There are two aspects of this that are relevant here. The first is the scale of avoidance and its routine character and the second is the complicity of the state in the avoidance. Reportedly, as a result of company structures and practices, Amazon had UK sales of £3.35bn in 2011 but paid only £1.8m in tax, while Starbucks made £400m of sales in the UK in 2011 but paid no corporation tax at all (Barford and Holt, 2013). The *Telegraph* reported in 2011 that Google funnelled £6bn or 80% of its global revenues through Bermuda, reducing its overall tax burden by £1bn and its tax contribution in the UK to £6m (Warman, 2013).These activities appear to fall outside the HMRC's estimate of avoidance and have become normalised as standard corporate practices.

In each instance, corporations defend their practices in terms of their legality – that is, they comply with the tax laws.Thus, a situation in which some of the largest revenue raisers pay little or no tax arises not just from the practices of companies but also from the actions and inactions of the state or supra-national rule-making bodies. Reduced levels of staffing in HMRC (HM Treasury, 2010) and the closure of tax offices, the practice of seconding individuals to the Treasury to advise on tax law from the four big accounting firms that design many of the tax avoidance vehicles, and a failure to modify tax rules to reflect the way corporations now operate globally and through the internet all contribute to complicity in undermining the tax contribution of corporations that have benefitted the most from globalisation (PAC, 2013).

The Gini coefficient has risen to 34 (OECD, 2013) and, between 1983 and 2005, redistribution in the UK *both through taxation and through cash transfers* declined, and the UK reduced its redistributive effort by more than all 19 other countries examined in a study by Caminada et al (2012).The reduction in overall tax rates between 1978 and 2011/12 has itself reduced the redistributive impact of the tax system (Caminada et al, 2012).The 27% share of national income held by the top decile in 2011/12 (Table 4.2) is up from 21% in 1978, with the middle deciles having noticeably lost out. Inequality, driven by the rising incomes of those in the top decile, is in part the outcome of the unequal strength of different groups to secure control over resources.

As the UK's place in the global economy is refashioned, expropriation is being increased not only through the lowering of wages measured as a share of national income (the 'wages squeeze') but also through the reduction in the contribution of employers to the social wage enjoyed by all, including workers.The former has been achieved largely through financialisation, economic restructuring and the weakening of trade unions; and the latter has been achieved through a restructuring of the tax system and through the growing sophistication of the very affluent and large corporations in legal tax avoidance and illegal evasion.

Proposals for a more progressive personal tax system

There are a number of ways in which the tax system can be modified to ensure that those who have benefitted most from the restructuring of production and distribution on a global basis and from the increasing financialisation of the economy pay a greater contribution in taxes. The proposals that follow give just an indicator of these and are far from comprehensive; they derive from existing work (for example Murphy, 2008; Irvin et al, 2009; Murphy and Reed, 2013; Unite, 2013). The first entails the introduction of a 40% minimum rate of income tax for those earning £100,000 and of 50% for those earning £150,000, by clawing back allowances and providing measures to tackle tax avoidance. Reducing the rate of VAT and exempting a wider range of essential items would benefit substantially those on lower incomes. NICs could be uncapped (that is, retain the initial allowance but then pay 12% throughout the income scale (rather than reducing NI payments to 2% of any income above the upper earnings limit). The levying of a surcharge on unearned income, that is investment income, would rectify a current anomaly whereby NICs are payable on the basis of income derived from the expenditure of effort, while income gained through no such effort attracts no such surcharge. This currently creates an incentive to translate earned income into unearned income. More radically, merging income tax and NICs would create one tax on income that could be reset as a progressive tax. This would simplify the tax system and remove inequitable anomalies, especially for those on more than one income. Provisions could be designed to protect pensioners on modest incomes, the registered disabled and those in receipt of associated benefits. Some avoidance could be addressed by making pension contributions free of only the basic rate of income tax, not of any higher rate levied.

These measures together would make direct taxation significantly more progressive and thus better able to counter the regressive effect of indirect taxes. They would also have a modest but discernible impact on the Gini coefficient of income inequality. However, they would have limited effectiveness in securing greater contributions from the rich without tackling avoidance or 'planning', that is, lawful ways of reducing tax liabilities. Capital gains could be taxed as income (after an allowance). This would reduce the incentive to recategorise income as capital gains, since CGT rates are substantially lower than the rate of income tax paid by the vast majority of those who benefit from this arrangement. A parallel reform would ensure that all gains arising from asset disposals when those assets have been held for less than a year would be subject to income tax. Similarly, dividend payments could be taxed as income, which would reduce incentives to pay individuals in dividends rather than salaries (which achieves avoidance of both income tax and NICs). A number of tax reliefs for investment, such as investment in Venture

Capital Trusts and the Enterprise Investment Scheme have also been used to avoid paying tax, despite the lack of evidence for the effectiveness of these schemes as a source of funds for innovative and entrepreneurial activity. Finally, a general anti-avoidance principle (rather than general anti-abuse rule) for more complex avoidance would transfer the burden to demonstrate that tax is not liable to the relevant individual (or corporation) by ignoring any step added into an otherwise commercial arrangement for the sole purpose of securing a reduction in tax liability.

Tax evasion could be tackled through greater international cooperation, collecting more relevant information and providing sufficient resources for effective enforcement. Important tax rules are set by the OECD and these shape, for instance, some of the practices of Google, Amazon and Starbucks. A requirement of multinational corporations to report economic transactions on a country-by-country basis would mean they must disclose where their sales (and purchases) are made to both third parties and other companies within the group, how many people they employ, what their profits are and how much tax they have paid. A comparison could then be made as to whether the location of profits matches the patterns of sales and location of staff and assets, with any mismatch subject to an investigation. Finally, cuts in HMRC staffing from 104,000 in 2005 to 71,000 in 2013 would need to be reversed, more specialists (for instance, in transfer pricing through which companies transfer money into other tax jurisdictions) would add to effectiveness and the retention and re-establishment of local offices would enable local economic activity (including the shadow economy) to be better monitored.

Conclusion

The position of labour has deteriorated through a combination of its weakened position in the workplace and the restructuring of a tax system so that it is less progressive and more proportional, as well as failing to capture around 20% of potential tax revenues. Labour's position is further threatened by constrained access to pensions, benefits and services through more stringent rules governing eligibility, rising or extended charges and the diversion of public funding into the costs associated with markets and privatisation. As we have shown in earlier work (Byrne and Ruane, 2008), because of our relatively flat tax system, not only gross but also net household incomes for the top decile move very steeply away from the deciles below them. Thus, it is the most affluent who have benefitted from recent social transformation, with the top

10% now accounting for an enormous share of national income (over 27%). Higher taxes on those who have most benefitted from economic restructuring in recent decades would ensure that they contributed more to corporate welfare, curtail the scope for dangerous speculation and reduce the expropriation of workers' labour power. While the bottom 20% of households bear a very heavy burden from indirect taxes, it is worth noting that the middle deciles have lost out to the top 10% not only through their smaller share of national income but also since they pay almost the same rate of total tax or even a higher one.

An informed debate about the distribution of the tax 'burden', as well as scrutinising tax avoidance and evasion, needs to shift the focus from individuals to households and from income tax to total tax rates, giving the inequitable distribution of indirect taxes proper prominence. In an era when adequate household incomes are so often dependent on the presence of two workers (or two pensions), and the loss of employment or a significant reduction in hours/pay for one can have a catastrophic impact, many 'middle' households are vulnerable. Many middle households rely on one or more public sector employment incomes and, although these households may be relatively modest recipients of cash benefits (they pay for the benefits of others and, particularly, for pensions and supplements to low wages), they do consume benefits in kind, and in particular education, for which, at the tertiary level, future prospective middle-income individuals have to incur debt to fund (other than in Scotland). A politics of tax and spending that was organised around no greater taxes for this group but much more public expenditure on services (and appropriate infrastructure) could be electorally attractive (see Irvin et al, 2009). Whether there is a political party that would be willing to engage in such a politics is another matter.

Note

[1] The Gini coefficient measures the degree of inequality in any distribution and is generally used in relation to inequalities in income or wealth. If there were perfect equality across all cases it would have a value of zero. If one case held all the income it would have a value of 1.0. Here, these values are converted to whole numbers on a 100-point scale.

References

Barford, V. and Holt, G. (2013) 'Google, Amazon, Starbucks: The rise of "tax shaming"', BBC News, 21 May.

Berruyer, O. (2010) *Evolution of the Gini coefficient for the United Kingdom 1960–2009*, Progress or Collapse, www.progressorcollapse.com/the-rise-of-income-inequality-during-thatcher-neoliberal-policies-in-britain/gini-index-uk/.

Beveridge, W. (1942) *Social insurance and allied services*, Cmd 6404, London: HMSO.

Boadway, R., Chamberlain, E. and Emmerson, C. (2011) *Taxation of wealth and wealth transfers: Appendix to the Mirrlees Report on reforming the tax system for the 21st century*, London: Institute for Fiscal Studies.

Boyer, G. (1990) *An economic history of the English Poor Law, 1750–1850*, Cambridge: Cambridge University Press.

Browne, J. and Roantree, B. (2012) *A survey of the UK tax system*, Briefing Note BN09, London: Institute for Fiscal Studies.

Bryson, L. (1992) *Welfare and the State*, London: MacMillan

Byrne, D. and Ruane, S. (2008) *The UK tax burden: Can Labour be called the 'party of fairness'?*, Thinkpiece No 40, London: Compass.

Caminada, K., Goudswaard, K. and Wang, C. (2012) *Disentangling income inequality and the redistributive effect of taxes and transfers in 20 LIS countries over time*, Munich Personal RePEc Archive Paper No 42350, November.

CIPD (2013) *Labour market outlook, summer*, London: Chartered Institute of Personnel and Development.

Farnsworth, K. (2012) *Social versus corporate welfare: Competing needs and interests within the welfare state*, London: Palgrave.

Fraser, D. (1984) *The evolution of the British welfare state*, Basingstoke: Macmillan.

Greif, A. and Iyigun, M. (2013) *What did the Old Poor Law really accomplish?*, Online only Discussion Paper No. 7398, Institute for the Study of Labour, Bonn, Germany.

HMRC (2012) *HMRC annual report and accounts 2011–12*, London: HMRC, www.hmrc.gov.uk/about/annual-report-accounts-1112.pdf.

HMRC (2013a) *Taxes, national insurance and stamp taxes*, London: HMRC, www.hmrc.gov.uk/rates/cgt.htm.

HMRC (2013b) *Measuring tax gaps – 2013 edition*, London: HMRC.

HM Treasury (2010) *Spending review 2010*, London: HM Treasury.

IFS (2013) *Summary of the main tax measures in each budget since 1979*, London: Institute for Fiscal Studies, www.ifs.org.uk/fiscalFacts.

Irvin, G., Byrne, D., Murphy, R., Reed, H. and Ruane, S. (2009) *In place of cuts*, London: Compass.

Matthiason, N. (2005) 'Where the rich stash their cash', *Observer*, 27 March.

Murphy, R. (2008) *The missing billions: The UK tax gap*, Touchstone Pamphlet, London: TUC.

Murphy, R. (2010) *Why HM Revenue and Customs have got the tax gap wrong*, Tax Research UK, www.taxresearch.org.uk/Documents/TaxGapResponse.pdf.

Murphy, R. and Reed, H. (2013) *Financing the social state: Towards a full employment economy*, London: Centre for Labour and Social Studies.

Nickell, S., Nunziata, L. and Ochel, W. (2005) 'Unemployment in the OECD since the 1960s. What do we know?' *The Economic Journal*, 115 (January): 1–27.

O'Connor, J. (1973) *The fiscal crisis of the state*, London: St James Press.

OECD (2013) *Statistical database: Income distribution and poverty by country*, Organisation of Economic Cooperation and Development, http://stats.oecd.org/index.aspx?queryid=46022#.

ONS (2013) *The effects of taxes and benefits on household income 1978 and 1911–12, Table 14*, London: Office for National Statistics.

PAC (2013) *Tax avoidance: the role of large accountancy firms*, Public Accounts Committee: Forty-Fourth Report, London: House of Commons, 15 April.

Paul, R. (1947) *Taxation for prosperity*, New York: Bobbs Merrill.

Polanyi, K. (2001) *The great transformation: The political and economic origins of our time*, Boston, MA: Beacon Press.

Reed, H. and Himmelweit, J. (2013) *Where have all the wages gone? Lost pay and profits outside the financial sector*, Touchstones Pamphlet, London: TUC.

Sabine, B. (1980) *A short history of taxation*, London: Butterworths.

Unite (2013) *Submission to the Labour Party policy review*, London: Unite.

Warman, M. (2013) 'Google's £6billion Bermuda tax shelter', *Telegraph*, 2 January.

Wells, H.G. (1922) *A short history of the world*, London: Cassell and Company.

FIVE

Occupational and fiscal welfare in times of crisis

Bent Greve

Introduction

In the period following the 'golden age' of welfare states, discussion turned towards the crisis of the welfare state, both in the academic literature (O'Connor, 1973; Crozier et al, 1975) and beyond, most notably in the Organisation for Economic Co-operation and Development's (OECD) *The Welfare State in Crisis* (OECD, 1981). Later on, several contributions such as Mishra (1984), Offe (1984) and Klein (1993) discussed the ongoing crisis of the 1980s from different perspectives. The issue of crisis largely disappeared from the literature (at least in a general sense) between 2000 and 2008. In the wake of the financial crisis of 2008 several books and many articles have dealt with the topic of the crisis (Farnsworth and Irving, 2011; Richardson, 2011; Greve, 2012). It has even been labelled a double crisis, in the sense that the pressures from immediate cuts – especially on the most vulnerable and dependent – and longer-term pressures on health and social care, linked to demographic pressures and rising healthcare costs, combine to create greater challenges for welfare states (Taylor-Gooby, 2013). Further, the ongoing reductions in welfare expenditure may, as has been argued, have a negative impact on health in Europe as there is a relation between welfare spending and health (Karanikolos et al, 2013). Crisis or not, there is also evidence of remarkable stability in social policy over the long run (Pierson, 2011) and even, perhaps, an increase in services, such as care for children.

Besides direct retrenchment and gradual changes in welfare spending, although these have varied among different welfare states (Table 5.2), there have been debates in many countries on the 'Big Society' and the use of voluntary work as a way of responding to the demand for more welfare. Developments in the Big Society, albeit direct or indirect cuts in spending do have an influence on civil society and voluntary work, are outside the scope of this chapter (cf. for the UK, Ishkanian and Szreter, 2012). At the same time there has been less focus on what has been labelled the more hidden part of the welfare state (Howard, 1997; Greve, 1994), for example the fiscal and occupational side of welfare delivery in Titmuss's understanding of the social division of welfare (Titmuss, 1987).

This chapter probes into changes in the more hidden area of the welfare state during the recent crisis period and how they can be described and measured, given the gaps in official data and the familiar problems of comparing data across states in the absence of coherent and systematic national reporting (European Commission, 2013). The chapter first develops a greater understanding of fiscal and occupational welfare, before debating changes in spending on welfare in recent years. Other ways in which private sector companies are dependent on public sector spending are not covered (see instead the work on corporate welfare by Farnsworth, 2013a).

What is fiscal and occupational welfare?

The concepts of 'fiscal welfare' and 'occupational welfare' were popularised in 1955 by Richard Titmuss, whose work identified the three different routes to welfare: public, fiscal and occupational. Public welfare is direct public sector spending on welfare, and the area of welfare states that is most frequently analysed. The three routes were also labelled as the social divisions of welfare, and Titmuss argued that fiscal welfare 'deserves as much analysis as public spending on social services' (Sinfield, 2013, p 20). This is due to the fact that the main difference between the two is that public welfare is paid directly as a cash transaction or delivered directly through welfare services paid for by the state, whereas fiscal welfare is indirect, via a reduction in public sector income by means of a tax rebate. However, the impact can vary and the size of tax expenditures depends on empirical analysis. The empirical analysis that follows will try to encapsulate the size of fiscal welfare and, thereby, the often more hidden part of the welfare state.

Fiscal welfare is often labelled as tax expenditure. The classical way of depicting and calculating the content and size of fiscal welfare is deviations from the normal tax system. Tax expenditure on welfare can take a number of forms, including allowances, exemptions, deferrals, tax credits and rate reductions. They can be in all or part of the system, can be more or less transparent and can be utilised to increase savings, to create work incentives and incentives for employers to take on additional workers (via wage subsidies) and to increase investments. There is a lack of general agreement on how precisely to calculate the size of tax expenditures, because both the benchmark tax structure and how to account for possible changes in behaviour if a change in tax system takes place are not clear. This may also help to explain the difficulty in getting comparable international data.

What we do know is that tax expenditures reduce public sector income and they have an upside-down effect, given that those people with the highest incomes can use fiscal welfare to a greater degree than others. Thus, fiscal welfare has a negative impact on the distribution of welfare because high-income earners benefit more from fiscal and occupational welfare than do low-income earners (Sinfield, 2013). Arguments for using fiscal welfare have often revolved around giving incentives for individuals or groups of people to behave in a specific manner, including to increase saving for pension purposes, investment and job creation.

The net effect of fiscal welfare is a reduction in tax revenues. A further problem is that it is often hidden, it increases the complexity of the tax system and is likely to be difficult to control. It may even lead to higher than expected spending in that individuals may adjust their behaviour so that they become eligible for tax benefits (Burman and Phaup, 2011). The existence of tax expenditure therefore also reduces the transparency and efficiency of the tax system; the EU even calls it a 'substantial challenge with efficiency in the tax-benefit system (e.g. a large amount of tax-expenditure)' (European Commission, 2012, p 12), and an EU directive (2011/85/EU) now ensures that from 2014 all EU member states will publish relevant information.

Titmuss's conceptualisation of occupational welfare included 'pensions for employees, wives and dependants; child allowances; death benefits; health and welfare services; personal expenses for travel, entertainment, residential accommodation; children's school fees; cheap meals, unemployment benefits; medical bills and an incalculable variety of benefits in kind' (Titmuss, 1987). Although this description of occupational welfare is not very precise it gives an indication of the content, but without being very clear as to whether it is a supplement or a substitute for public welfare (Greve, 2007). The boundaries and varieties are great, ranging from pensions to minor fringe benefits such as company clothing and cheaper company goods. Important examples of occupational welfare include pensions and sickness benefits. For a list and the variety, also indicating that some will be taxed, some not, see Kirk (2008), who also gives an overview of the social division of welfare. That such a wide range of possibilities is involved, ranging from benefits that are taxable (and for which, in principle, data should be available) to benefits that figure only as part of a company's balance sheet, indicates the difficulty in getting good data; or, more precisely, that 'occupational welfare tends to be treated as "non-wage labour costs" by employers and this is not disaggregated in a manner that enables researchers to find out precisely who gets what' (Kirk, 2008, p 13). At the same time, occupational welfare can be linked to fiscal welfare in the sense that the use of occupational welfare may be encouraged as a means to reduce the tax bill either of the company or of the individual taxpayer. Such problems with the 'relatively sketchy' (Farnsworth, 2013 p 35) inevitably get in the way of comparative analysis, although it is possible to draw general conclusions from the data that is available, as it 'sheds some useful light onto the key forms of occupational welfare' (Farnsworth, 2013, p 35).

Fiscal welfare used to achieve a direct purpose can be beneficial for society if, after successful intervention, it results in a return of income. However, it has been argued that 'the tax system was not conceived to support innovation systems, which are disproportionately driven by actors who are willing to invest decades before returns appear on the horizon' (Mazzucato, 2013, p 187). Mazzucato also points to tax avoidance and tax evasion as problems connected to the argument in favour of the benefits of tax expenditure for investment purposes. Besides the possible direct impact, there may also be an indirect negative impact on distribution, as mentioned above.

Occupational welfare is driven by different factors. These range from employers' expectations that occupational provision will increase workers' productivity, to government's hopes that it will reduce the pressure on state welfare. And employees may have an interest in these goods if they can switch from taxable income to tax-exempt benefits. This is on the assumption that occupational welfare has the same value to the individual as what can be purchased with taxed income.

The development of pension systems in many countries is based upon defined contributions rather than on defined benefits. This increases the importance of regular employee contributions, decreases the costs for employers and increases the risks to employees, since the value of pensions is highly dependent on the performance of stock markets. Viewed from this perspective, the development of the pension system implies a reduced pressure on the welfare state, while at the same time increasing the risk of a higher level of inequality. Government policies to make work pay by using a variety of incentives within the tax system can also be argued to be a form of fiscal welfare, as they can be used to ensure higher disposable incomes for those in work, thereby reducing their risk of poverty – while at the same time increasing inequality with those outside the labour market. Occupational and fiscal welfare are thus, either alone or in combination, another part of the welfare state that is often delivered and financed by an alternative means, and also for rationales that differ from those of the traditional welfare state. At the same time, not all tax expenditure may be directly related to welfare provision, as it can have many and varied purposes, ranging from work incentives, health, housing and pensions to research and development and business incentives (OECD, 2010). Finally, the distributional impact of fiscal and occupational welfare tends to increase inequality in access to welfare.

What do we know?

Given its often hidden and indirect character, our information about fiscal and occupational welfare is often limited. Adding up the different forms of fiscal and occupational welfare is therefore problematic, especially when it comes to comparative analysis. This limits our ability to estimate the total size and distributional impact of their use. However, some data is available and it does provide some information. For example, there seems to be a growing use of tax expenditure (OECD, 2010), especially in liberal welfare countries like the US (where tax expenditures were estimated to be worth 5.97 % of GDP in 2008) and the UK (where they were worth 12.79 % of GDP) (OECD, 2010, p 224). However, a problem for comparative welfare state analysis is that it is not always clear from the data which aspects of tax expenditures relate specifically to the social policy area. Furthermore, tax expenditures often include tax breaks for social purposes, where any reduction may be temporary and/or deferred; for example, tax rebates for pension contributions may be fully or partly paid when the pension is eventually paid out. However, this is not necessarily very comprehensive and still seems to indicate an upside-down impact, and thereby increasing inequality (Sinfield, 2013). The development of greater fiscal and occupational welfare is not new and seems to be part of a long-term development, with more individual and market responsibility (although see also the Conclusions to this chapter), especially through the growth in private pensions (Taylor-Gooby, 2001). However, recent years have seen some reduction in the use of tax expenditure in many countries as part of attempts to broaden the tax base (European Commission, 2013).

Occupational welfare is broadly understood as welfare provided by employers to employees. However, this does not make its cost very clear, nor how it can be more precisely defined (Farnsworth, 2013). Here the main point is to try to look into those benefits that employees receive that have an affinity to the welfare that could have been provided by the state. Whether these are supplementary to (or top up) state benefits or a substitute for state welfare is not central to the argument and to understanding of the concept and development. Thus, receiving a normal wage during sickness instead of a state sickness benefit could be considered as a form of occupational welfare that often goes unrecorded. Still, it might be that collective agreements, and thereby, in principle, fiscal as well as occupational welfare, 'have a role in compensating the declining welfare state' (Järvi and Kuivalainen, 2012, p 22).

Again, this points to the hidden elements related to welfare and welfare state developments. It is not easy to get a clear and comprehensive picture, although the OECD has attempted this in its publication of tax expenditures (OECD, 2010), having data up to 2009 and estimates for the US to 2014, alongside estimates of net social expenditures[1] (Adema and Ladaique, 2009). These analyses also show that the differences among countries in the overall level of spending on social welfare are much less dramatic than is often assumed.

Table 5.1 shows public expenditure on social welfare for a selected number of countries in the EU. Countries have been chosen to represent the various welfare models, the north, south, east and west of Europe and countries with different positions in the wake of the financial crisis.

Since 2000, in all countries with the exception of Germany, there has been an increase in spending measured as a percentage of GDP, so that, when it is understood in this way, it is difficult to argue that there has been a strong crisis of the welfare state. One could argue that this development implies a large reduction in spending on welfare as a consequence of falling GDP. Table 5.2 tries to shed some light onto this by measuring real growth in expenditure on social welfare since 2000.

Table 5.1: Percentage of GDP spent on social expenditure in selected EU-countries since 2000

	2000	2005	2009	2010	2011	2012	2013
Czech Republic	19.1	18.7	20.7	20.8	20.8	21.0	21.8
Denmark	26.4	27.7	30.2	30.6	30.6	30.8	30.8
France	28.6	30.1	32.1	32.4	32.0	32.5	33.0
Germany	26.6	27.3	27.8	27.1	25.9	25.9	26.2
Greece	19.3	21.1	23.9	23.3	24.4	24.1	22.0
Italy	23.1	24.9	27.8	27.7	27.5	28.0	28.4
Norway	21.3	21.6	23.3	23.0	22.4	22.3	22.9
Spain	20.2	21.1	26.0	26.7	26.4	26.8	27.4
Sweden	28.4	29.1	29.8	28.3	27.6	28.1	28.6
United Kingdom	18.6	20.5	24.1	23.8	23.6	23.9	23.8
United States	14.5	16.0	19.2	19.8	19.6	19.7	20.0
OECD – total	18.9	19.7	22.1	22.1	21.7	21.8	21.9

Note: Data extracted on 3 October 2013 13:10 UTC (GMT) from OECD.Stat. Note that the data from 2010 to 2013 is OECD projections.

Source: OECD, SOCX.

Table 5.2: Development in spending on social policy (year 2000 prices = 100)

	2000	2005	2009	2010	2011	2012	2013	Change in spending 2009–2013 (%)
Czech Republic	100.0	119.6	147.2	152.1	154.6	154.4	158.5	11.3
Denmark	100.0	111.7	119.5	122.7	123.9	124.1	124.6	5.1
France	100.0	114.0	123.3	126.5	127.1	129.1	130.8	7.5
Germany	100.0	105.7	110.6	111.9	110.1	110.9	112.7	2.1
Greece	100.0	133.3	158.5	149.3	145.1	134.2	116.5	-42.0
Italy	100.0	113.2	122.7	124.6	124.1	123.5	123.1	0.4
Norway	100.0	113.1	126.2	125.3	123.4	126.8	132.0	5.8
Spain	100.0	122.6	158.1	162.1	161.1	161.1	162.1	4.1
Sweden	100.0	117.0	121.9	122.9	124.1	128.2	132.3	10.4
United Kingdom	100.0	126.8	149.5	150.5	150.2	152.7	153.3	3.8
United States	100.0	124.6	152.8	160.1	160.6	165.1	171.3	18.5

Source: Author's own calculations based on OECD data on spending on social welfare and growth in GDP in fixed prices.

Table 5.2 shows that in all countries over a 13-year period there has been a real-terms increase in spending on welfare, although it has been highest in the classical liberal welfare economies such as the US and the UK, and has also been high in Spain and the Czech Republic. This indicates that the trend has been one of convergence, or of movement by low-spending countries towards the level of high-spending countries, rather than of retrenchment. Since 2009, the data seems to indicate that, with the exception of Greece, which shows a dramatic cut, there has been more money available for public welfare than before the crisis began. The data stands in contradiction with the arguments of severe cuts in most European states, including the UK (Taylor-Gooby, 2013).

Naturally, the amount of money available to deliver the same level of services is blurred by the fact that there has also been an increase in the numbers of unemployed and people dependent on public welfare. In some countries there has been pressure on public sector spending due to demographic transitions, which implies that a real growth in public sector spending can be compatible with a reduction in benefits or coverage, given changes in the level and composition of the population in need of support from the welfare state. Thus, there might be and have been cuts in public sector spending. These might have been even larger if there had been no economic growth at all. If the numbers of people in need of welfare transfers or services had remained the same, then it would have been possible to provide better and more welfare. This implies also that welfare states' difficulties may in part be due to the need to cover more areas and to the fact that expectations are constantly increasing as we adapt to what we have (Greve, 2012a). Given that the welfare state is seemingly no longer able to provide both for new and for existing welfare benefits and services, the pressures on and for even more occupational and fiscal welfare are higher: pressure on occupational welfare from employees as this can be financed by the market itself, and fiscal welfare due to its more hidden nature.

Table 5.3 shows private social spending, which can be seen as equivalent to at least partial occupational welfare (Farnsworth, 2013), and indicates its importance and development until 2009.

Table 5.3 confirms a picture of more hidden welfare in liberal welfare states such as the US and the UK, in particular. Over time there has been a general, albeit slight, increase in the use of occupational welfare, with some differences among countries. Unfortunately the data does not enable discussion about changes in the wake of the financial crisis. However, it does show that the changes are of a considerable size in the

UK and US and, perhaps surprisingly, also in France and the universal welfare states of Denmark and Sweden.

Table 5.3: Private voluntary social spending as a percentage of GDP

	2002	2003	2004	2005	2006	2007	2008	2009
Czech Republic	0.1	0.1	0.1	0.1	0.1	0.1	0.1	0.2
Denmark	2.2	2.3	2.4	2.4	2.3	2.3	2.5	2.7
France	2.5	2.5	2.5	2.7	2.6	2.6	2.6	2.8
Germany	1.7	1.8	1.8	1.9	1.8	1.8	1.8	2.0
Greece	2.1	1.9	1.8	1.7	1.6	1.5	1.7	1.8
Italy	0.6	0.6	0.6	0.6	0.6	0.6	0.7	0.7
Norway	0.9	1.0	0.8	0.8	0.8	0.8	0.7	0.8
Spain	0.3	0.5	0.5	0.5	0.5	0.5	0.5	0.5
Sweden	2.3	2.4	2.3	2.5	2.4	2.5	2.6	2.8
United Kingdom	5.6	5.5	5.3	5.5	5.5	4.6	4.8	5.3
United States	9.4	9.6	9.7	9.8	10.0	10.3	10.3	10.2

Source: Social expenditure: Aggregated data, OECD Social Expenditure Statistics (database), doi: 10.1787/20743904-2012-table6 (Last UPDATED 16 November 2012; disclaimer: http://oe.cd/disclaimer)

Given that only limited international comparative data is available, a case will be presented. What follows is an attempt to give more detailed information on the UK, which is a liberal welfare state with a seemingly high level of fiscal and occupational welfare. Given that, as argued above, pensions are a central area of provision, Table 5.4 shows developments in the cost of tax relief in respect of pension contributions.

Table 5.4 shows a considerable increase in the use of tax relief related to pension schemes, even after the start of the financial crisis, when one would have expected companies to be less willing to pay into pension schemes. Relief for registered pension schemes in the UK in 2012/13 is estimated to be 1.4 % of GDP.[2] That the UK has a high level of such relief is also clear, as it is argued to be around 20% of revenue from personal income taxation in 2007/08 (European Commission, 2012, p 67). Such relief may even be increasing, as it is also argued that several countries use it as an employment incentive, and also many countries, including the UK, have substantial reduction in taxes, including in relation to corporation tax. Thereby, in at least 12 countries, according to the EU Commission, there is a 'room for tax-expenditure review' (European Commission, 2012, p 69). Furthermore, the EU argues that tax expenditures 'increase the complexity of the tax system and thus compliance costs' (European Commission, 2013, p 56).

Table 5.4: Cost of registered Pension Scheme Tax Relief in the UK

	2001/02	2005/06	2009/10	2011/12
£m/year	10,000	17,600	20,100	23,300

Source: http://www.hmrc.gov.uk/statistics/pension-stats/pen6.pdf (accessed 1 October 2013)

In the UK there has historically been an increase in the use of tax and other reliefs. From a value of £29,050 million in 1994/95 they rose to £52,820 million in 2009/10.[3] For 2012/13 the amounts in structural relief are: £68,300 million for personal allowances, £15,000 million for income tax and corporation tax and £20,000 million for national insurance contributions. Tax expenditures for 2012/13 are shown in Table 5.5.

Table 5.5: Tax expenditures in the UK in £ million, 2012/13

	£ million
Income tax	
Of which registered pension schemes	21,600
Other	10,055
Corporation tax	915
National Insurance contributions	9,790
Capital gains tax	11,600
Inheritance tax	1,180
VAT	
Of which zero rate on food	15,450
Other	25,900
Climate change levy	520
Total	97,010

Note: One needs to be aware of the risk of double counting.

Source: http://www.hmrc.gov.uk/statistics/expenditures.htm.

Table 5.5 suggests that tax expenditures have not been reduced either during or after the fiscal crisis; rather, there has been a continuous expansion of expenditures, thus indicating that the hidden welfare state has seemingly survived, at least in the UK, and even expanded slightly. Further, tax expenditures still cover the key areas and are large in size. Given the trend towards a higher degree of inequality through the use of tax expenditures and occupational welfare, this contributes to increasing levels of inequality. Furthermore, the expenditures are substantial and thereby reduce public sector income, accounting for up to 20% of income tax in the UK, thus also reducing the option of using public sector spending to improve welfare and achieve a more equitable society.

In the US also, it was argued already in 2011 that reduction of tax expenditures is necessary in order to deal with the budget deficit (http://economics21.org/commentary/navigating-tax-expenditures-minefeld). It is argued that the cost of tax expenditures in 2012 is equal to US$1,101,260 billion, and expected to be US$6,465,280 billion for the period 2012–16. It is also argued therefore that welfare spending in the US is on a par with Europe, the same conclusion reached by Adema and Ladaique (2009). That this spending in the US is close to the relatively high spending of the Nordic countries is not a new development, and is also apparent over a longer period (Fishback, 2010). Tax expenditures in the US are expected to continue to increase, while at the same time there are budget proposals to make a cut in 2014 of US$24,568 million (Office of Management and Budget, 2013, p 212).

However, recent studies do indicate that as part of the broadening of the tax base some reduction in tax expenditures has taken place, although 'only the low hanging fruit has been gathered to date and the political economy of base broadening remains difficult' (LeBlanc et al, 2013, p 7), while at the same time countries have been under pressure to 'introduce new tax reliefs to try to stimulate investment or increase employment' (LeBlanc et al, 2013, p 30).

Possible patterns of changes in the wake of the crisis

Welfare states have, in the ways in which financing has taken place, moved toward a gradual broadening of the tax base over the last 30 years at least (OECD, 2011). In a way this can be looked upon as, in principle, a possible reduction in the support for fiscal and occupational welfare, as it has reduced the state's economic incentives to make companies spend more in these areas. Reduction in the income tax rate also reduces the value of fiscal welfare, and on this basis one could expect the hidden welfare state to have become reduced in size. However, as the data above indicates, this seems unlikely to have been the case.

Furthermore, one could expect companies to have a stronger position in relation to their employees in times of economic crisis, leading to a reduction in the different kinds of welfare delivered and financed by them and, especially, a diminution in the use of occupational welfare. On the other hand, the use of fringe benefits, on the basis that they can increase employees' productivity, in particular non-cost fringe benefits such as flexible working time, in-house training and so on (Weathington, 2008), can mean that the costs of occupational welfare may be quite low, given the gains that can be made from increased productivity and tax benefits. However, when employers are in a more favourable position to attract employees, as in a time of a high unemployment, they can be expected to cut down on expenditures and to anticipate increases in productivity to come instead from people's fear of being made redundant. So, during times of high unemployment we should, all things being equal, expect a downward trend in occupational welfare. A possible reason why there has been no downward trend is that unemployment is unequally distributed among labour market groups, such that those who have kept their jobs have continued to have access to occupational welfare.

This is indirectly confirmed by a survey by Aon Hewitt in the UK that estimates that more than half of respondents spend more than 15% of payroll on benefits and more than one third spend more than 20% (Aon Hewitt, 2013). Although one can debate the overall validity of the survey, it emphasises that, despite the crisis, benefits are still a central and important element of expenditure and are used as a means to improve the recruitment and retention of employees. So expenditure remains an important issue for companies.

While the risks and costs of occupational welfare may be low for employers, employees may bear a higher risk. This is especially the case where employers can access pension pots, as happened in the case of Robert Maxwell in 1991.[4] The most significant risk for employees is losing entitlement to occupational welfare when they lose their job. In general, in occupational-based contributory pension schemes the risk also depends on the rules regarding where it is allowed to invest the fund. Following on the crisis of the Fannie Mae mortgage corporation and others in the US, the value of some pension savings funds was hit hard as bonds turned out to be junk. The risk depends on the rules, but naturally is also about the effectiveness of the pension investors. Still, individual savings will often carry a higher risk, as pension funds can pool the risk and by this means yield on average a higher overall level of income and, thereby, ability to pay out pensions. Nonetheless, occupational-based schemes are vulnerable in times of crisis.

A possible reason for expectations of a reduction in fiscal and occupational welfare is that changes can, at the same time, improve the efficiency of the tax system (see also the European Commission's viewpoint above) and can reduce the pressure on public sector spending without the need to make cuts in directly delivered welfare. It is presumably for the same reason that there has been increased focus internationally on how to reduce the negative impact on public sector income of tax havens, and international cooperation to ensure that multinational companies pay more in tax.

A counter argument to the suggestion that the crisis should reduce fiscal and occupational welfare prevails in the area of pensions, where not only employers may have an interest in occupational-based pension schemes (Trampusch, 2013), but also employees, who might see an increase in their pension levels. Such schemes may have been developed historically, either as part of previous fiscal retrenchment or as part of industrial relations bargaining, and will therefore be very difficult to change even in the wake of a fiscal crisis. In this respect, for those in stable jobs, occupational-based pension schemes presumably have a greater degree of security than do state pensions. Finally, also as a consequence of the use of occupational welfare, if this continues at the same or even an increasing level, further increases in the dualisation of the labour market are a possibility (Wiss, 2013).

Conclusions

The welfare state is seemingly here to stay. Spending on public welfare in real terms is still above the level of 2000, although since 2009 the rate of increase has been much lower and there has been a large reduction in Greece. Further, the lower rate of increase, combined with the growth in unemployment and in numbers in need of welfare support, implies that welfare benefits and service per person in need have been reduced across Europe.

Further, although little data is available, it does not seem to imply that the same approach has been taken towards the more hidden part of the welfare state, for example, fiscal and occupational welfare, where only the low-hanging fruit has been picked. This is despite the fact that even international bodies, like the EU have argued for a reduction in fiscal welfare in order to improve the transparency and efficiency of the tax system and reduce its complexity and at the same time reduce the public sector deficit, but with a less detrimental impact on the welfare state. So, even today Titmuss's appeal for better information on the different pathways to welfare has not been met and those who are better positioned in society still seem to be the ones most supported by the more hidden elements of the welfare state.

To this one might add that a reduction in fiscal and occupational welfare could ensure a more equitable welfare state, as they both tend to imply that those with the highest incomes get the most out of these approaches to welfare. The existence of a large hidden welfare state reduces the welfare state's ability both to redistribute and to support a more expansive economic policy in times of crisis.

Notes

[1] This refers to the fact that the possible impact of the tax system is taken into account, as some social security benefits are taxable income in some countries.

[2] Here from power points by Gilles Mourre: The use of tax expenditures in times of fiscal consolidation. Lessons from the 2013 report: Tax Reforms in EU Member States, Brussels, 23 October 2013.

[3] Data kindly provided by Adrian Sinfield, including revision for 2010, where the data from 1994–95 is from Sinfield (2006).

[4] See a short account of the case here: www.theguardian.com/media/greenslade/2011/nov/03/pressandpublishing-daily-mirror.

References

Adema and Ladaique (2009) *How Expensive is the Welfare State? Gross and Net Indicators in the OECD Social Expenditure Database (SOCX)*, OECD Social, Employment and Migration Working Papers No 92, 13 November, Paris: OECD.

Aon Hewitt (2013) *Benefits administration survey 2013*, www.aonhewitt.cou.uk/administration.

Burman, L. and Phaup, M. (2011) *Tax expenditures, the size and efficiency of government, and implications for budget reforms*, Working Paper 17268, www.nber.org/papers/w17268, National Bureau of Economic Research.

Crozier, M., Huntingdon, S. and Watanuki, J. (1975) *The crisis of democracy: Report on the governmentality of democracies to the Trilateral Commission*, New York: New York University Press.

European Commission (2012) *Tax reforms in EU Member States: Tax policy challenges for economic growth and fiscal sustainability. 2012 report*, Brussels: European Union.

European Commission (2013) *Tax reforms in EU Member States 2013. Tax policy challenges for economic growth and fiscal sustainability. 2013 report,* European Economy 5, 2013, Brussels: European Union.

Farnsworth, K. (2013) 'Occupational welfare', in B. Greve (ed) *The Routledge handbook of the welfare state,* Abingdon: Routledge.

Farnsworth, K. (2013a) 'Bringing corporate welfare in', *Journal of Social Policy,* 42(1): 1–22.

Farnsworth, K. and Irving, Z. (eds) (2011) *Social policy in challenging times. Economic crisis and welfare systems,* Bristol: Policy Press.

Fishback, P.V. (2010) *Social welfare expenditures in the United States and the Nordic countries: 1900–2003,* Working Paper 15982, Cambridge: National Bureau of Economic Research.

Greve, B. (1994) 'The hidden welfare state, tax expenditure and social policy: a comparative overview', *Scandinavian Journal of Social Welfare,* 3: 203–11.

Greve, B. (2007) *Occupational welfare,* Cheltenham: Edward Elgar.

Greve, B. (ed) (2012) *The times they are changing: Crisis and the welfare state,* Oxford: Wiley-Blackwell.

Greve, B. (2012a) *Happiness,* Abingdon: Routledge.

Howard, C. (1997) *The hidden welfare state: Tax expenditures and social policy in the United States,* Princeton, NJ: Princeton University Press.

Ishkanian, A. and Szreter, S. (eds) (2012) *The big society debate. A new agenda for social welfare,* Cheltenham: Edward Elgar.

Järvi, L. and Kuivilainen, S. (2012) *Does occupational welfare matter? Measurement and the importance of collectively negotiated sickness benefit in cross-national social policy analyses: Case of the Nordic Countries,* paper presented to ESPANET conference, Edinburgh.

Karanikolos, M. et al (2013) 'Financial crisis, austerity, and health in Europe', *Lancet,* 381: 1323–31.

Kirk, M. (2008) 'Remembering and rethinking the social division of welfare', *Journal of Social Policy,* 39(1): 1–18.

Klein, R. (1993) 'O'Goffe's tale' in C. Jones (ed) *New perspectives on the welfare state,* London: Routledge.

LeBlanc, P. et al (2013) *The tax policy landscape five years after the crisis,* OECD Taxation Working Papers no 17, Paris: OECD Publishing.

Mackenzie, M. et al (2013) 'Is "candidacy" a useful concept for understanding journeys through public services? A critical interpretive literature synthesis', *Journal of Social Policy & Administration,* 47(7): 806–25.

Mazzucato, M. (2013) *The entrepreneurial state: Debunking public vs private sector myths,* New York, NY: Anthem Press.

Mishra, R. (1984) *The welfare state in crisis*, Oxford: Oxford University Press.

O'Connor, J. (1973) *The fiscal crisis of the state*, New York: St. Martin's Press.

OECD (1981) *The welfare state in crisis*, Paris: OECD.

OECD (2010) *Tax expenditures in OECD countries*, Paris: OECD.

OECD (2011) *OECD's current tax agenda*, Paris: OECD.

Offe, C. (1984) *The contradictions of the welfare state*, ed. J. Keane, London: Hutchinson.

Office of Management and Budget (2013) *Analytical perspectives: Budget of the US Government*, Budget.gov.

Pierson, P. (2011) *The welfare state over the very long run*, ZeSArbeitspapier, No 02/2011, Bremen: Universitat Bremen.

Richardson, J. (2011) *From recession to renewal: The impact of the financial crisis on public services and local government*, Bristol: Policy Press.

Sinfield, A. (2006) 'Tax welfare', in Martin Powell (ed) *Understanding the mixed economy of welfare*, Bristol: Policy Press, pp 129–146.

Sinfield, A. (2013) 'Fiscal welfare', in B. Greve (ed) *The Routledge handbook of the welfare state*, Abingdon: Routledge.

Taylor-Gooby, P. (ed) (2001) *Welfare states under pressure*, London: Sage.

Taylor-Gooby, P. (2013) *The double crisis of the welfare state and what we can do about it*, Basingstoke: Palgrave.

Titmuss, R.M. (1987) *The philosophy of welfare. Selected writings of R.M. Titmuss*, London: Allen & Unwin.

Trampusch, C. (2013) 'Employers and collectively negotiated occupational pensions in Sweden, Denmark and Norway: promoter, vacillators and adversaries', *European Journal of Industrial Relations*, 19(1): 37–53.

Weathington, B. (2008) 'Income level and the value of non-wage employee benefits', *Employee Responsibilities & Rights Journal*, 20: 291–300.

Wiss, T. (2013) *From countries to sectors: The explanatory power of trade unions' and employees' skills for sector differences in occupational pensions*, Paper for the 25th Annual Meeting of SASE in Milan, 2013.

Part Two

The Social Policy Association Conference 2013

Better to satisfy the coroner than the auditor: social policy delivery in challenging times

Michael Hill

Introduction

This chapter is a very personal examination of issues about social policy delivery, rooted in my early experience in the National Assistance Board (NAB) and a subsequent academic career in which much of my research and writing has been about aspects of the place of discretionary decision making in public policy implementation.

In 1960, on my first day as an executive officer (EO) in a local office of the NAB I was called in to meet the manager. He had been a Poor Law relieving officer before the Board was formed and was within a few weeks of retirement. The only thing I recall from that conversation was the statement I have used as my title: 'Better to satisfy the coroner than the auditor'. This memory sums up my surprise at the emphasis placed upon satisfactorily meeting need by many of those who trained and managed me in the NAB. I do not want to exaggerate this; of course there was also a considerable amount of cynicism and stereotyping of poor people from many of my superiors and colleagues. But there was a clear identification that we could not pass on our responsibility to meet need to anyone else. Indeed, before being selected as an EO, I had been a temporary clerk in a Labour Exchange where the 'social insurance culture' involved a view that the role played by the NAB sometimes undermined the rules about unemployment entitlement.

In the House of Commons debate on the 1948 National Assistance Act, the Minister of National Insurance, James Griffiths, said in his response to the debate:

In the field in which the Assistance Board will make cash payments after July, there will be an infinite variety of human needs to meet – such an infinite variety that I am certain it cannot be met by any general scale or special standard scales, however generous. It is, therefore, essential that from the beginning the Board should realise that they will not be able to fulfil their tasks adequately unless they exercise a wide measure of discretion in their payments over and above the standard scales. (Hansard, 1947)

One cannot imagine such a statement being made today as political parties compete with each other to demonstrate their tough attitudes to public support for poor people.

We need to contest strongly the expectation of modern government that those in economic distress may have to look beyond the statutory social benefit system. The growth of food banks should be regarded with particular horror in this regard. I recall, from the period when I worked on the NAB office counter dealing with emergency payments, when charities or the local mayor's office would phone about someone in need, that my understanding of my duty was to tell them to send the person to our office. Similarly, specifically bearing in mind the need to 'satisfy the coroner', it is appalling that in winter 2012–13 cases were reported of deaths among people who were sleeping rough. While in the NAB we were expected to be wary of 'itinerant fraud'; we were also expected to make emergency payments to those presenting as homeless and to direct them to places where they might find accommodation (exceptionally in the NAB-run 'reception centres'). And while vouchers could be used, this was very rarely done.

Before I am dismissed as a nostalgic old fool who has simply forgotten all the things that were wrong about the NAB, may I say that I stand by the critical views I set out in an article I wrote after I left the NAB and became an academic. I wrote there of 'tensions and conflicts that inevitably accompanied such a personalized and decentralised system of administration' (Hill, 1969, p 89). I exemplified them with illustrations of the inconsistencies in decision making and the inevitable biases against our less socially acceptable clientele. In retrospect, I could have said more about the racism in a London office encountering the early waves of migration from the Caribbean and about the appalling treatment of single mothers.

So my objective is not to offer an idealised view of the past. I do recognise that it was 'another country'. Nevertheless I hope, from my own distant starting point, to offer observations on the social policy of today that are helpful and perhaps provocative.

The trouble with devising a catchy title for oneself long before writing the article is that you are then trapped in the underlying assumptions embodied in your title. There are various pitfalls in respect of the approach I am adopting. The contrast between the role of the coroner and that of the auditor probably overstates that of the coroner. The interventions of coroners secure little attention in discussions of social policy delivery. Perhaps they should be given more attention; there is a research topic for someone there. Death *directly* caused by unreasonable social policy decisions is fortunately rare. It is not easy to identify death which is *indirectly* the product of policy implementation systems. Mention was made above of deaths of people sleeping rough, as a specific example of where the use of emergency powers could have prevented them; but the wider incidence of high levels of winter deaths has to be attributed to a complex collection of factors. Hence, in what I will have to say the contrast is perhaps better drawn as between 'caring' and 'counting'.

Another pitfall is that I want to discuss a range of issues about social policy delivery, not just about the evolution of social assistance since that time. Yet it is that issue in which I have most expertise. What I am going to do therefore is move through the issues of social assistance discretion to wider questions about the role of discretion in social policy delivery in various areas of policy. I will then return to the underlying issues about caring and counting, to make it clear that my critique is not of 'auditing' per se but of many of the forms it takes.

Social policy delivery issues in context

Before going on, there is a need to say more about the concern to avoid nostalgia: a danger of disregarding all that was wrong then (taken-for-granted sexism, racism, homophobia and so on). I must beware the vision of myself as riding out on my bike (like the middle- and upper-class women in the TV series *Call the Midwife*) to minister to the poor. But the irony is that the world of the late 1950s and early 1960s was one in which efforts to sustain communities were occurring in a context of much lower levels of inequality than we have today and very low levels of unemployment.

Next there is a danger that discussion of how policies are delivered may be seen to by-pass the crucial issues about lack of resources. Michael Lipsky argued that street-level bureaucrats will 'never be free from the implications of significant restraints' and that 'demand will always increase to meet the supply of services' (1980, p 81). There is a case for this realism, but it translates all too easily into fatalism. A debate about delivery models has to be carried out in the context of questions about overall resourcing. We certainly do not want to get into a situation in which models from the past are extolled, when in fact, whatever the quality of service, they were inadequate to meet need. The related issue here is that official social policy discourse tends to by-pass resourcing problems to see better policy delivery as solving those problems. It is important to not stress solutions to weaknesses of the delivery system as if they are, in themselves, all that is needed.

However, the most serious pitfall of this analysis lies in the fact that it seems to extol the virtues of the high-discretion approach to social policy (and of course specifically social assistance) of the NAB. This is something that needs to be carefully qualified, and is the topic of the next section.

For or against discretion?

While much that I wrote in the past was specifically about discretion in social assistance, the aim here to try is to review the debate in ways that widen it out to more than this. The crucial point here is that discretion is ubiquitous and cannot be entirely eliminated. When he was engaged, as Chair of the Supplementary Benefits Commission, in trying to eliminate the most problematic forms of discretion in social assistance, David Donnison argued for a distinction between 'discretion' and 'judgement' (1977). That usage, important in Donnison's concerns at that time, separates very specific powers, then existing in social assistance, to add or subtract amounts after the application of an assessment formula from decisions required in the interpretation of rules. But it does not accord with the way the concept of discretion is used in the varied academic literature on the topic. Rather, it is recognised that in public policy unfettered discretion is rare but 'discretion, as the translation of rules into action, is inevitable' (Hawkins, 1992, p 11). Hawkins clarifies this, noting that 'Discretion is heavily implicated in the use of rules: interpretative behaviour is involved in making sense of rules, and in making choices about the relevance and use of rules' (Hawkins, 1992, p 13). Such a view is reinforced in Lipsky's examination of the work of street-level bureaucrats. He says of discretion: 'Policy makers and economists might wish it were otherwise, but it seems clear that in the implementation of social welfare programs there remains an irreducible extent to which worker discretion cannot be eradicated' (Lipsky, 1980, p 28).

My 1969 article mentioned above was noticed by both Peter Townsend and Richard Titmuss. Peter Townsend cited it as a contribution to the evidence against means testing (1975). Titmuss cited it as evidence that 'officials like claimants are people who reflect the limitations of their particular cultural environment', in an article that was to prove to be rather controversial (Titmuss, 1971, p 130). That essay by Titmuss was seen as an attack on the newly developing welfare rights movement. It was critical of arguments for the elaborate itemisation of needs in order to constrain discretion. But his argument needs to be seen in relation to quite specific observations about the need to limit discretion, and in particular his reiteration of the case for universal benefits (particularly social insurance-based ones), which had been a key theme in much of his work. This goes to the very core of the issues about discretion today.

What is crucial here is to separate what may be called the 'welfare rights' case against discretion, with its close links to concerns about professional patronage, from arguments deriving from the fact that policies with highly discretionary elements within them are expensive to administer. Cutting down on administration is the leading theme for all who think they can cut social expenditure without endangering benefits and services. There is a need for scepticism about these arguments.

I left the NAB convinced of the case for the strengthening of the universal benefits (family allowances – Child Benefit as it is now – together with the social insurance benefits extended well beyond the limits of any simple interpretation of the insurance principle). I joined the many social policy scholars who took that view. Subsequently of course, what happened was the reverse, the systematic weakening of universalism. In its place mass means testing has developed, with at the same time continuous efforts to give this a shape which cannot be described as simplification, but has involved efforts (in this electronic age) to minimise expenditure on the staffing of its administration.

Two particular problems follow from the modern approach. One is that, with a 'mass' approach to means testing, choices have had to be made been two alternative versions of the 'rough justice' that flows from a routinised scheme often dependent on form-filling without any human contact with the social security agency. One approach is to adopt comparatively generous assumptions, recognising that some people will do comparatively well out of the scheme, that there will be overpayments and potentially quite a lot of fraud (something that, of course, was kept in check by home visiting in the past). The other is to draw tight assumptions, creating hardship where people's actual circumstances diverge from the standard assumptions. It is not necessary to spell out here the direction taken in the UK system. Just two aspects of this will be briefly explored further: support for housing costs and support for unemployed people.

Significantly, the problems about simplistic assumptions have been rendered particularly problematical by the way in which the relationship between the social security system and the subsidy of housing has been allowed to develop. The issues about the impact of variable housing costs upon a simple social security system were interestingly discussed in the Beveridge report (1942). Beveridge largely evaded the problem, since variations between the housing costs of the poor were low at that time. In the period up to the end of the 1960s two solutions to this issue operated: one was the subsidy of local authority housing (as opposed to the subsidy of tenants), the other was the rent costs addition to social assistance. The former was systematically abandoned, and complicated – particularly in the 1980s under the Thatcher governments – by the selling of council houses without any corresponding effort to feed the income back into social housing. The latter was integrated into means-tested housing benefit. Following the logic of this policy development we have had therefore the development of a benefit, separate from the other means-tested benefits, to assist with the rental costs of all low-income tenants. This had at least the merit that it meant that housing support did not necessarily stop people moving off social assistance.

But in the context of a dramatic rise in housing costs, the virtual abandonment of rent regulation and the emasculation of the only organisations that could have managed a rational and fair rental system (the local authorities), the administration of housing benefit has proved a far from simple matter. Local authorities have been forced down the route of simplification and computerisation, often involving the delegation of administration to private companies. Costs have risen dramatically and two related rough-justice issues have become salient, and the subject of draconian solutions: firstly, the extent to which claimants can make housing choices regardless of costs, and secondly, the acceptability of under-occupation. In both cases the rough-justice remedy has been to cut benefit so that actual rented costs are disregarded, regardless of whether other cheaper accommodation is available or whether it is reasonable to expect families to move.

While the issues about support for housing costs have arisen in critical forms fairly recently, the issues about support for workless people go much further back. There is a wonderful quotation from a memo written by the young Winston Churchill in 1909 in respect of the planned unemployment insurance scheme for the UK, arguing that issues about behaviour should not affect benefit entitlement:

> he has insured himself against the fact of unemployment, and I think it arguable that his foresight should be rewarded irrespective of his dismissal ... I do not like mixing up moralities and mathematics. (Quoted in Fulbrook, 1978, pp 137–8)

That view was not accepted, and the UK unemployment insurance scheme was hedged by rules entailing benefit-loss punishments for those who were considered to blame for their job loss and, in the long run perhaps more importantly, not making adequate efforts to obtain work. However, the unemployment insurance system Churchill was helping to set up would have worked well only in a context where unemployment was essentially an occasional interlude in working life. In practice, widespread and prolonged unemployment has undermined strict unemployment insurance rules. Governments have had to determine how to deal with hardship stemming from prolonged unemployment, way beyond the limits initially imposed to protect insurance funds, and from difficulties in getting into the workforce in the first place. So today, with 'jobseeker's allowance', the original insurance element is of minor significance.

So, contrary to Churchill's hope, 'moralities' have inevitably entered into the treatment of unemployed people, linking concerns about job search with the issues about support. This development has further been influenced both by views that, regardless of the demand for labour, the qualifications, attitudes and behaviour of the labour supply matter too. Hence three related policy issues – support for unemployed people, labour market policy and education and training policy – come together in the modern world.

That has then been given a further twist by two things. One of these has been female labour market participation, leading on to issues about whether benefit support should be conditional if there are children in the household. The other has been, in recent times, the systematic elimination of one of the main pillars in the Beveridge scheme for people below pension age: social insurance support for long-term sick and disabled people. In respect of all workless people, 'morality' preoccupations dominate. The consequence has been the development alongside routinised benefit administration of corps of people required to operate in modes that are of necessity highly discretionary, with the aim of securing labour market participation. Here, of course, we are seeing some of the most worrying manifestations of delegation to private agencies: to encourage and perhaps coerce labour market participation, to make distinctions between disabled people in terms of work capacity and so on. Despite a background of limited work opportunities, contracts to these agencies necessarily set performance targets. Routine people processing to fill contractual targets is a long way away from the discretion to which James Griffiths was referring.

While discretionary decision making in social policy, and particularly social security policy, takes rather different forms than it did in the 1960s, when there was a very lively debate about discretionary powers in social assistance, it has certainly not gone away. What we have seen is the development, obviously very influenced by technological change, of ways in which means testing may be administered that minimise personalised and face-to-face decision making. But these throw up new problems for which automated solutions are difficult, without a great deal of rough justice. Simplifications that did not involve means testing have been abandoned – in particular, social insurance and the direct subsidy of social housing – leaving behind new kinds of administrative dilemmas. The next two sections discuss remedies for this situation.

Ways to minimise discretion?

Since the end of the 1970s the thrust of government policy has been to try to develop means testing in forms that will facilitate mass production and minimise discretion (note Donnison, 1977). There are questions here about just how sophisticated such systems can be. Bovens and Zouridis (2002) suggest that with electronic resources there can be a shift of discretion from 'street level' to 'screen level', but then of course much hinges on how information collection is structured. At the time of writing, a particularly puzzling question faces social policy analysts trying to interpret the controversy about the implementation of the new Universal Credit scheme: can programming expertise solve all the problems relating to the operation of a routinised mass system so that error correction and information updating can be done quickly enough to avoid hardship? Behind this lie two issues, one about the feasibility of designing user-friendly application forms, the other concerning the need for these to be contextualised by clear rules. In Jewell's comparative study of social assistance (2007) a comparison of the high discretion levels in Sweden with the rule-dominated German system suggests that in the latter, the corpus of rules is so considerable that officials cannot keep up with all the considerations they should take into account. In that sense discretion and differential rule use are functional equivalents. In the UK maybe we can say that extensive discretion has been replaced by error rates. We come back here therefore to Titmuss's objection to detailed rules.

There are ways of extending universalist policies on, at least, the academic agenda. The problem is the likelihood that any political adoption of them would probably leave unmet needs. The revival of social insurance is one such possibility. The problem, as far as the UK is concerned, is that after the sustained dismantling of social insurance, it is probably too late to revive it. The cynical way in which past governments have manipulated the residual system has led to a recognition that social insurance contributions are a tax (and a fairly regressive tax at that) by another name. Revivals of the system are bound to involve increasing contributions, which would be seen as tax increases that politicians are pretending they are not. In any case in the UK, what might be called the Bismarck/Beveridge dilemma has never been solved. I mean by this that the drawback of the Bismarck model tends to be its relative closeness to commercial insurance, with benefits dependent on contributions and those who have had difficulty in making contributions excluded, while the drawback of the Beveridge model is that inclusiveness tends to come at the price of inadequate benefits. The success of the Scandinavians in combining the two approaches is unlikely to be emulated in these 'challenging times'. On the contrary, politicians are even there engaged in dismantling their systems.

Another option is the development of 'citizens' income' (see Torry, 2013). There is much to be said for this approach to income maintenance, particularly inasmuch as full employment is likely to remain hard to achieve. However, consideration of the politics of the introduction of such a scheme leads to sceptical conclusions. The great virtue of such a scheme, its inclusiveness, will continue to make its adoption by mainstream politicians very unlikely. It resolves the 'mathematics/moralities' issue by a total rejection of the latter. If it were to get on the agenda, the very incremental nature of policy making would probably produce a tentative scheme with various caveats and exclusions. To be satisfactory it has to be generous; if it is not, then it needs to be supplemented in various ways. This is particularly highlighted by the housing support issue discussed above. In short, we need to imagine a citizens' income scheme not framed in the terms set out by its advocates but one introduced by Iain Duncan Smith!

In any case, as suggested above in the discussion of what is meant by discretion, problems about discretion as a residual issue will remain with us, even if only in terms of issues about the interpretation of rules. Hence the next section explores issues surrounding how to minimise the problems with the role of discretion in policy delivery.

Towards better approaches to discretion?

It is easier to be negative rather than positive about the issues concerning how to structure discretion in social policy. There is an argument deserving consideration that supports the delegating of discretionary powers to a level relatively close to those they affect. Here of course there is a relevant contemporary policy: the shifting of the social assistance 'social fund' responsibilities to local government. This is reminiscent of another issue much debated in the 1960s and 1970s: the money-giving powers vested in local authority social services. Bill Jordan (1974) cogently attacked the development of these powers as entailing a return to the 'poor law' in which help came with conditions and controls. In the short run Jordan's predictions did not come about, but the issue has now emerged by a different route.

There is a general tendency for a lack of trust in the capacities of local government. This is often over-stated. Like other questions about trust, distrust tends to be self-fulfilling. A local government system that is tightly centrally controlled and with limited discretion over its own funding is unlikely to be a creative policy innovator. The history of social policy action by British local government, going back to Poplarism in the 1920s (Branson, 1979), is one in which generous and creative action by local government is likely to be undermined by central government. The problem about delegation of social fund powers is that local discretion will tend to operate in a downwards direction. Some local authorities will do less than they could; it is unlikely that any will do significantly more than they could.

In the earlier discussion some concerns were expressed about delegation of discretionary aspects of social policy to private agencies. Similar remarks are likely to be appropriate about the involvement of voluntary agencies. It is important to be clear about the logic of delegation. It involves a contract to carry out a specific task with specific rewards guaranteed if it is done as required. Such a contract has to specify an expected performance, and the 'principal' will need to collect evidence to ensure that this performance occurs. While the expectation will be only about the performance of the agency as a whole it will hardly be surprising if there is some carry-through to expectations about the duties of the staff of the agency. This can then in various ways affect the interaction between the staff and the public with whom they are required to work. Of course, much depends upon the task (see the exploration of this in terms of the relationship between 'modes of governance' and tasks, in Hill and Hupe, 2009, pp 183–93). We are talking here of situations in policy implementation where success needs to be evaluated in terms of outcomes, and in which 'co-production' is involved. What this means is that staff require certain kinds of collaborative actions from the public. This is of course particularly evident in the case of job seeking and training.

However, even if the policy product does not depend upon co-production there are grounds for concern about the ways in which agencies are rewarded for the work that they do. This is, of course, the general problem about a need to satisfy 'the auditor' but it takes on an additional dimension in a situation in which there is delegation. There is an issue here about the extent to which, in contracts, quantitative performance expectations are accompanied by qualitative ones. There is a need not to pursue this argument as if the inclusion of the latter in contracts is impossible (look here at the success of governments in getting local governments to secure improvements in refuse collection and disposal, despite extensive privatisation). But there are great dangers if tasks are delegated without strong and enforceable qualitative standards set out in contracts (look here at the case of social care for adults). A somewhat alarming variant of this is embodied in the current examination of ways of extending payment by results, where perverse incentives are particularly likely. Can we get beyond these negative considerations? One consideration here is whether systems can be devised that enable the exceptional to be highlighted among the system-based decisions. In the context of the heavy pressure to cut the size of government departments, this has not been satisfactorily tackled. There seems to be a need for systems to analyse computerised data to identify cases where a more personal approach may be appropriate.

Looked at also from the other side there must surely be issues about 'voice'. Crucial here are the difficulties people face in getting access to *actual people* in government agencies (and indeed elsewhere) as opposed to automatic answering systems, either by phone or computer. A related issue is difficulties about making complaints. There is a massive growth in routine questionnaires, but these do not necessarily offer an easy way to complain. Appeals are an important element in the voice agenda. There is not the space here to explore the issues about the extent to which appeal systems are accessible and useable. The argument that there is a need to have systems that identify issues where routine solutions are not appropriate and then have officials required to exercise discretion raises an argument, much debated in social policy analysis, about professionalism. To what extent is it feasible, through selection, training and sympathetic management, to inculcate a quasi-professionalism in which officials take pride in careful decision making in respect of exceptional circumstances. This is a much contested issue, but there is some evidence – largely from outside the UK (Hupe, Hill and Buffat, forthcoming 2015) – that this is possible. The debate about professional discretion occurs, of course, primarily in other policy contexts, notably health. But there is no clear boundary between strong and weak forms of the case for professionalism. The notion that some public functionaries (namely those typically labelled 'professionals') necessarily exercise discretion better than others is rightly a contested one. Hence the issues about routinisation explored here have equivalents in those other contexts too.

The routine and the exceptional: a wider issue

Much of the discussion above has concerned the implications of routinisation in social security in general and in means testing in particular. But the issues about routinisation extend to much more than this. In health and social care policy, the discretionary elements are, as suggested above, particularly complex. Denial of service comes indirectly through forms of queuing, waiting lists or simply delays in places like accident and emergency units. Political leaders hide 'under-resourcing' behind allegations about managerial inefficiency or professional protectionism. The focus then is upon the provision of an efficient service, using measurement to curb the discretionary freedom of professional decision makers.

In practice, damage to the actual service – even events that will not satisfy the coroner, as in the Stafford Hospital case – have followed from some of the forms of managerialism used to try to increase control. Ian Greener's (2013) discussion of the Francis Report on the Mid Staffordshire NHS Foundation Trust takes this argument further and sees that 'the recommendations from the Report, being based on the imposition of care standards on nurses and doctors, ... seem more likely to repeat the gaming and professional disengagement reported in research than [to result] in creating an environment which promotes transparency, openness and learning'. Greener's argument has been powerfully reinforced by Baroness Neuberger introducing her report on the misuse of the 'Liverpool Care Pathway' for end-of-life care, significantly titled 'More Care, Less Pathway' (2013), with a comment to the press that 'caring for the dying must never again be practised as a tick box exercise'.

The rather polarised debate in which professional self-protection and performance-oriented management are seen as being on opposite sides is not very helpful. Le Grand's (2010) 'knights' and 'knaves' analysis raises issues about how 'knavish' tendencies within professions may be curbed by regulatory systems. However, it tends, particularly because of his advocacy of competition and choice, to give too little attention to the way these same systems may actually reward self-interested behaviour. Rather more attention could be given to ways to enhance 'knightish' behaviour. Trust is fundamental to this, as Peter Taylor-Gooby has suggested: 'Competitive and target-driven approaches direct provider interests outwards to the market or upwards to the target-setter. Trust becomes vulnerable' (2009, p 106).

At this point there is a need to go back to my own warning against 'nostalgia'. It is all too easy to argue for an age in which no attention was given to the measurement of performance. There is a case to be made for relaxed professionals: for example, the GP who recognises that someone needs to talk and should not be constrained by an awareness of the size of the slot in the appointments system. The question is about how to make this possible in a situation in which time rationing is a necessary response to high levels of demand. The GP needs to be seen as 'accountable' not just to the patient in the surgery but also to the patients 'queuing' outside the door. The solution to this problem must surely lie in developing ways to differentiate the routine and the exceptional. For example, for most of us, most of the time, the timed GP slot is sufficient. Indeed sometimes it is even the case that the routinised face-to-face GP appointment is not the right way to meet our need. Telephone consultations are possible, there may be others who can help, or indeed we may be able to self-diagnose.

I am conscious that here it is easier to provide polemic than to offer solutions. Securing those solutions depends on careful analysis to which we as social scientists can contribute. I am not offering a post-modernist diatribe against all forms of audit.

Satisfying the coroner *and* the auditor

The manager who supplied my title quote almost certainly had an image of the auditor in his mind as a person who responds retrospectively to judge a payment as extravagant, or even as illegal. But there are many forms that auditing can take. Clearly in the contemporary context, as indicated already in various ways here, there must be particular concerns about the use of very specific performance indices. Eleanor Brodkin (2011), in an ethnographic study of welfare policy implementation in Chicago, provides a horrendous illustration of the kinds of practice that become adopted when policy 'success' is measured in terms of caseload reduction by any means, and workers are rewarded for doing so. While this academic source is American, in the UK newspapers stories are increasingly surfacing that suggest that there are similar problems deserving of research attention here, for example:

- Secret filming of training given to doctors recruited by the private company Atos to assess whether sickness and disability benefit applicants are fit for work suggests that staff are monitored to ensure they do not find excessive numbers of claimants eligible (*Guardian*, 27 July 2012).

- An internal inquiry at the Department for Work and Pensions into the covert regime of welfare targets at jobcentres says it has found no evidence of the practice – yet it accepts that action is taken against those jobcentres that do not sanction benefits as much as others. The report also says some jobcentre staff are sometimes given personal targets, but only after being disciplined (*Guardian*, 15 May 2013).

Both from the perspective of practical politics and from our point of view as social scientists there is a need to avoid a perspective that seems to reject efforts to monitor and measure. While Ian Greener (2013), in his comments on the Francis report, raises issues about the weaknesses of 'universal measures', he recognises a requirement for 'a careful negotiated approach' to measurement rather than assuming that demanding improvements in universal measures will make things better.

Measuring, and in the process identifying high and low performers in respect of any activity, should be driven by a commitment to understanding delivery processes. What that means for the regulation of those processes needs to follow on sophisticated analysis of measures. That is a very different approach from the auditing of activities driven by targets. It matters that there are differential death rates, for example, and it matters that variations in official behaviour affect these. Le Grand is justified in labelling as 'paternalist', or worse as 'knaves', those professionals who want to prevent the investigation of those issues. Professionalism should entail a continuing commitment to appraisal, but an appraisal where the decision makers are partners in the investigation. In this respect, however, the widespread publication of 'raw' indices before attention is given to explanations of variation is undesirable (see Taylor, 2013 for an examination of the use of death rates to measure hospital performance). From the perspective of an advocate of realistic analysis of the public policy process, that may be regarded as a naive remark. Political leaks, the behaviour of the media and the public interest in 'league tables' make the prevention of this difficult. However, the point still needs making.

I end up thus with perhaps an ambivalent perspective on counting and measurement, as I have indeed on the cruder forms of positivist social science. I can only conclude by going back to the coroner/auditor contrast to argue that measurement needs to be in the service of the prevention of harm, and that there is a need to ensure that those who deliver public policy see their own commitments in that direction to be supported by the management system, not threatened by it. But I must add to that the reiteration of one of my qualifications to my own theme set out at the beginning. Delivery resources cannot be addressed without reference to overall resource issues. It is very hard to produce concrete evidence to prove that the spate of concerns about poor performance by public services (particularly health services) is a product of under-resourcing. Nevertheless, all that we know about the difficulties of securing efficiency gains in services in an effort to meet rising demand must lead us to questions about whether public social services are being squeezed too hard. Just as we identify political 'blaming of the victim', we must recognise that another kind of blaming goes on: blaming the public agencies and their staff who deliver public policy without the resources to do it properly.

References

Beveridge, W. (1942) *Social insurance and allied services*, Cmd 6404, London: HMSO.

Bovens, M. and Zouridis, S. (2002) 'From street-level to system-level bureaucracies: how information and communication technology is transforming administrative discretion and constitutional control', *Public Administration Review*, 62(2): 174–84.

Branson, N. (1979) *Poplarism 1919–1925*, London: Lawrence and Wishart.

Brodkin, E.Z. (2011) 'Policy work: street-level organizations under new managerialism', *Journal of Public Administration and Research*, 21(2): 253–77.

Donnison, D.V. (1977) 'Against discretion', *New Society*, 15 September, 534–6.

Fulbrook, J. (1978) *Administrative justice and the unemployed*, London: Mansell.

Greener, I. (2013) 'The NHS in crisis? The problematization of failure in the report of the Francis public inquiry into the Mid Staffordshire NHS trust', paper presented to the SPA Annual Conference, Sheffield, 9 July.

Hansard (1947) Second Reading of the National Assistance Bill, 24 November, 444: cols 1603–716.

Hawkins, K. (ed) (1992) *The uses of discretion*, Oxford: Clarendon Press.

Hill, M. and Hupe, P. (2009) *Implementing public policy* 2nd edn), London: Sage.

Hill, M.J. (1969) 'The exercise of discretion in the national assistance board', *Public Administration*, 47: 75–90.

Hupe, P., Hill, M. and Buffat, A. (eds) (forthcoming 2015) *Understanding street level bureaucracy*, Bristol: Policy Press.

Independent Review of the Liverpool Care Pathway (2013) *More care, less pathway*, www.gov.uk/dh.

Jewell, C.J. (2007) *Agents of the welfare state*, New York and Basingstoke: Palgrave Macmillan.

Jordan, B. (1974) *Poor parents*, London: Routledge and Kegan Paul.

Le Grand, R. (2010) 'Knights and knaves return: public service motivation and the delivery of public services', *International Public Management Journal*, 13(1): 56–71.

Lipsky, M. (1980) *Street-level bureaucracy: Dilemmas of the individual in public services*, New York: Russell Sage Foundation.

Taylor, P. (2013) 'Rigging the death rate', *London Review of Books*, 11 April: 12–16.

Taylor-Gooby, P. (2009) *Reframing social citizenship*, Oxford: Oxford University Press.

Titmuss, R.M. (1971) 'Welfare rights, law and discretion', *Political Quarterly*, 42(2): 113–32.

Torry, M. (2013) *Money for everyone: Why we need a citizen's income*, Bristol: Policy Press.

Townsend, P. (1975) *Sociology and social policy* (first published 1972), London: Allen Lane.

SEVEN

Social Impact Bonds: shifting the boundaries of citizenship

Stephen Sinclair, Neil McHugh, Leslie Huckfield, Michael Roy and Cam Donaldson

Introduction

One result of the reforms pursued by governments across the world to reduce public expenditure deficits since the 2008 financial crisis has been a growing interest in outsourcing the funding and delivery of welfare services. In the UK context, austerity measures and the demand for greater policy innovation have been strongly associated with the application of market incentives and business principles to social welfare provision. For example, the UK Cabinet Office's Green Paper *Modernising Commissioning* (Cabinet Office, 2010) reaffirmed the government's commitment to extending payment by results (PbR) mechanisms across public services. The UK government has declared that 'new forms of commissioning and contracting ... improve both the outcomes derived from delivery of public services and the value for money achieved by public expenditure' (Cabinet Office, 2013a).

Social Impact Bonds (SIBs) are the most recent example of this policy trend. According to their supporters, 'SIBs offer an answer to a question all policy makers are facing in these difficult fiscal times: How do we keep innovating and investing in promising new solutions when we can't even afford to pay for everything we are currently doing?' (Azemati, et al 2013, p 24). SIBs harness private investment to finance innovative welfare services, and the strength of the UK government's interest in them is testified to in its creation of a Centre for Social Impact Bonds within the Cabinet Office and the establishment of a £20 million Social Outcomes Fund designed to support the development of PbR methods and SIBs (Cabinet Office, 2013b). However, interest in SIBs is international – they are currently being considered or developed in the US, Canada, New Zealand, Australia, Columbia, India, Ireland and Israel in relation to a wide range of policy areas, including reducing offending and recidivism, tackling homelessness, employability and active labour market measures and provision of early years education (Robinson, 2012). The possibility of extending the SIBs model to create Development Impact Bonds to fund social and medical programmes in the developing world has also been proposed (Rosenberg, 2013).

SIBs are certainly an interesting idea, but they are also a significant innovation in how social welfare services are funded and provided. They constitute a boundary shift in the nature of social welfare and raise fundamental questions about what makes a service 'public' and what, if anything, is changed in the nature of a welfare service when it is incentivised by profit (Spicker, 2009). Answers to these questions have important implications for our understanding of the role and accountability of social services and for users' rights. This chapter explores these issues, firstly by discussing how it is proposed that SIBs operate and outlining what their advocates have claimed are their benefits for financing and delivering welfare services. This discussion principally draws upon the UK experience, where SIBs were first introduced. Secondly, the potential limitations that SIBs share with more familiar PbR funding mechanisms (such as the Flexible New Deal, the Work Programme and Troubled Families programme in the UK) are examined. The third section of the chapter analyses how SIBs relate to more conventional forms of welfare service funding and delivery and explains why they represent a significant departure from previous practice. The chapter concludes by considering what SIBs imply for the principles that guide social welfare provision.

Social Impact Bonds and payment-by-results systems

The UK coalition government's *Open Public Services* White Paper (HM Government, 2011) was explicit about the intention to expand and extend the use of PbR in financing and delivering public services and welfare policies (HM Government, 2011). PbR was introduced into UK welfare provision by the previous Labour government as part of the Flexible New Deal (FND) employment activation programme in 2009. The system was based on the recommendation of the Freud Report (2007), which proposed that (following practice in Australia, some Scandinavian countries and states in the US) employment training and placement support should be provided by private and third sector organisations. It was argued that these could provide more personalised and innovative support through competition and by rewarding providers for the outcomes they achieved rather than focusing on inputs (Hayman, 2008). As the subsequent report from the Department for Work and Pensions (DWP), *Raising Expectations and Increasing Support: Reforming Welfare for the Future*, argued, 'we believe there is value in having different providers competing for contracts. This contestability will raise standards. The contracts will be based on payment by results, so as to give incentives to providers to focus on getting people in to work … our approach is based on a "black box" method, where we specify what is wanted, not how it should be done' (DWP, 2008, p 11). The FND would also introduce what the government called an 'Invest to Save' approach, which allowed the DWP to switch the financing of employment activation programmes from annual to departmental budgets and to 'invest' the savings from future benefit payments in current employment support programmes – anticipating that these measures would reduce unemployment and therefore expenditure in the longer term. There is of course a potential gamble in this approach in that the anticipated reductions in unemployment might not be achieved (particularly since the supply of jobs fell in the subsequent prolonged recession); however, there was cross-party support for PbR, which was further extended in the UK Coalition government's Work Programme, which replaced the FND from June 2011. The Work Programme is designed to incentivise service providers by paying them in three stages: first, an 'Attachment fee' paid when the service provider engages with the user; this is followed by a 'Job Outcome payment' when the client secures employment; finally a 'Sustainment fee' is paid to the service provider if the client retains employment for a time specified in the DWP contract. Each of the three payments also varies, depending on the extent of support required by different clients (DWP, nd).

The Audit Commission (2012, p 4) has stated that the experience of the FND and Work Programme has demonstrated that PbR has 'significant benefits', including delivering savings and generating new resources. This assumed success underpins the current enthusiasm to extend the principle using Social Impact Bonds. There are various forms that SIBs can take; however, the most developed and analysed model is that implemented in the UK, where over a dozen now operate; for the purposes of clarity, this is the model discussed here. An SIB is a method of funding public services though a multi-stakeholder arrangement between government and a service provider with finance provided by private investors, brokered by a third sector intermediary. The arrangement enables private investors to pay for innovative public services and recoup their capital investment, along with an additional financial return paid by the government if the service achieves outcomes superior to those delivered by conventional providers (Bolton and Savell, 2010). Any additional dividends are financed from savings made in future welfare and other public expenditure that could be attributed to the impact of the innovative provision financed by the SIB; for example, a reduction in recidivism among offenders leading to reduced welfare and criminal justice service costs (Azemati et al, 2013). The rate of return paid to investors varies in relation to the outcomes attained, with an agreed base level below which investors forsake their investment. As SIBs repay investments only when specified outcomes are met, the investor faces an element of risk, so that, strictly speaking, SIBs are not 'bonds' but resemble an equity product[1] (Greenhalgh, 2011). For example, in the world's first SIB, introduced in Peterborough in September 2011 to finance measures to reduce reoffending among short-term prisoners, the investor will receive a return of 2.5% on their investment if there is a 7.5% reduction in reoffending in relation to a comparator group; higher reductions in reoffending will generate greater financial returns, up to a ceiling of 13%. The rationale of SIBs is therefore that they provide private investors with a financial return while delivering innovative public welfare services (Kingston and Bolton, 2004).

Although implemented under a Conservative Minister of Justice, the Peterborough SIB was initially announced by the Labour government in March 2010. The level of cross-party support for SIBs in Britain suggests that they appear as an unideological and technical response to the problem of recidivism, and their advocates have claimed that they, and related PbR measures, promote greater efficiency and innovation and will achieve greater impact. Other advantages claimed for SIBs in particular include that they:

- focus agencies' efforts on outcomes rather than inputs
- transfer costs from the public to the private sector
- generate new resources by increasing incentives for private investment in social welfare services
- inspire innovation by incentivising service providers to improve performance.

In short, advocates of SIBs portray them as a 'win-win' option for all involved. A particularly attractive feature of SIBs is that they enable public services to be delivered, while the risk of providing the capital required to finance services is borne by private investors rather than service providers, as in other PbR arrangements (Scott, 2012). Therefore SIBs allow governments 'to privatize the up-front costs of social innovations and the associated risks, thus reducing taxpayer expenditure in the short-term and eliminating the risk of government money being spent on interventions which do not deliver the desired outcomes' (Fox and Albertson, 2012, p 356). In the Peterborough SIB, funding was provided by various foundations and charities and brokered by Social Finance, a quasi-public wholesale funder (Disley et al, 2011). The first SIB in the US (funding a recidivism programme in New York) is funded by loans from Goldman Sachs underwritten by Bloomberg Philanthropies (Azemati et al, 2013).

The UK Minister for Civil Society, Nick Hurd, described SIBs as 'opening up serious resources to tackle social problems in new and innovative ways' (quoted in Wintour, 2012). Stimulating innovation is a virtue frequently claimed for SIBs and other forms of PbR. Proponents argue that public service providers tend to be risk averse and have incentives to stick to established practices even when these have limited effectiveness. In contrast, it is argued that PbR and SIBs can 'encourage new ideas, new forms of service delivery and new entrants to service provision' (Audit Commission, 2012, p 4). In particular, the Centre for Social Impact Bonds argues that, as 'payment is based on results rather than process, there is more room for innovation and greater freedom to demonstrate solutions that work', as the costs of under-performance or failure are not borne by accountable public officials (Cabinet Office, 2013b). It has also been claimed that both PbR and SIBs facilitate early intervention and preventive social policies, as the risks of investing in long-term preventive measures to address complex social problems are shifted from the public sector to private investors or providers (Mulgan et al, 2011). This enables experimentation and the benefits of improvement over time to be realised, as those providing services can adapt to change and emerging lessons without this being perceived as failure. As a result, policy makers may feel less compelled to intervene and micro-manage delivery. Nevertheless, for all their attested benefits, there are a number of familiar risks posed by PbR, as well as some potential drawbacks that are distinctive to SIBs, which must also be considered.

The risks of Social Impact Bonds

The *Open Public Services* White Paper stated that PbR will 'provide a constant and tough financial incentive for providers to deliver good services' (HM Government, 2011, p 33). However, the evidence for this belief is at best incomplete: the Audit Commission noted that 'schemes that make a large part of the payment dependent on performance are still largely untested and their overall effectiveness is not yet proven' (2012, p 3). Fox and Albertson (2012) identify three methodological and practical challenges to PbR: unintended consequences due to perverse incentives and gaming; the difficulty of measuring outcomes and attributing these to particular policies; and identifying savings from interventions. Other potential drawbacks of PbR and SIBs are the risk that they will narrow the supply of potential service providers, due to the investment costs and cash-flow challenges which they pose for smaller organisations, and that they might lead to speculation as derivatives. Each of these hazards will be discussed in turn.

Both PbR and SIBs require the ability to determine that outcomes have been achieved and that results are attributable to the actions of service providers. This poses multiple challenges, not least in specifying appropriate outcomes, which can be both complex and controversial. Even the ostensibly straightforward outcome of reduced reoffending requires selecting between alternative indicators, and the UK Ministry of Justice alone has identified six different ways to measure reoffending (Fox and Albertson, 2012). Establishing systems to collect the robust evidence required to assess performance can be a resource-intensive and time-consuming task. SIBs and payment in relation to outcomes are in part a reaction to the perceived heavy-handed monitoring and control associated with new public management approaches to enforcing accountability and measuring performance. However, there is no reason to believe that SIBs will reduce performance monitoring and reporting requirements, quite the contrary; as the Audit Commission noted, 'Developing the data, and the payment model linked to it, can involve considerable analytical resource' (Audit Commission, 2012, p 25).

Even assuming that it is possible to specify outcomes and the means of measuring performance in relation to these, there are still considerable problems in attributing the accomplishment of outcomes to policy inputs and rewarding organisations appropriately for their respective performances. It is questionable in some cases how far particular organisations can actually deliver outcomes, as results may depend upon conditions and the responses of users to the services and opportunities offered to them. For example, can a school alone ensure that pupils achieve particular grades, find employment or proceed to further education or training? Perhaps what should be expected in such cases is that agencies help create conditions that enable individuals to achieve particular outcomes, rather than assume that policies can produce results that are mediated by numerous factors. Many complex public health interventions have this indirect impact (Craig et al, 2008). Conversely, some outcomes may occur irrespective of the actions of those providing services; for example, due to wider economic or other changes. These challenges are well known in the policy evaluation literature but there is no evidence that SIBs resolve them (Pawson, 2006).

A further problem of attribution is how to match any savings to the respective contributions of different service providers. Attaching payment to outcomes creates an incentive for providers to claim credit for results that might be attributable to the actions of others. Similarly, the consequences of outcomes might not be shared equally: it is not necessarily the case that positive outcomes for one agency benefit others; in fact, successfully reducing demand for one service might increase demand and costs elsewhere (Audit Commission, 2012, p 8). Even if positive outcomes are achieved without generating additional demand elsewhere, there is no guarantee that these will produce longer-term savings; for example, by how much would reoffending have to fall to justify reducing probation services, let alone closing a prison? It seems unlikely that, even if it achieves its contracted outcomes, the Peterborough SIB will deliver significant savings in other service areas (Fox and Albertson, 2012). Establishing the relationship between actions and outcomes is most straightforward for interventions where there is already robust evidence of impact and an understanding of causality, but it is not clear how such familiarity and experience will encourage innovation.

There are numerous familiar perverse incentives produced by PbR systems, and these are shared with – and in some cases exacerbated by – SIBs. For example, performance measurement systems encourage providers to focus their activity on meeting whichever indicators are measured at the potential expense of other, perhaps equally important issues that are not included among metrics. Attaching payment to results reinforces this tendency. Often what is neglected are 'soft' outcomes that are more difficult to measure – what has been described as 'that horrible touchy-feely thing that you don't want to go near', such as enhancing service users' confidence, self-esteem or more general well-being (Davies, 2009, p 86). Assessing performance in relation to outcomes rather than narrower indicators does not resolve this problem nor address the incentive to games playing – focusing on meeting formal performance targets rather than substantive issues – and shaping services to meet the terms of a contract rather than the needs of clients (Hudson et al, 2010; Batmanghelidjh, 2012). SIBs could encourage investors to focus on policy areas that have more readily measurable results but not necessarily address the underlying causes of the most serious cases, and encourage a focus on the 'low hanging fruit' (Davison, 2013). This can lead to 'mission-drift' (or shift) as investors pressure service providers to prioritise outcomes that are more readily measured and away from the most needy (Starr, 2012).

SIBs also run the risk of excluding smaller organisations from funding and delivering services, as the investment required may be affordable only for larger organisations with ready capital. Social Finance was required to raise £5 million to fund the Peterborough SIB (Local Government Association, 2013), and it has been estimated that a SIB contract would need to be worth at least £12 million to cover such overheads as legal fees, evaluation expenses and investor's due diligence costs (Azemati et al 2013, p 27). Such sums are beyond the majority of British third sector organisations. The principal contractors in welfare services funded by PbR, such as the Work Programme, have been large private sector corporations (such as Atos, A4E and Serco) that possess sufficient capital to enable them to wait until payments are triggered (Social Enterprise UK, 2012). Neither do SIBs address the 'principal-agent problem', which is a standard neoliberal criticism of conventional public services and state-owned enterprises; that is, the challenge of ensuring that those who deliver policies serve the public interest rather than their own (Chang, 2007: 105). In the case of the Peterborough SIB, for example, it is investors rather than the service providers who are paid in relation to results; the latter are paid up front, which raises the question of what incentive they have to improve performance. The current reliance upon quasi-public and philanthropic funders to finance SIBs indicates their questionable attractiveness to private investors. Investors motivated by profit may be discouraged by the long lead times before SIBs demonstrate evidence of impact, and also may be reluctant to fund untried and more innovative interventions if this involves them facing 'equity-like risk with bond-like returns' (Liebman, 2011, p 5) – that is, uncertain investments that produce low rates of return.

SIBs reflect the assumption that non-state providers are more effective and efficient in delivering services. However, in some areas (such as employment training and support) there is little evidence that the sector from which the service provider comes has much independent effect on its impact or benefit to users, and there is certainly no evidence that the private sector is superior in terms of improving employment outcomes (Damm, 2012). In relation to this, 'What does appear to be important is the quality, enthusiasm, motivation and commitment of the staff providing the service' (Hasluck and Green, 2007, p 22). There is no reason to believe that SIBs will enhance any of these qualities. If anything, the quality of service is more likely to be promoted by measures that support the professional commitment and public service ethos of service providers (Bartley, nd).

A final risk posed by SIBs is that a secondary market could emerge in which investors could divest themselves of their initial investment by selling on to speculators (Disley et al, 2011). The recent experience of derivatives markets and their central role in the continuing financial crisis might be a basis for being wary of the repackaging and resale of social investments as assets, not least because this would attenuate the relationship between those who legally own the SIB and those responsible for delivery, thereby reducing transparency and accountability (Acharya et al, 2009). The technical challenges posed by SIBs are therefore significant, but they also have implications for citizenship rights that are not considered by their advocates.

Social Impact Bonds: a boundary shift

Social welfare is big business: it has been estimated that the 'public service industry' in the UK (that is, the value of public services provided by private contractors) amounts to more than £100 billion annually (Gosling, 2011). However, SIBs raise the question of what qualifies as a 'public' or 'private' welfare service, and indeed whether this distinction is anything other than a technicality. Reflecting on the implications of SIBs for service users suggests that this distinction is both important and significant. Burchardt and Hills' (1999) classification of public and private welfare services is an appropriate starting point for considering this issue. This proposes that welfare activity should be analysed using three dimensions:

1. Provision – whether the provider is a public or private sector body
2. Finance – whether the public sector pays for the service either directly or indirectly
3. Decision – whether service users personally choose the provider or amount of service.

This approach defines a service by considering who pays for and delivers it and how it operates. However, a further service dimension that should be considered is what it is run *for*; that is, what purposes it fulfils, and what the defining values are that it promotes. Whether a service is motivated to achieve public benefits or private profit is not incidental to its character, but influences how it is delivered, its quality as an entitlement and the experience of those receiving it. This is not to suggest that a service that has the ostensible purpose of addressing social needs or promoting well-being, and that is directly provided by public servants, is necessarily of higher quality, by any measure (as the experience of many UK social security claimants will testify; see Walker et al, 2012). Nevertheless, the market relationship between a customer and a seller is qualitatively different (which is not to say necessarily 'worse') from that between a public service user and provider, even if the service provider is incentivised, wholly or in part, by targets, league tables, sanctions and other performance measures. There is evidence that a public service ethos exists among many officials employed to provide welfare support to claimants, and this distinguishes their orientation in some measure from those whose principal motivation is profit (Taylor-Gooby, 2008). Therefore a further dimension can be used to classify services as more or less public or private: whether the essential motivation for the provision of the service is recognised social need or profit. SIBs alter the character of services in this respect.

SIBs can be regarded as a boundary shift, that is, a reform that alters the character of a service in a qualitative manner beyond mere quantitative or incremental adjustment (Bolderson, 1982, pp 290–1). The nature of such a shift can be illustrated by comparing SIBs to the PbR funding of the FND and Work Programme, both of which maintained direct public funding of provision and control over services even though these were delivered by private or third sector agents. In contrast, SIBs entail private finance, provision and control over delivery (perhaps with a third sector partner). A conventional probation and offender-rehabilitation service would be classified as purely public, using Burchardt and Hills' criteria, that is, publicly provided and financed, and allocated and delivered by public officials. In contrast, the corresponding service funded by the SIB in Peterborough is privately financed, privately provided, allocated and delivered by public agencies but profit oriented. Table 7.1 illustrates the several degrees of difference between these services.

A boundary shift, as opposed to an incremental development, could be defined as a change in at least two dimensions of the public-private classification, and represents a fundamental adjustment of the responsibility for a service from one sector to another. While a move in one cell could be regarded as what Hall (1993) describes as a routine 'first order' reform, a shift in two dimensions corresponds to a 'second order' policy change, that is, a reform that goes beyond routine incremental adjustment and develops new policy instruments. Such shifts could either diminish or enhance the quality of welfare (in terms of claimants' entitlements and/or capabilities), and this is an empirical question. However, social policies are (or ought to be) concerned with more than instrumental ends – why and how they are provided are important for the experience of service users, and are also statements about ideals of citizenship, fraternity and solidarity that mark the social fabric of a society (Spicker, 2006). Such features as the enforceability of service users' entitlements, their right to appeal decisions and to receive redress for poor service, and other qualities that distinguish social rights from mere benefactions must be considered when analysing and comparing welfare services (Veit-Wilson, 2012).

Table 7.1: Illustration of public and private services

Service format	Finance source		Service provider		Decision making		Motivation	
	Public	Private	Public	Private or third sector	Public	Private	Need	Profit
Conventional probation and rehabilitation service	✓		✓		✓		✓	
HM Prison Peterborough SIB		✓		✓	✓			✓

In outsourcing funding, service delivery and the responsibility for selecting a provider, SIBs erode direct public and democratic accountability for welfare entitlements. The Centre for Social Impact Bonds has proposed that in the case of SIBs, 'where payments are wholly dependent on outcomes … it is appropriate that the specification does little more than identify the target outcomes and any statutory and regulatory requirements that must be met in engaging with the target user groups' (Cabinet Office, 2013a). Therefore, funding, selection of service providers and responsibility for delivery will all be shifted to private or third sector agencies, and 'the government … has no direct relationship with the service provider' (Audit Commission, 2012, p 14). The UK government has declared that any private or third sector organisation can become an investor in a SIB, and that the 'contract should contain limited rights only for the [public] authority to intervene in how it is being performed, given that the contractor will be taking on the risk that outcomes may not be achieved and that, as a result, payments may not be made' (Cabinet

Office, 2013b). The UK government considers it entirely reasonable that investors or intermediaries 'may want some influence over the way the project is delivered, given that they're taking much of the risk', and suggests that taking seats on a project board or asserting the right to assume control over 'or terminate the project in the event of sustained under-performance' are unproblematic (Cabinet Office, 2013b). This is another way in which SIBS do not resemble a conventional bond, as such loans do not grant lenders the right to assume control of the borrower's operations. It also reinforces the point that SIBs mark a shift in the boundary of public policy. It is assumed that a welfare service should be accountable to those who pay for it rather than those who use it, let alone the wider community or their elected representatives, who might be thought to be the ultimate stakeholders. Cabinet Office guidance on designing contracts for SIBs suggests that 'There may be significant value in the commissioner engaging with current or past users of the service and/or service providers, to understand better what is likely to be effective' (Cabinet Office, 2013a). Such user engagement (for example, consulting with released offenders) is motivated by technical considerations and the desire to ensure that appropriate outcomes and measurements are in place, not through any impulse to empowerment nor citizen democracy. The lack of serious consideration of what SIBs imply about citizens' rights raises more basic questions about the role of markets in public welfare provision.

Markets, morality and motivation

It has been pointed out that, from the point of view of private investors, the most attractive SIBs will be those that appear most likely to provide secure and substantial returns, rather than risky innovative projects (Davison and Heap, 2013). However, if it is possible for private investors to distinguish between such options, the question arises as to why governments simply do not finance the most attractive projects themselves (Fox and Albertson, 2012, p 367). The question suggests that a compelling motivation for SIBs, in the UK case at least, is not to improve policy outcomes per se but to increase private involvement in financing and delivering public services. An initiative that might achieve better outcomes for service users but that would not produce dividends for investors would not be funded through SIBs, which therefore limits what counts as a valuable outcome to only those that generate savings. In this respect SIBs are a further expression of what Kynaston described as 'City cultural supremacy' in the UK: the incorporation of the values of financial markets throughout institutions and areas of life that were previously governed by other principles (Kynaston, 2002, p 879).

SIBs represent a further extension of the belief that self-interest activated by means of the profit motive can be harnessed to achieve collective benefit (Ruane, 2013). SIBs shift the motivation for, and therefore the morality of, welfare provision: services and support are no longer provided through a desire to help those in need as a valuable end in itself; rather, changing the circumstances of service users is valued as a metric to trigger payments to investors. This changes the status of the service user from a citizen entitled to support into a commodity processed for profit. SIBs take the pseudo-technical principle that 'what matters is what works' to a new level by dismissing the purposes and intentions of policy as irrelevant to achieving narrowly conceived outcomes. However, such dry instrumentality fails to reflect upon what counts as a service 'working' and how the pursuit of outcomes is shaped by the motivation that prompts them. Receiving a service that is provided by the desire to turn a profit, and where the service user is not even a consumer in their own right but a product accountable to an investor, is a different experience from receiving a service provided out of solidarity. The fact that conventional public services have not always met the standards of quality and respect that they ought to does not alter the purposes and intentions that distinguish them from those provided in order to generate profit.

SIBs are part of a process that de-moralises social policies. Markets are motivated in accordance with considerations of exchange, incentives, profit and reward; their function is to distribute resources. Public welfare policy is about delivering a vision of the Good Society and how to achieve this in an acceptable way (Galbraith, 1997). The process of how this end is accomplished is more than a merely technical matter. Social policies are (or are supposed to be) propelled by beliefs about right and wrong; such principles as entitlement, desert, need, dignity and fairness should inform delivery, not merely a focus on the accomplishment of technical (let alone financial) outcomes. SIBs imply that, for example, the rehabilitation of offenders is no longer prompted by moral motivations but is incentivised by the prospect of profit, and this changes its normative nature. For example, would it be acceptable for a SIB to meet a recidivism target by *paying* ex-offenders not to reoffend? If expense-saving outcomes are all that matters, is it important how they are accomplished? Arguably, there should remain a sphere of social policy and services that are beyond the reach of markets, and debate around the pros and cons of SIBs should be informed by such considerations (Sandel, 2011).

Conclusion

In the face of recession and changing demand for public welfare services there is a need in many societies to consider new operating models and potential funding sources. The persistence of deprivation, exclusion and inequality demonstrates that public services are far from perfect and there are undoubtedly lessons to be learned from the private and third sectors. SIBs are an imaginative response to these challenges and demands; however, they face significant practical challenges themselves. SIBs do not resolve the difficulty of attributing outcomes to inputs; they narrow what is counted as a 'successful' policy; and they risk encouraging service providers to manipulate how their performance is measured and reported. There is also no evidence that SIBs will encourage innovative delivery or widen the pool of service providers. These technical challenges are more significant than those who advocate SIBs often acknowledge.

A more fundamental feature of SIBs is that they alter the moral character of the services that they provide and change the nature of citizenship rights; features which do not seem to have occurred to, let alone trouble, their supporters. Nevertheless, it is important not to lose sight of the ultimate purpose of welfare services when pursuing additional resources and improved ways of delivering services. The distinction between the principles that propel markets and those that ought to guide the provision of support to citizens in need is significant and should be maintained. Rather than pursuing the current vogue for 'innovation' it might be more effective to build upon effective practice and defend existing welfare rights, such as they are. This is perhaps less glamorous, but more likely to produce substantial outcomes.

Note
[1] A bond is a form of security in which debtors borrow from creditors and pay a predetermined rate of interest until the bond is redeemed when it matures. In principle, bonds guarantee repayment, unlike equity products, where the investor can lose their investment.

References

Acharya,V., Philippon,T., Richardson, M. and Roubini, N. (2009) 'The financial crisis of 2007–2009: causes and remedies', *Financial Markets, Institutions & Instruments*, 18(2): 89–137.

Audit Commission (2012) *Local payment by results. Briefing – payment by results for local services.* http://archive.audit-commission.gov.uk/auditcommission/sitecollectiondocuments/Downloads/20120405localPbR.pdf (accessed 10 June 2013).

Azemati, H. et al, (2013) 'Social Impact Bonds: lessons learned so far', *Community Development Investment Review*, 9(1): 22–32.

Bartley, M. (ed) (nd) *Capability and resilience: Beating the odds*, London: UCL Department of Epidemiology and Public Health/ESRC, www.ucl.ac.uk/capabilityandresilience/beatingtheoddsbook.pdf (accessed 15 December 2013).

Batmanghelidjh, C. (2012) 'Address to NCVO trustee conference', London. www.civilsociety.co.uk/finance/news/content/13788/batmanghelidjh_social_impact_bonds_wont_work_for_everyone (accessed 10 June 2013).

Bolderson, H. (1982) 'Ambiguity and obscurity in policy-making for social security', *Policy & Politics*, 10(3): 289–301.

Bolton, E. and Savell, L. (2010) 'Towards a new social economy: blended value creation through Social Impact Bonds', *Social Finance*, www.socialfinance.org.uk/resources/social-finance/towards-new-social-economy-blended-value-creation-through-social-impact-bonds (accessed 10 June 2013).

Burchardt, T. and Hills, J. (1999) *Private welfare and public policy*, York: Joseph Rowntree Foundation.

Cabinet Office (2010) *Modernising commissioning: Increasing the role of charities, social enterprises, mutuals and cooperatives in public service delivery*, London: Cabinet Office.

Cabinet Office (2013a) *Guidance on the template contract for Social Impact Bonds and payment by results*, www.gov.uk/government/publications/guidance-on-the-template-contract-for-social-impact-bonds (accessed 10 June 2013).

Cabinet Office (2013b) *Social Impact Bonds*, www.gov.uk/social-impact-bonds (accessed 10 June 2013).

Chang, H.-J. (2007) *Bad Samaritans: Rich nations, poor people and the threat to the developing world*, London: Random House.

Craig, P. et al (2008) *Developing and evaluating complex interventions: New guidance*, Medical Research Council, www.mrc.ac.uk/Utilities/Documentrecord/index.htm?d=MRC00487 (accessed 15 December 2013).

Damm, C. (2012) *The third sector delivering employment services: An evidence review*, Third Sector Research Centre, Working Paper 70.

Davies, J.S. (2009) 'The limits of joined-up government: towards a political analysis', *Public Administration*, 87(1): 80–96.

Davison, R. (2013) *Does social finance understand social need?* Liverpool: Can Cook. www.cancook.co.uk/wp-content/uploads/2013/01/Does-Social-Enterprise-Understand-Social-Need.pdf (accessed 10 June 2013).

Davison, R. and Heap, H. (2013) *Can social finance meet social need?* Liverpool: Can Cook. www.tomorrows-people.org.uk/files/blog/can-social-finance-meet-social-need-heap-and-davison-june-20131.pdf (accessed 25 July 2013).

Disley, E., Rubin, J., Scraggs, E., Burrowes, N. and Culley, D. (2011) *Lessons learned from the planning and early implementation of the Social Impact Bond at HMP Peterborough*, London: RAND Europe, Research Series 5/11, Ministry of Justice.

DWP (Department for Work and Pensions) (2008) *Raising expectations and increasing support: Reforming welfare for the future*, Cm 7506, London: DWP.

DWP (nd) *The Work Programme: Invitation to tender specification and supporting information, version 5.0*, www.dwp.gov.uk/docs/work-prog-itt.pdf (accessed 10 June 2013).

Fox, C. and Albertson, K. (2012) 'Is payment by results the most effective way to address the challenges faced by the criminal justice sector?' *Probation Journal*, 59(4): 355–73.

Freud, D. (2007) *Reducing dependency, increasing opportunity: Options for the future of welfare to work: an independent report to the Department for Work and Pensions*, London: DWP.

Galbraith, J.K. (1997) *The good society: The humane agenda*, London: Sinclair-Stevenson.

Gosling, P. (2011) *The rise of the 'public services industry' updated*, London: UNISON.

Greenhalgh, R. (2011) '"New" models of social finance', *Centre for Local Economic Strategies, Bulletin*, 86, www.cles.org.uk/wp-content/uploads/2011/10/No-86-New-models-of-social-finance.pdf (accessed 10 June 2013).

Hall, P. (1993) 'Policy paradigms, social learning and the state: the case of economic policymaking in Britain', *Comparative Politics*, 23(4): 275–96.

Hasluck, C. and Green, A.E. (2007) *What works for whom? A review of evidence and meta-analysis for the Department for Work and Pensions*, Research Report No 407, London: DWP.

Hayman, A. (2008) 'Three million jobless: could we cope?' *Regeneration & Renewal*, 14 November.

HM Government (2011) *Open public services*, White Paper, London: Cabinet Office.

Hudson, M., Phillips, J., Ray, K., Vegeris, S. and Davidson, R. (2010) *The influence of outcome-based contracting on provider-led pathways to work*, Research Report No. 638, London: Department for Work and Pensions.

Kingston, J. and Bolton, M. (2004) 'New approaches to funding not-for-profit organisations', *International Journal of Nonprofit and Voluntary Sector Marketing*, 9(2): 112–21.

Kynaston, J. (2002) *The city of London – Volume 4: A club no more, 1945–2000*, London: Pimlico.

Liebman, J.B. (2011) *Social Impact Bonds: A promising new financing model to accelerate social innovation and improve government performance*, Center for American Progress, www.americanprogress.org/issues/open-government/report/2011/02/09/9050/social-impact-bonds/ (accessed 25 July 2013).

Local Government Association (2013) *An introduction to social investment*, London: Local Government Association/Social Finance.

Mulgan, G., Reeder, N., Aylott, M. and Bo'sher, L. (2011) *Social Impact investment: The challenge and opportunity of Social Impact Bonds*, London: The Young Foundation.

Pawson, R. (2006) *Evidence-based policy: A realist perspective*, London: Sage.

Robinson, J. (2012) *Better public services through social impact bonds: Lessons from the US, Canada, New Zealand and Australia*, London: Winston Churchill Fellowship, www.wcmt.org.uk/reports/1074_1.pdf (accessed 9 November 2012).

Rosenberg, T. (2013) 'An investment strategy in the human interest', *New York Times Opinionator*, 19 June, http://opinionator.blogs.nytimes.com/2013/06/19/an-investment-strategy-in-the-human-interest/?_r=0 (accessed 25 July 2013).

Ruane, S. (2013) '"Bringing corporate welfare in" – and pushing further at the boundaries of social policy: a reply to Farnsworth', *Journal of Social Policy*, 42(1): 23–9.

Sandel, M.J. (2011) *What money can't buy: The moral limits of markets*, London: Allen Lane.

Scott, L. (2012) 'Social Impact Bonds: what's that coming over the hill?', acquiringbusiness4good, 16 May, www.senscot.net/view_art. php?viewid=12318 (accessed 10 June 2013).

Social Enterprise UK (2012) *The shadow state: A report about outsourcing of public services*, London: Social Enterprise UK.

Spicker, P. (2006) *Liberty, equality, fraternity*, Bristol: Policy Press.

Spicker, P. (2009) 'The nature of a public service', *International Journal of Public Administration*, 32(11): 970–91

Starr, K. (2012) 'The trouble with impact investing: P1', *Stanford Social Innovation Review*, 24 January, www.ssireview.org/blog/entry/ the_trouble_with_impact_investing_part_1 (accessed 10 June 2013).

Taylor-Gooby, P. (2008) 'Assumptive worlds and images of agency: academic social policy in the twenty-first century?' *Social Policy and Society*, 7(3): 269–80.

Veit-Wilson, J. (2012) 'Heading back to the Poor Law?' *Poverty and Social Exclusion Survey*, http://www.poverty.ac.uk/articles-attitudes-benefits-welfare-editors-pick/heading-back-poor-law (accessed 10 June 2013).

Walker, R., Chase, E. and Lødemel, I. (2012) 'The indignity of the Welfare Reform Act', *Poverty*, 143 (Autumn): 9–12.

Wintour, P. (2012) 'Social Impact Bond launched to help teenagers in care and the homeless', *Guardian*, 23 November.

EIGHT

Creating a legacy of long-term indebtedness: the toxic impact of payday loans in Wolverhampton

Steve Iafrati

Introduction and context

At a time when UK poverty is increasing as both benefits and incomes fail to keep pace with inflation, payday loans (PDLs) are an expanding market in terms of the value and number of loans. Payday loan companies offer short-term unsecured loans repayable on the borrower's next payday, with annual interest rates often in excess of 3,000%. The increasing number of adverts on television (Ofcom, 2013) and their heightened presence on high streets in lower-income areas provides an initial, if somewhat unscientific, barometer of their target audience.

As the popularity of PDLs increases, the impact of this expensive debt is falling disproportionately on the poorest neighbourhoods. Recently, there has been increasing alarm from MPs, the Church of England and voluntary sector organisations regarding the impact of PDLs on neighbourhoods experiencing the brunt of recession and unemployment. Against this background, there have been calls for policy interventions and alternative financial services to limit their impact.

While proposals to use planning regulations to limit the presence of PDL companies on high streets (Smith, 2013), caps on the interest rates and a review of the use of Continuous Payment Authority will have some impact (Personal Finance Research Centre, 2013), this chapter argues that proposed interventions focus too heavily on limiting the *supply* of PDLs. While the supply and impact of PDLs in poorer neighbourhoods is problematic, there is a need for greater focus on factors fuelling *demand* for PDLs. Significantly, demand factors of relative poverty and real-term decline in living standards for many people have fuelled the increase in numbers of PDLs and value of the market.

In addition to existing evidence, this chapter is informed by dialogue with the local authority and debt advice agencies in Wolverhampton regarding their evidence of the PDL market in the city. Wolverhampton, a city in the West Midlands, has suffered from a decline in its traditional manufacturing and industrial economy, with there being above-average unemployment, low skills and low-paid work.

Evidence will be presented of PDLs being most popular in the poorest areas of cities such as Wolverhampton, coupled with evidence that PDLs are being used for everyday expenses rather than one-off, unforeseen expenses. Though their tempting presence and advertising may contribute to their growing popularity, they represent a product that clearly thrives on poverty-led demand. The chapter concludes that we will see a decline in PDLs only through policies that address demand for such credit.

Poverty, demand for debt and payday loans

Dominant discourses relating to poverty have traditionally looked at poverty in terms of relative income, though this can be problematic, as it is ultimately a measure of inequality rather than of ability to meet needs (Spicker, 2012). Recently, understandings of poverty have developed a holistic understanding of people's experiences of not just income, but also living standards and essential expenses, including fuel poverty (Hirsch et al, 2011; Hills, 2012; De Haro and Koslowski, 2013), food poverty (Lambie-Mumford, 2012; 2013; Griffith et al, 2013) and water poverty (Bradshaw and Huby, 2013).

Leading to a more detailed understanding, this recognises a lived experience of poverty amid increasing fuel and energy prices alongside reductions in relative income. Importantly, this more holistic understanding of poverty demonstrates a relative balance between income and consumption that can be a catalyst to debt when savings and cutbacks become impossible, leading to households either borrowing or not paying bills. Evidence shows that 63–79% of PDLs are taken out to cover the cost of 'everyday expenses' or 'to pay household bills', with a further 8–13% of PDLs being used for other debts, including rent/mortgage arrears (Personal Finance Research Centre, 2013). Furthermore, for many low-income households the 'only opportunity for borrowing comes from PDL companies for everyday living expenses and housing costs' (Burton, 2010; YouGov, 2011; OFT, 2012; Personal

Finance Research Centre, 2013), with the result that '13% of the population in Britain have prioritised paying back the [payday] loans over essentials such as buying food and paying gas and electricity bills' (R3, 2012).

PDLs represent a market whereby demand is not prompted by '[temporary] financial difficulty but rather long-term poverty' (Personal Finance Research Centre, 2013, p 110). As such, evidence suggests no 'widespread profligate use of credit to acquire a high materialistic standard of living amongst people on persistent low incomes', with debt being 'a function of persistent low levels of income' among working and unemployed people, and many people 'churning' between work and welfare dependency (Whitfield and Dearden, 2012, p 88). This can be placed in the context of many low-income families having limited access to alternative financial services and being at risk of experiencing financial exclusion (Leyshon et al, 2008; Kempson and Collard, 2012; Banks et al, 2013; Flaherty and Banks, 2013). At the same time, policies to tackle financial exclusion are 'at great risk of being reversed as the current economic situation is placing huge pressures on household budgets' (Rowlingson and McKay, 2013).

During the late 1990s and 2000s, the UK had a period of sustained economic growth that saw increases in both GDP and real-terms income levels. However, since 2008, economic contraction and a double-dip recession have resulted in increased unemployment, and lower real-terms incomes for those in work (Clayton and Brinkley, 2011; Savage, 2011; Pennycook and Whittaker, 2012). Many of the poorest families failed to fully benefit from the 'boom' years and were also the most affected by economic decline (Whitfield and Dearden, 2012).

While economic stagnation and contraction have been consistent since 2008, this period can be split into two distinct phases defined by differences in social policy. Since the 2010 general election there has been a sustained policy of cutting public spending, reducing benefits and pursuing a target of 'small government'. The result of this is a 'double whammy' of both social and economic policy contributing towards increasing and sustained levels of poverty as prices increase at a faster rate than incomes (Crib et al, 2013; DWP, 2013a; Hirsch, 2013), with a total average drop in earnings of 7.1% in real terms since 2008 (Rhodes, 2013). Significantly, price increases have been highest in childcare, rent, public transport, food and energy (Hirsch, 2013), essential areas of expenditure for many households. For those experiencing poverty, a growing proportion of income will be devoted to these essentials. The result for the West Midlands is that it has some of the lowest average pay in the country as well as the highest levels of fuel poverty (Department of Energy and Climate Change, 2012).

Amid such trends there is a political rhetoric of blaming the poor for their poverty (Bochel, 2011; Mooney, 2011; Newman, 2011) and a government belief that poverty is caused by individual choices rather than socio-economic factors (Social Justice Policy Group, 2007). The Chancellor's claims at the 2013 Conservative party conference that some people are 'sleeping off a life on benefits' and choosing a 'lifestyle to sit on out of work benefits' underpin a belief that cuts in welfare will encourage people back into work.

However, despite rising levels of unemployment and increasing poverty in the UK, evidence suggests that poverty is not rooted in a dichotomy of those in work and those on benefits, with the rhetoric of 'workers and shirkers' failing to accurately define poverty in the UK (Aldridge et al, 2012; Lawton and Thompson, 2013; Social Mobility and Child Poverty Commission, 2013). While unemployment has risen to over three million, there has been an increase in zero-hour contracts to include up to one million people, while underemployment of people working part-time when they want to work more hours has also increased by over one million since 2008 (Aldridge et al, 2012; Beatty et al, 2012; ONS, 2012, 2013a; Pyper and McGuinness, 2013). Such changes in the labour market, coupled with wages growing slower than inflation, have led to 6.1 million working people becoming reliant on benefits (Aldridge et al, 2012), amid the 8.3 million classed as 'benefit reliant' (Resolution Foundation, 2013).

Amid disappointing economic growth and rising levels of poverty, households are faced with increasing difficulties in paying bills, managing rent/mortgage payments and covering everyday expenses. With declining relative living standards and an immediate demand for money, PDLs offer a temporary solution that is quick and easy to access. Over the last few years, PDL companies have seen a significant growth in demand for loans, as well as increased profits (R3, 2012; Personal Finance Research Centre, 2013). The Office of Fair Trading (OFT, 2010) estimates that PDLs in 2008 totalled £900m and that by 2012 this figure had grown to £2.2bn (OFT, 2013a). Increasingly, loans are being extended (rolled over) for an average of 3.2 months rather than being paid back in the initial loan period (House of Commons, 2012), with an estimated 36–41% of PDL company revenue coming from rolling over loans and late-payment fees (OFT, 2013a). Problematically, lengthening periods of debt and transferring between debts is most prevalent among borrowers on the lowest incomes and those with least access to family and friends from whom to borrow (Hall and Perry, 2013).

Currently, over 50% of the PDL market is accounted for by three companies, with one of those companies recently announcing a 35% increase in profits between 2011 and 2012 and a 68% increase in loans (Wonga Group Limited, 2013). In the wake of such commercial success, the government is increasingly identifying PDL working practices as problematic (OFT, 2012), with market competition based on speed of PDL decisions leading to PDL companies not carrying out affordability checks in a market that is described as 'not working very well for consumers' (OFT, 2013b).

Amid such trends, understanding of the demand for debt has, in the case of poverty, become more complex since the credit crunch and recessions (Dearden et al, 2010). Rather than studying debt solely in a quantitative cross-sectional manner, there has been greater recognition of particular groups at risk, as well as understanding of the motives for and experiences of debt in a more qualitative manner (Dearden et al, 2010; Flaherty and Banks, 2013). Experiences of debt are heavily influenced by the socio-economic factors leading to growing levels of debt during and following recession (Patel et al, 2012), which increasingly affects younger people with financial vulnerability (Financial Inclusion Centre, 2011). Additionally, subjective analyses of poverty identify those on the lowest incomes being as 13 times more likely to understand their own debt as being a 'heavy burden' (ONS, 2013b) rather than manageable. Research identifies a significant overlap between debt and poverty with an understanding of its causes through price increases and low wages (Collard et al, 2012).

Despite government claims that poverty is an individual issue (DWP, 2011; Harkness et al, 2012), poverty and debt are actually structural rather than agential phenomena. While the politics of the current government emphasise an 'untested' agenda of personal responsibility and agency (Wright, 2012; Peeters, 2013), the PDL market demonstrates a structural link between poverty, geography and financial opportunity, with people in the poorest neighbourhoods being the least geographically mobile (Kelly, 2013). With the PDL problem understood in poverty and structural terms, it follows that policy interventions should be similarly matched.

Potentially, in terms of social policies, economic inequalities and poverty may well be exacerbated by the introduction of Universal Credit, changes to Housing Benefit, reduction in Council Tax Benefit and changes to disability benefits, prompting need for greater understanding of the relationship between welfare and debt (Brewer, Browne and Wechao, 2011; Brewer, Browne and Joyce, 2011; Bushe et al, 2013). There are already concerns that PDL companies will capitalise on such welfare changes to target the poorest households (CAB, 2013).

The biggest step forward in addressing the spread of PDLs will consequently come through addressing demand-side factors, most particularly price inflation experienced by those on low income that is notably above mainstream inflation rates (Levell and Oldfield, 2011), and reversing welfare reforms. Greater controls on energy price increases and other areas of necessity that are highlighted as being drivers for PDL applications will also reduce demand. In relation to energy prices, identified by Hirsch (2013) as rising faster than average inflation, recent price rises of 8–10% have led to the Labour opposition proposing a price freeze, should it be elected in 2016, and the current government looking to lower prices by reducing the green levy on energy companies.

Wolverhampton: a case study

Debt advice agencies in Wolverhampton are identifying a rapidly growing use of PDLs in the city that are contributing to debt problems. By the start of 2013, there were over 32,000 active PDLs in Wolverhampton, a city with a working-age population of 159,418 living in 102,177 households. Of these loans, most were concentrated in the city's poorest wards, with wards featuring unemployment rates exceeding 10% having the highest numbers of PDLs. In one particular ward, with some of the highest levels of deprivation, there were nearly 2,200 active PDLs among a working-age population of 7,700. With the national average for a PDL being £270–£294 (Burton, 2010; OFT, 2013a; 2013b), that would mean a possible PDL debt of nearly £650,000 in this ward alone. According to methodology used by Burton (2010) and data from the OFT (2013a; 2013b), the added interest costs of the loans is likely to be in the region of £170,000–£200,000, making total PDL debt in the ward in excess of £800,000 and possibility possible £4m of PDL debt in the five city wards with unemployment persistently over 10%.

This debt can be added to rent arrears (likely to rise with changes to Housing Benefit), debt to the city council (which may increase as Council Tax Benefit is abolished), and other significant debts. The collective impact will be to further push down standards of living for a group of people who are likely to be the least geographically and socially mobile. With PDLs having APR interest rates often in excess of 3,000%, the poorest neighbourhoods in the city are experiencing not only the largest burden of hyper-expensive debt, but also the fastest growth of such debt. Ultimately, this will undermine attempts to address poverty and will stifle economic recovery and regeneration currently identified by the city council (Wolverhampton City Council, 2013a).

With an economy traditionally reliant on industry, Wolverhampton has experienced a range of difficulties in its transition to a post-industrial economy. Traditional areas of work, including steel works, tyre manufacturing and small manufacturing companies, have closed, and while there has been some development of high-value manufacturing, 'many high-paying jobs have either been replaced by lower-paying consumer service positions or are taken by in-commuters with higher skills' (Wolverhampton City Council, 2010, p 6). While other areas of the country were 'better prepared to respond to the shock of recession', the limited range of businesses, skills and 'innovative capacity' has disadvantaged Wolverhampton's ability to regenerate (Wolverhampton City Council, 2010, p 6). The result is a 'gap in economic performance between Wolverhampton and other areas [that] has widened, as the decline of traditional industries has left concentrations of inter-generational unemployment, high levels of deprivation and low skills' (Wolverhampton City Council, 2010, p 6). However, the socio-economic position of the city, its skills profile, demographics and patterns of deprivation make Wolverhampton far from unique among those post-industrial regions in the UK experiencing high levels of multiple deprivation, recession, and unemployment persistently higher than national and regional averages.

Even for those in employment, Wolverhampton has above-average concentration of low-paid jobs and numbers of people with low or no qualifications. Additionally, the city has seen a growth in the percentage of children in jobless households, indicators of poverty have worsened and the city council sees little prospect of these trends being reversed (Wolverhampton City Council, 2009; Wolverhampton in Profile, 2013). Looking in greater detail, the effects of economic stagnation have most seriously affected the poorest parts of the city, with 5 of the city's 20 wards experiencing unemployment persistently over 10% and even higher among certain demographic groups such as young people, where it can be over 20% (Wolverhampton in Profile, 2013).

Furthermore, welfare reforms such as limiting benefit increases to 1%, abolition of the spare room subsidy ('bedroom tax') and changes to disability benefits will exacerbate the situation and, by definition, negatively impact on those already affected by economic downturn. For the poorest neighbourhoods in Wolverhampton that have seen a decline in living standards since 2008 (Wolverhampton City Council, 2010), the bedroom tax will affect 2,000 households; limiting benefit increases to below inflation will intensify demand for supplementary sources of income; and changes to Council Tax Benefit mean that even the poorest in the city will pay at least 8.5% of their Council Tax. Wolverhampton City Council estimates that even those on low incomes will have to pay in excess of £700 towards their Council Tax in the financial year 2013/14 and over £1,000 in 2014/15 (Wolverhampton City Council, 2013a).

The government's proposal to pay Housing Benefit directly to tenants has been shown in pilot studies elsewhere in the country to lead to additional debt (Wilson, 2013). This exacerbates the fears of organisations such as Shelter that people are taking out PDLs to pay their rent (YouGov, 2011), and evidence from the Personal Finance Research Centre's (2013) study prompts a similar conclusion that tenants will turn to PDLs to pay off rent arrears so as to avoid eviction.

Policy solutions

Ultimately, success in addressing the spread of PDLs will come only when responses focus on the factors fuelling demand rather than solely on regulating the supply of such loans. To date, the main calls for regulation of PDLs have been to limit interest rates, to control the number of roll overs and to limit administration charges. Subsequently, on 25 November 2013, the Chancellor of the Exchequer proposed amendments to the Banking Reform Bill to create 'much stronger powers to protect consumers in financial services' by placing 'a cap on the total cost of credit ... not just the interest fee, but also the arrangement fees as well as the penalty fees'.

In the search for solutions, there have also been calls for alternative financial services that are not characterised by causing unnecessary 'misery and hardship' (OFT, 2013b). For many, the natural choice is the expansion of credit unions as a way of providing mutual financial support coupled with financial literacy and community involvement (DWP Credit Union Expansion Project, 2012; Glasgow City Council, 2012; Guardian, 2013).

However, despite credit unions' appeal as providers of 'affordable credit' and 'suitable financial services to those on low incomes' (DWP Credit Union Expansion Project, 2012), they are unlikely to be the solution. Not only do they maintain a focus on supply-side solutions of enabling better debt, rather than addressing the demand for debt, but credit unions also demand a period of regular saving before borrowing, which may prove difficult for those already experiencing poverty. Additionally, credit unions are a financial model that has not proved popular, with fewer than 2.5% of the population having a credit union account (World Council of Credit Unions, 2012). Consequently, credit union loans do not represent a product that is able to meet the financial immediacy of debt/poverty that is capitalised upon by PDLs. Furthermore, should there be a significant expansion of credit unions in terms of membership, evidence suggests that this would still see 'riskier' loans being rejected if credit unions were to maintain low or even market interest rates (Stango, 2012). In essence, credit unions provide a different financial product than PDLs, which makes comparison problematic. While many credit unions risk being financially 'unsustainable', their strength lies in providing a saving and subsequent loan service to those excluded from mainstream financial services (DWP Credit Union Expansion Project, 2012), while many PDL customers already have bank/building society accounts to receive PDLs.

From a local perspective, some neighbourhoods might benefit from the lower-cost finance available from credit unions. This could be through relaxation of regulations or through proactive targeting of credit unions to prospective members at an early age, as seen in Glasgow, which has the largest credit union membership in the UK and proposals for every teenager to be given a credit union account (Glasgow City Council, 2012; Wright, 2013). Similarly, it is beneficial for people in poorer neighbourhoods to have a choice of financial services other than PDLs. Problematically, this means that the issue of risk needs to be addressed or underwritten in a way that does not involve exorbitant interest rates. However, greater supply of financial services and the expansion of credit unions cannot sustainably address the problem of increasing poverty in cases of incomes not being able to cover expenditure. Essentially, cities such as Wolverhampton, and especially the poorest neighbourhoods in Wolverhampton, need to break free from an increasing cycle of low-pay/low-demand economies, by increasing employment rates and government interventions to limit increases in the prices of essential items identified by Hirsch (2013), including transport, energy and childcare.

Part of the problem for many low-income neighbourhoods is the persistently high levels of unemployment in these areas, coupled with a concentration of workers in low-paid employment and underemployment. In certain geographical areas there exist a range of social and economic barriers to employment that can be best addressed through targeted responses (Joyce et al, 2010). Job creation has to be seen as a priority, with new employment opportunities being concentrated on benefiting the poorest wards; problematically, this comes at a time when cuts in local government budgets mean that local authorities such as Wolverhampton City Council will make cuts to economic development that will 'significantly reduce [Wolverhampton's] ability to stimulate economic growth' (Wolverhampton City Council, 2013b; 2013c). Similarly, for those in employment, the introduction of a 'living wage', which is estimated to place only an additional 1% on company wage costs, would ensure benefits for both the company and the employees (Bennett and Lister, 2010; Pennycook and Lawton, 2013). In addition to paying a living wage, it is important to ensure that work is seen to be secure and that wages are negotiated through a strong wage bargaining structure; currently, this seems to be an unlikely possibility, as previously mentioned trends in the labour market, including zero-hour contracts and underemployment, highlight rising insecurity and low pay for those in work.

Additionally, the restriction of benefit increases to a below-inflation 1% – a real-terms cut in income – and other welfare reforms will serve only to increase debt, poverty and, ultimately, the use of PDLs for the eight million people previously identified as relying on social security benefits (Resolution Foundation, 2013). On a national level, the Chancellor's commitment to cutting annually managed expenditure and public spending through areas such as the 'bedroom tax', reduced Council Tax benefits and changes to disability benefits will reduce their effect as automatic stabilisers in the economy. Thus, there is a chance that cutting benefits will reduce the economy's ability to recover and will also reduce economic demand in those neighbourhoods most reliant on benefits.

While solutions may seem costly and politically difficult to achieve, the alternative is a spiral of debt and deprivation that is gradually gaining momentum in many low-income neighbourhoods. The more this gains in momentum, the harder it will be to reverse the direction of travel and the more it will cost to do so. The cost of addressing poverty through benefits is currently high and will increase, with greater levels of rent arrears and unrecovered Council Tax. In essence, addressing PDLs as an element of financial indebtedness and the demand emanating from poverty is, in real terms, a form of social and economic investment, of one bears in mind their structural dimension. Government aims to develop greater social investment in lower-income areas represent a particular, business-like vision (Cabinet Office, 2011), although it is hard to envisage this prospering in low-income neighbourhoods without greater market intervention and incentives to investment. This stands in contrast with previous Labour governments' more social attempts, which focused on neighbourhoods with the highest needs (Churchill, 2011).

Labour's mooted concept of predistribution (Miliband, 2012) represents a strategy in which some of the demand-led factors might be addressed. Continuing New Labour's logic of social investment, there is a belief that it is better to address the problems of inequality than for government to intervene to compensate for poverty. Clearly, the vagueness of the concept in current UK political rhetoric and its limited examination in social policy allows for varied responses and policy directions. If the outcome of predistribution is a model of responsible capitalism (Martell, 2012), then it is likely that we will see a continued focus on managing the supply side of PDLs by ensuring that they present a more ethical product. This in itself would be no bad thing, given the findings of the Citizens Advice Bureau regarding the sector's working practices, although it would not alone produce an approach that 'addresses inequalities at source, through state interventions into the operation of market systems to reduce income inequalities and shift power towards the lower paid' (Taylor-Gooby, 2012, p.13).

Conclusion

In conclusion, while the government has become increasingly keen on less market intervention and smaller government, it is important to realise the nature of debt not only as a force that damages the lives of individuals, but as something increasingly affecting specific neighbourhoods and that will exacerbate differences between the 'haves' and 'have nots' in many cities. This will reinforce geographical patterns of poverty, limit economic development in the city and diminish strategic attempts to address poverty and its outcomes.

It can be assumed that any legal or policy intervention in the PDL market will be based on limiting and placing new conditions on the supply of such loans. However, if policies are based solely on supply-side limits, they will fail to address the poverty and debt of which PDLs are an increasing element. In fact, in terms of the supply of financial services, the problem for many low-income areas is that there is an already limited and declining supply of financial services, and supply-side policies should be aiming to increase rather than decrease financial services. That way, there would be lower-priced loans as more reputable companies such as banks and building societies were enticed back into the high streets of poorer areas. This would involve possible support from local authorities through planning and incentives. The UK government's current interest in the financial sector through part-ownership of Royal Bank of Scotland and, to a lesser extent, Lloyds Bank might allow the government to encourage or even underwrite financial services in poorer neighbourhoods.

Despite the possibility that we might see some increased market regulation and perhaps an even larger and more user-friendly market, the bottom line is that the PDL market, as well as the lack of mainstream financial services in certain neighbourhoods, is fuelled by poverty. Only by addressing the fundamental problem of poverty will we see a sustainable and significant decrease in demand for PDLs. Evidence of the reasons for taking out loans and the geographical spread of loans shows that persistent poverty and low incomes are the driving forces in the PDL market's expansion.

Local authorities, with support from central government, need to develop strategies that will address poverty. These need to involve implementing a living wage, increasing employment levels and identifying the reasons for low employment (such as lack of necessary skills), and looking at how new jobs can be located in poor areas. Without question, this might be a costly option, but it can be argued that the cost of not doing this might be even higher. Labour's concept of predistribution is one possible way of creating awareness of demand factors, by addressing problems in the economy rather than problems in the PDL market.

References

Aldridge, H., Kenway, P., MacInnes, T. and Parekh, A. (2012) *Monitoring poverty and social exclusion 2012*, York: Joseph Rowntree Foundation.

Banks, S., Brown, G., Flaherty, J., Herrington, T. and Waters, M. (2013) *Debt on Teeside: Pathways to financial inclusion. Final report*, Durham: Centre for Social Justice and Community Action, Durham University.

Beatty, C., Fothergill, S. and Gore, T. (2012) *The real level of unemployment 2012*, Sheffield: Centre for Regional, Economic and Social Research, Sheffield Hallam University.

Bennett, F. and Lister, R. (2010) *The 'living wage': The right answer to low pay?*, London: Fabian Society.

Bochel, H. (ed) (2011) *The Conservative Party and social policy*, Bristol: Policy Press.

Bradshaw, J. and Huby, M. (2013) 'Water poverty in England and Wales', *Journal of Poverty and Social Justice*, 21(2): 137–48.

Brewer, M., Browne, J. and Joyce, R. (2011) *Child and working-age poverty 2010–2020*, London: Institute for Fiscal Studies.

Brewer, M., Browne, J. and Wenchao, J. (2011) *Universal credit: A preliminary analysis*, Briefing Note 116, London: Institute for Fiscal Studies.

Burton, M. (2010) *Keeping the plates spinning: Perceptions of payday loans in Great Britain*, London: Consumer Focus.

Bushe, S., Kenway, P. and Aldridge, H. (2013) *The impact of localising Council Tax Benefit*, York: Joseph Rowntree Foundation.

Cabinet Office (2011) *Growing the social investment market: A vision and strategy*, London: HM Government.

Churchill, H. (2011) 'Wither the social investment state? Early intervention, prevention and children's services reform in the new policy context', paper presented at the Social Policy Association conference, University of Lincoln, 4–6 July.

CAB (Citizens Advice Bureau) (2013) 'Citizens Advice warns payday lenders could prey on universal credit claimants', press release, 25 November.

Clayton, N. and Brinkley, I. (2011) *Welfare to what? Prospects and challenges for employment recovery*, London: Work Foundation.

Collard, S., Finney, A. and Davies, S. (2012) *Working households' experiences of debt problems*, London: StepChange Debt Charity.

Crib, J., Hood, A., Joyce, R. and Phillips, D. (2013) *Living standards, poverty and inequality in the UK: 2013*, Report R81, London: Institute for Fiscal Studies.

Dearden, C., Goode, J., Whitfield, G. and Cox, L. (2010) *Credit and debt in low-income families*, York: Joseph Rowntree Foundation.

De Haro, M. and Koslowski, A. (2013) 'Fuel poverty and high rise living: Using community based interviewers to investigate tenants' inability to keep warm in their homes', *Journal of Poverty and Social Justice*, 21(2): 109–21.

Department for Energy and Climate Change (2012) *Annual Report on Fuel Poverty Statistics*, London: Department of Energy and Climate Change.

DWP (Department for Work and Pensions) (2011) *A new approach to child poverty: Tackling the causes of disadvantage and transforming families' lives*, London: HM Government.

DWP (2013) *Households below average income*, London: Department for Work and Pensions.

DWP Credit Union Expansion Project (2012) *Project steering committee feasibility study report*, London: Department for Work and Pensions.

Financial Inclusion Centre (2011) *Debt and the family series: Report 2: Debt and the generations*, London: Consumer Credit Counselling Service.

Flaherty, J. and Banks, S. (2013) 'In whose interest? The dynamics of debt in poor households', *Journal of Poverty and Social Justice*, 21(3): 219–32.

Glasgow City Council (2012) *Strategic Plan 2012–2017*, Glasgow: Glasgow City Council.

Griffith, R., O'Connell, M. and Smith, K. (2013) *Food expenditure and nutritional quality over the great recession*, Briefing Note BN143, London: Institute for Fiscal Studies.

Guardian (2013) 'Archbishop of Canterbury wants to "compete" Wonga out of existence', 25 July.

Hall, S. and Perry, C. (2013) *Family matters: Understanding families in an age of austerity*, London: Family and Childcare Trust.

Harkness, S., Gregg, P. and MacMillan, L. (2012) *Poverty: The role of behaviours, institutions and culture*, York: Joseph Rowntree Foundation.

Hills, J. (2012) *Getting the measure of fuel poverty: Final report of the Fuel Poverty Review*, CASE Report 72, London: Centre for Analysis of Social Exclusion, London School of Economics.

Hirsch, D. (2013) *A minimum income standard for the UK in 2013*, York: Joseph Rowntree Foundation.

Hirsch, D., Preston, I. and White, V. (2011) *Understanding fuel expenditure: Fuel poverty and spending on fuel*, London: Centre for Sustainable Energy.

House of Commons Business Innovation and Skills Committee (2012) *Debt Management*, Fourteenth Report of Session 2010–12.

Joyce, K., Smith, K., Sullivan, C. and Bambra, C. (2010) '"Most of the industry's shutting down up here …": Employment initiatives to tackle worklessness in areas of low labour market demand', *Social Policy and Society*, 9(3): 337–53.

Kelly, B. (2013) *The process of socio-economic constraint on geographical mobility: England 1991 to 2008*, Working Paper 2013-08, Manchester: Centre for Census and Survey Research, University of Manchester.

Kempson, E. and Collard, S. (2012) *Developing a vision for financial inclusion*, Bristol: University of Bristol.

Lambie-Mumford, H. (2012) 'Regeneration and food poverty in the United Kingdom: learning from the New Deal for Communities programme', *Community Development Journal*, 48(4): 540–54.

Lambie-Mumford, H. (2013) '"Every town should have one": emergency food banking in the UK', *Journal of Social Policy*, 42(1): 73–89.

Lawton, K. and Thompson, S. (2013) *Tackling in-work poverty by supporting dual earning families*, York: Joseph Rowntree Foundation.

Levell, P. and Oldfield, Z. (2011) *The spending patterns and inflation experience of low-income households over the past decade,* London: Institute for Fiscal Studies.

Leyshon, A., French, S. and Signoretta, P. (2008) 'Financial exclusion and the geography of bank and building society branch closure in Britain', *Transactions of the Institute of British Geographers,* 33(4): 447–65.

Martell, L. (2012) 'Can predistribution deliver responsible capitalism?' *Social Europe Journal,* [online] http://www.social-europe.eu/2012/09/can-predistribution-deliver-responsible-capitalism/.

Miliband, E. (2012) Speech to Policy Network: 'Labour's New Agenda', 6 September.

Mooney, G. (2011) *Stigmatising poverty? The 'broken society' and reflections on anti-welfarism in the UK today,* Oxford: Oxfam GB.

Newman, I. (2011) 'Work as a route out of poverty: a critical evaluation of the UK welfare to work policy', *Policy Studies,* 32(2): 91–108.

Ofcom (2013) *Trends in advertising activity: Payday loans,* London: Ofcom.

OFT (Office of Fair Trading) (2010) *Review of high cost credit final report. Annexe D – Theories of harm and consumer detriment,* London: Office of Fair Trading.

OFT (2012) *Payday lending compliance review – interim report,* London: Office of Fair Trading.

OFT (2013a) *Payday lending compliance review – final report. Annex A: Quantitative findings,* London: Office of Fair Trading.

OFT (2013b) *Payday lending compliance review – final report,* London: Office of Fair Trading.

ONS (Office for National Statistics) (2012) 'Underemployed workers up 1 million since onset of downturn', news release, 28 November.

ONS (2013a) *Estimating zero-hour contracts from the Labour Force Survey,* London: Office for National Statistics.

ONS (2013b) *Wealth in Great Britain wave 2: The burden of household debt in Great Britain,* London: Office for National Statistics.

Patel, A., Balmer, N. and Pleasence, P. (2012) 'Debt and disadvantage: the experience of unmanageable debt and financial difficulty in England and Wales', *International Journal of Consumer Studies,* 36(5): 556–65.

Peeters, R. (2013) 'Responsibilisation on government's terms: new welfare and the governance of responsibility and solidarity', *Social Policy and Society,* 12(4): 583–95.

Pennycook, M. and Lawton, K. (2013) *Beyond the bottom line: The challenges and opportunities of a living wage,* London: Resolution Foundation & Institute for Public Policy Research.

Pennycook, M. and Whittaker, M. (2012) *Low pay Britain 2012*, London: Resolution Foundation.

Personal Finance Research Centre (2013) *The impact on business and consumers of a cap on the total cost of credit*, report by University of Bristol for Department for Innovation, Business & Skills.

Pyper, D. and McGuinness, F. (2013) 'Zero hour contracts', House of Commons Library, standard note SN/BT/6553.

R3 (2012) *Personal debt snapshot: 'Zombie' debtors emerge*, London: Association of Business Recovery Professionals.

Resolution Foundation (2013) *Squeezed Britain 2013*, London: Resolution Foundation.

Rhodes, C. (ed) (2013) *Economics indicators, September 2013*, Research Paper 13/52, House of Commons Library.

Rowlingson, K. and McKay, S. (2013) *Financial inclusion annual monitoring report 2013*, Birmingham: University of Birmingham.

Savage, L. (2011) *Low pay Britain*, London: Resolution Foundation.

Smith, L. (2013) 'Planning use class orders', House of Commons Library, standard note SN/SC/1301.

Social Justice Policy Group (2007) *Breakthrough Britain. Ending the costs of social breakdown*, London: Conservative Party Social Justice Policy Group.

Social Mobility and Child Poverty Commission (2013) *State of the nation 2013: Social mobility and child poverty in Great Britain*, London: Social Mobility and Child Poverty Commission.

Spicker, P. (2012) 'Why refer to poverty as a proportion of median income', *Journal of Poverty and Social Justice*, 20(2): 163–75.

Stango, V. (2012) 'Some new evidence on competition in payday lending markets', *Contemporary Economic Policy*, 30: 149–61.

Taylor-Gooby, P. (2012) *A left trilemma: Progressive public policy in the age of austerity*, London: Policy Network.

Whitfield, G. and Dearden, C. (2012) 'Low income households: Casualties of the boom, casualties of the bust?' *Social Policy and Society*, 11(1): 81–91.

Wilson, W. (2013) 'Paying the housing element of Universal Credit direct to tenants in social rented housing', House of Commons Library, standard note SN/SP/6291.

Wolverhampton City Council (2009) *Window on Wolverhampton*, Wolverhampton: Wolverhampton City Council.

Wolverhampton City Council (2010) *Wolverhampton economic assessment – 2010*, report prepared by GHK, Wolverhampton: Wolverhampton City Council.

Wolverhampton City Council (2013a) *Council Tax reduction scheme consultation. How the new proposals affect you*, Wolverhampton: Wolverhampton City Council.

Wolverhampton City Council (2013b) 'Rationalisation of economic development and Black Country working', Cabinet paper, 23 October, Wolverhampton: Wolverhampton City Council.

Wolverhampton City Council (2013c) 'Transitioning from Local Neighbourhood Partnerships to community led economic development – stage two', Cabinet paper, 23 October, Wolverhampton: Wolverhampton City Council.

Wolverhampton in Profile (2013) *Wolverhampton in Profile* [online], http://www.wolverhamptoninprofile.org.uk/profiles/profile?profile Id=14&geoTypeId=26&geoIds=Wolverhampton.

Wonga Group Limited (2013) *Annual report 2012*, London: OpenWonga.

World Council of Credit Unions (2012) *2012 statistical report. Credit Unions Worldwide*, Washington: World Council of Credit Unions.

Wright, J. (2013) *Credit unions: A solution to poor bank lending*, London: Civitas.

Wright, S. (2012) 'Welfare to work, agency and personal responsibility', *Journal of Social Policy*, 41(2): 309–28.

YouGov (2011) 'Millions rely on credit to pay for home', http://england. shelter.org.uk/news/previous_years/2012/january_2012/millions_ rely_on_credit_to_pay_for_home and also http://cdn.yougov.com/ cumulus_uploads/document/h3ln9mpb40/YG-Archives-Shelter-PayingMortgageCreditLoans-170112-WebsiteEdit.pdf.

NINE

No future to risk? The impact of economic crises and austerity on young people at the margins of European employment and welfare settings

Marion Ellison[1]

Introduction

The imposition of austerity measures on global labour markets already severely damaged by economic crises is estimated to have increased global unemployment levels by 202 million, with 5.9 million jobs being lost in Europe since 2008 (O'Higgins, 2010; ILO, 2013). Young people have borne the brunt of a heavily depleted and debilitated European jobs market (Dicken, 2007; Carlson, 2013). In 'liberal competitive' employment and welfare settings such as the UK, this has been exacerbated by deterioration in working conditions and withdrawal of employment rights over the previous two decades (Hogarth, 2009; Kompier, 2009; Hurley, 2011; Kersbergen and Hemerijck, 2012). For young people at the margins of European labour markets the lived experiences of crises and austerity are often defined by personal despair, deterioration in mental and physical health and the perception of a hopeless future. In the UK these brutal realities have been documented in a major survey carried out by The Prince's Trust (2014). The survey found that more than 'three quarters of a million young people between the age of 16–25 believe they have nothing to live for', with 40% of young people suffering 'devastating symptoms of mental illness', including suicidal thoughts, self-loathing and panic attacks, as a direct result of unemployment. With nearly one million young people who are not in employment, education or training and 430,000 young people facing long-term unemployment, the situation is critical in the UK (The Prince's Trust

Macquarie, 2014).These findings are echoed by *The World of Work Report* (ILO, 2012), which found that fiscal austerity and labour market reforms across Europe have had 'devastating consequences' for employment while mostly failing to cut deficits, and warned that governments risked fuelling unrest unless they combined tighter spending with job creation. Lower employment levels, higher unemployment, more marginally attached workers and growing levels of underemployment pervade the lived experiences of young people (between ages of 16 and 25) across a number of European societies (ILO, 2013; OECD, 2013).The combined impact of a labour market increasingly permeated by precarious, poorly paid, unstable jobs and reductions in public and welfare expenditures has exacerbated the levels of poverty and marginalisation endured by young people across a number of European societies. In particular, the growth in the number of part-time, temporary jobs and the alarming rise of zero hours contracts has deepened financial and personal insecurity for young people, particularly within competitive labour markets such as the UK's (Bell and Blanchflower, 2013). Concern with these developments resonates in recent communications from the EU Commission with a call for increases in job opportunities for young people as a priority, which should not be achieved at the cost of 'lower job quality and increased levels of insecurity'. Launching the Youth Guarantee scheme in December 2012, the EU urged member states to ensure that all young Europeans have access to good-quality employment, continued education, training or an apprenticeship within four months of leaving school or becoming unemployed (EU, 2012). Drawing upon evidence from the UK, Greece, Netherlands, Germany, Denmark, Sweden, Finland, Scotland and Norway, this chapter analyses the impact of austerity and social investment strategies specifically designed to enable young people to enter, strengthen and sustain their position within the labour market. Adopting a 'Varieties of Capitalism' approach, the chapter examines evidence relating to the experience of young people within distinct labour market settings and welfare settings (Kitschelt, 2012). Following the Varieties of Capitalism approach, distinct labour market and welfare settings are considered in terms of the dichotomy between liberal competitive and coordinated cooperative market economies (Hall, 2001). Liberal competitive labour market settings are characterised by flexible labour market arrangements underpinned by the rationale that the efficient working of the market relies upon flexibility and the de-regulation of social, employment and labour market policies. In contrast, coordinated labour market settings are characterised by cooperative arrangements with a commitment to the protection of workers against structural inequalities arising from the operation of the market. Integrated services and programmes involve both employers and the state. Importantly, in cooperative labour markets both employers and employees share the costs and future benefits of investments in integrated services such as education and training, and more targeted labour market programmes. This level of integration is of particular relevance to the quality of provision available to young people from disadvantaged backgrounds, as programmes compensate for social exclusion and often lead to permanent employment. In addition, coordinated cooperative labour markets are usually characterised by more generous provision of social protection. As this chapter will reveal, this dichotomy of labour market and welfare arrangements becomes very significant when applied to the outcomes for disadvantaged young people within Europe. In particular, whilst the level of investment in education, training and ALMPs in coordinated cooperative labour markets is found to be of significance for young people at the margins of European labour markets, of equal significance is the level of integrative capacity of these investments in terms of the relationship between work, education and training. For example, apprenticeship systems that entail a substantial commitment between employers and the state, involving the completion of full professional qualifications, are found to have long-term value for the individual, the economy and society. The impact of austerity and distinct labour market arrangements on inequality and the stratification of social risks are also addressed within the chapter. In particular, it is argued that in liberal market economies such as the UK, characterised by the dominance of the market, financial services and individualism, there is a growing 'tension between social protection measures and economic competition' (Hay, 2005, p198). This tension exacerbates the feedback loop between socio-economic conditions of the stratification of life chances and social risks and economic inequality. Using this theoretical approach and a framework for understanding youth transitions within distinct youth employment and welfare systems (Figure 9.3), the chapter critically evaluates the impacts of austerity and social investment measures upon employment outcomes, inequality and the social stratification of social risks for young people at the margins of European labour markets as they undertake transitions between education and employment within 'liberal competitive' and 'coordinated cooperative employment and welfare settings'.

The economic and social cost of recession and austerity for young Europeans

Following the economic and financial crises of 2008, the gap between total unemployment rates and youth unemployment rates across the EU 27 increased by 2.6 times by the end of 2012 (Eurostat, 2013). As Table 9.1 indicates, this upward trend has continued in most European countries. At the time of writing, recovery of the youth employment market to pre-crisis levels has eluded all European states apart from Germany and Austria. The impact of the economic crisis in 2008 on the stratification of social risks for disadvantaged young people has been mediated by economic conditions, the severity of austerity measures and the principles underlying social investment approaches, particularly with regard to the level, form and degree of strategic integration of investments in education and training, labour market programmes, minimum-income support, employment law and job security (Sinfield, 2011; Grusky and Kricheli-Katz, 2012; Taylor-Gooby, 2013). Critically, youth employment is particularly sensitive to fluctuations and changes in labour market conditions and youth unemployment rates are usually much higher than unemployment rates for all ages. The economic crisis has had a more severe impact on the young (defined as between 16 and 25 years old) than on any other age group. As Table 9.1 reveals, youth unemployment rates and ratios have shown an increasingly upward trend in most European countries. An important caveat to these recent indicators is that overall youth unemployment rates include young people who are studying full time and therefore not actively looking for work. Recent data from the Organisation for Economic Co-operation and Development (OECD) (2013) shows that education is still the best protection against long-term unemployment, despite the recession. The youth unemployment ratio may be regarded as a more accurate measurement of the long-term prospects for young people within specific settings, as it calculates the proportion of unemployed young people for the whole population. Another key issue, however, relates to rising levels of underemployment amongst young people. This issue is more pronounced within 'liberal competitive' markets.

For young people living at the margins of the European job market the long-term personal, social and economic cost of crisis and austerity is significant, with an estimated 7.5 million young people (between the ages of 15 and 24) not in employment, education or training (NEET) across the EU (Eurostat, 2013). As Figure 9.1 reveals, NEET rates vary significantly across countries, from 5.5% of young people in the Netherlands to 15.1% in the UK and 22.7% in Italy. Critically, most young people within this category have low levels of education. Addressing this, the EU 2020 Strategy 'Youth on the Move' focuses upon the vulnerability of young people with low levels of education and calls for sustainable support measures to aid the transition from education to work within a global knowledge economy. Bolstering this, the EU has implemented social investment measures aimed at supporting Europe's 'lost generation' of young unemployed, including a €5 billion programme of apprenticeships and training based upon an integrated approach to youth transitions. Recognising the 'social aspects of education in fostering sustainable development, active citizenship and personal fulfilment', the European Commission has identified youth transitions from education to employment as pivotal within complex and long-term attachment to the labour market and society itself (Council of the European Union, 2013, p 3).

Table 9.1: Youth unemployment rate, ratio between 2008 and 2012

	Youth unemployment rate				Youth unemployment ratio		
	2010	2011	2012	2012Q4*	2010	2011	2012
EU-27	21.1	21.4	22.8	23.2	9.0	9.1	9.7
Euro area	20.9	20.8	23.0	23.7	8.7	8.7	9.6
Belgium	22.4	18.7	19.8	22.0	7.3	6.0	6.2
Bulgaria	21.8	25.0	28.1	28.4	6.7	7.4	8.5
Czech Republic	18.3	18.1	19.5	19.3	5.7	5.4	6.1
Denmark	14.0	14.2	14.1	14.2	9.4	9.6	9.1
Germany	9.9	8.6	8.1	7.9	5.1	4.5	4.1
Estonia	32.9	22.3	20.9	19.3	12.6	9.1	8.7
Ireland	27.6	29.1	30.4	29.4	12.0	12.1	12.3
Greece	32.9	44.4	55.3	57.9	10.0	13.0	16.1
Spain	41.6	46.4	53.2	55.2	17.8	19.0	20.6
France	23.6	22.8	24.3	25.4	8.9	8.4	9.0
Italy	27.8	29.1	35.3	36.9	7.9	8.0	10.1
Cyprus	16.6	22.4	27.8	31.8	6.7	8.7	10.8
Latvia	37.2	31.0	28.4	24.7	13.9	11.6	11.4
Lithuania	35.3	32.2	26.4	24.2	10.4	9.0	7.7
Luxembourg	15.8	16.4	18.1	18.5	3.5	4.2	5.0
Hungary	26.6	26.1	28.1	28.8	6.6	6.4	7.3
Malta	13.1	13.8	14.2	14.5	6.7	7.1	7.2
Netherlands	8.7	7.6	9.5	9.8	6.0	5.3	6.6
Austria	8.8	8.3	8.7	8.7	5.2	5.0	5.2
Poland	23.7	25.8	26.5	27.5	8.2	8.7	8.9
Portugal	27.7e	30.1	37.7	38.4	8.2	11.7	14.3
Romania	22.1	23.7	22.7	22.2	6.9	7.4	7.0
Slovenia	14.7	15.7	20.6	23.2	5.9	5.9	7.1
Slovakia	33.9	33.5	34.0	35.1	10.4	10.0	10.4
Finland	21.4	20.1	19.0	19.3	10.6	10.1	9.8
Sweden	24.8	22.8	23.7	24.1	12.8	12.1	12.4
United Kingdom	19.6	21.1	21.0	20.7	11.6	12.4	12.4

Notes: *The quarterly youth unemployment rate is seasonally adjusted.

e = estimate

Figure 9.1: Young people not in education, employment or training in Europe

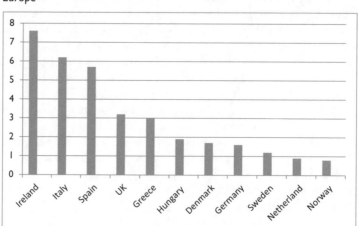

Source: Eurostat: Most recent data, last updated 5 December 2013: Young people not in employment and not in any education and training, by age and sex (NEET rates) [edat_lfse_20].

Despite this, in some European states austerity has signalled reductions in government expenditure in education, training, labour market programmes and social protection, with absolute decreases in levels of expenditure at local rates in 10 European countries, including Ireland, Greece, Spain, Italy and the United Kingdom (Eurostat, 2013). In the UK, for example, government expenditure on tertiary/further education (following completion of secondary education) has decreased from £16 billion in 2010 to £14 billion in 2012 and is estimated to fall to £11 billion in 2014 (ONS, 2013). The multi-faceted nature of youth transitions is captured by the long-term 'scarring effects' of negative experiences of early unemployment or substandard employment. Young people face a European jobs market that is increasingly characterised by substandard employment relationships. In particular, the growth in part-time, temporary work and zero hours contracts has been legally sanctioned by the withdrawal of key employment rights within some European settings, and young people are more vulnerable to the impacts of precarious labour market arrangements than are other age groups (O'Higgins, 2010). Their employment disadvantage is also mirrored by higher increases in poverty levels since the crisis, in comparison to older age groups (Figure 9.2).

This vulnerability emerges from a dynamic relationship between personal development and socio-economic factors. Several key facets

Figure 9.2: Differential impact on poverty rates for children 0–17, young people 18–25 and the elderly (over 65) in OECD 33 between 2007 and 2010

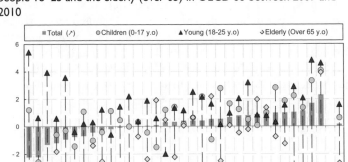

Note: Percentage point changes in relative poverty rates between 2007 and 2010, by age groups. Income poverty measured using relative poverty rate based on 50% of current median equivalised household disposable income Poverty rose among children and youth and fell among the elderly, confirming earlier trends.

Source: OECD Income Distribution Database (www.oecd.org/social/income-distribution-database.htm)..

are interwoven within this tapestry of vulnerability. Firstly, at a personal level young people are more vulnerable to the effects of crises because they are at a critical developmental stage, and social and psychological developmental processes are forming from youth into early adulthood. Deprivations during early youth can have lifelong impacts. Positive early transitions between education and the labour market are critical, for this reason. Secondly, young people are more likely to be income poor than other age groups. This structural disadvantage arises from immediate labour market factors such as disproportionately lower wages and also from structural inequalities, particularly within neoliberal competitive employment and welfare settings (Leventi et al, 2010). In other settings, recent austerity measures instituted in Greece, for example, have resulted in a reduction of the minimum wage for young people (Kousta, 2013). Rising levels of child poverty across Europe also mean that a substantial number of young people may have experienced relative or even absolute poverty, with related health problems, including undernourishment, and limited education (Fahmy, 2007; Arie, 2013). These cumulative impacts merge to form dynamic drivers of the stratification of life chances, shaping both the lived reality of the present and perception of future (Arie, 2013; The Prince's Trust Macquarie, 2014). Demonstrating this, unemployment and sub-standard working conditions have been evidenced as leading to mental health problems. In a recent report, the World Health Organisation observed that in EU countries an increase of 1% in the general unemployment rate leads to a rise of 0.8% in the suicide rate (World Health Organisation, 2011). Suicide levels in Europe since the crises have increased significantly in European men aged between 15 and 24, with the highest increases being in Greece and Spain (Chang et al, 2013). Moreover, several studies have indicated a rise in the prevalence of depression and suicide since the crises, particularly for unemployed men in Greece, Spain and England (Stuckler et al, 2009; Katikireddi et al, 2012). Significantly, Stuckler et al's (2009) study also indicated that increased investment in active labour market programmes led to a reduction in the effect of unemployment on suicides. Thirdly, the impact of austerity measures on the stratification of life chances within different European countries is compounded by the nature of structural changes in global production, as many young people access employment in sectors that are especially vulnerable to the global recession, such as export-oriented manufacturing and small and medium enterprises (Dicken, 2007; World Health Organisation, 2011). Fourthly, as mentioned above, the current crisis has led to disproportionate numbers of young people being subjected to non-standard working conditions, temporary work and underemployment (Bell, and Blanchflower, 2011). The impact of the degradation of the labour process cannot be underestimated. The growing significance of social movements such as the Occupy movement and the strength and extent of demonstrations by young people across Europe reveal how precarious labour relations and social movements have coalesced, forming socio-labour movements of young workers protesting against socio-economic exclusion. Finally, young people may face a number of barriers to entering employment for the first time. This is due largely to lack of skills and experience, poor self-esteem, low education and bargaining power within the labour market (The Prince's Trust, 2010; Bell and Blanchflower 2012; Arie, 2013).

Theoretical considerations

Located at the axis of the relationship between the state and the market, the relationship between labour markets, institutions and welfare settings has been placed under considerable scrutiny across Europe in recent decades. As Adrian Sinfield argues, 'Unemployment and sub-employment are primary characteristics of society and its workings' (Sinfield, 2011). The Varieties of Capitalism approach is based upon the notion that advanced, affluent capitalist economies develop institutional arrangements that are constructed as either liberal market economies or coordinated market economies. These services include how workers are allocated to specific jobs, and the legal and contractual basis of employment, mobility, the distribution of wages and working conditions, training and transition between education and employment. Young people face a disproportionate risk of gaining access to short-term, precarious jobs with lower wages and poorer conditions. The level, form and degree to which government interventions in the labour market mitigate the stratification of social risks for young workers in European settings is mediated by the type of labour market and welfare setting.

As Bigos et al (2013) point out, the official definition of resilience in labour markets proposed by the OECD refers to 'labour markets that weather economic downturns with limited social costs or, more formally, limited losses in worker welfare' (OECD, 2012, p 57). Recent research highlights the critical influence of the levels and dynamics of 'societal risk', that is, the risk that societies will fail to provide adequate systems of education, health, housing or public infrastructure, which may in turn limit the well-being and potential of young people within European labour markets (Furlong, and Cartmel; 2004; Paull and Patel, 2012; Shildrick et al, 2012; Grusky and Kricheli-Katz, 2013). Within this context, and as noted above, the impact of austerity measures on the inclusion of young people within European employment and welfare regimes settings is mediated within a multi-faceted and complex relationship between socio-economic conditions and the stratification of social risks, particularly in relation to the accessibility and quality of education and training, employment and social security and levels of pay and the form and quality of active labour market measures. Underlining the value of coordinated state intervention strategies, a number of recent comparative studies have provided an evidential base to suggest that strongly interventionist labour market and welfare approaches are consistent with economic and social resilience (Schelkle, 2012; Whyman et al, 2012). In particular, it is argued that an emphasis on social investment in education at all levels, combined with proactive and sustained redistributive policies, is consistent with equitable income and skill distribution aiding productivity and economic growth within a global knowledge economy (OECD, 2012). Critically, there is substantive evidence that many young people remain constrained by background, origin and income inequality (Paull and Patel, 2012; Grusky and

Kricheli-Katz, 2013; Taylor-Gooby, 2013). Here it is argued that the 'social risks likely to induce poverty, including unemployment, illness and disability, early school dropout, low levels of education and family breakdown are socially stratified across all welfare states, including the Scandinavian ones' (Cantillon and Van Lancker, 2012; Ellison and Fenger, 2012; Grusky and Kricheli-Katz, 2013; MacDonald and Shildrick, 2013). Given this, it is contended that social investment and active labour market programmes designed to support and sustain young people in the labour market 'cannot and will not' enable social progress to occur unless combined with the implementation of adequate levels of social protection. 'Coordinated cooperative' and 'liberal competitive' employment and welfare arrangements significantly impact upon the experience of young people within distinct European employment and welfare settings. The four key domains impacted upon by these contrasting arrangements are set out in Figure 9.3.

Figure 9.3: A framework for understanding the experiences of young people with coordinated cooperative and liberal competitive welfare and employment settings in Europe

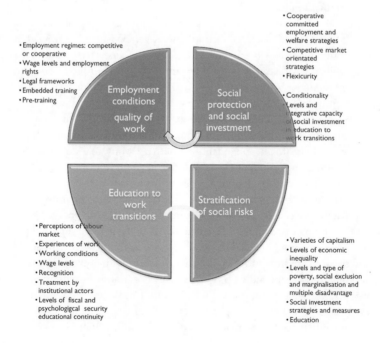

The impact of austerity on young people within 'liberal competitive' models of capitalism: the UK

Recent evidence reveals the complex personal dynamics of young people's transition to adulthood in the UK as being dominated by the interrelated dimensions of precarious employment, fragmented educational experiences, poverty, structural inequalities and employer discrimination against young people (Du Bois-Reymond and López-Blasco, 2003; Fahmy, 2007). The UK government has recently announced plans to reduce public spending by £25 billion between April 2016 and 2018. Within this context, some illustration of effects related to these dimensions can be explored. In England, the introduction of student fees and the marketisation of higher education, combined with an underfunded further education sector, have exacerbated the situation for young people, particularly those from socially deprived groups (Lynch, 2006; Dearden et al 2011; Vaitilingam, 2013). Moreover, existing support measures for students from the most disadvantaged backgrounds have been severely undermined by the UK government's recent spending review. The 'National Student Support Programme' is designed to provide help to the most economically disadvantaged students to apply to university, through direct financial aid and reduction in university fees. However, this budget will be reduced from £150 million to £50 million in 2015 to 2016. As has been previously evidenced in this chapter, the situational constraints created by inequality condemn a growing number of young people in Britain to a life of clinging onto temporary, insecure and often poorly paid part-time employment back and forth across the fluctuating rapids of macro-economic demand and pools of economic stagnation. Active labour market and welfare measures in the UK are characterised by an emphasis on individual pathology, with the work–welfare nexus being firmly focused upon adjusting the capabilities and motivations of individuals so as to enable them to become integrated in the labour market. Activation approaches involve rigid and severe sanctions on individuals who are not contributing to the formal economy.

The UK government's fiscal and economic policy remains resolutely focused upon an austerity agenda. As Peter Taylor-Gooby (2013) argues, it may be suggested that two key underlying objectives emerge from this approach. Firstly, to embed the cuts permanently, reframing the welfare state and rewriting the social contract in the UK, and secondly, to transform the political economy of the UK into a radical, competitive and individualistic liberalism. The vulnerability of young people in the

UK to the exigencies of this transformation centres upon wider cuts and the marketisation of higher education (although not in Scotland). Critically, the transition from education to employment may be fraught with obstacles, particularly for disadvantaged young people, rendering investment in tertiary and further education, training and active labour market policies (ALMPs) a priority. Despite this, as Table 9.2 reveals, UK public expenditure on labour market programmes, largely directed towards the provision of adult apprenticeships and the Work Programme, is less than that in all of the EU 27 states apart from Lithuania.

Table 9.2: Proportion of GDP allocated to labour market programmes within EU member states

	LMP services (category 1)	LMP measures (categories 2-7)	LMP supports (categories 8-9)	Total LMP expenditure	Unemployment rate
EU-27	0.21 e	0.50 e	1.24 e	1.95 e	9.7
BE	0.21	1.39	2.10	3.70	7.2
BG	0.04	0.13	0.42	0.59	11.4
CZ	0.10	0.18	0.28	0.56	6.8
DK	0.54 e	1.55 e	1.65 e	3.74 e	7.7
DE	0.35 e	0.45 e	1.04 e	1.84 e	6.0
EE	0.08 e	0.15	0.50	0.73 e	12.8
IE	0.14	0.74	2.74	3.63	14.9
ES	0.10 e	0.69	2.81	3.60	21.8
FR	0.25 b	0.68 e	1.41	2.34	9.3
IT	0.03 e	0.31	1.36	1.70	8.5
CY	0.03 e	0.31	0.69 p	1.04 p	8.1
LV	0.04	0.33	0.32	0.69	16.5
LT	0.08 e	0.18 e	0.30	0.56 e	15.7
LU	0.05 e	0.46 e	0.63	1.14	4.9
HU	0.01 e	0.35	0.66 e	1.01 e	11.0
MT	0.12	0.05	0.33	0.50	6.6
NL	0.37 e	0.70 e	1.63 e	2.70 e	4.4
AT	0.19 e	0.57	1.28	2.04	4.2
PL	0.08 e	0.33	0.30	0.72 e	9.8
PT	0.12	0.46 b	1.34	1.91	13.4
RO	0.03 e	0.02	0.24	0.28	7.7
SI	0.11	0.26	0.88	1.24	8.3
SK	0.07	0.22	0.50	0.79	13.7
FI	0.12	0.84	1.45	2.42	7.9
SE	0.25 e	0.80 e	0.63 e	1.68 e	8.0
UK	0.21 e	0.03 e	0.34	0.59 e	8.2
NO	:	0.46	0.41	:	3.2

Notes: LMP expenditure for EU27 excludes EL.

e = estimate

Source: Eurostat; Most Recent Data: LMP expenditure as % of GDP and the unemployment rate, 2011 (1)'- Source: Eurostat, LMP (lmp_expsumm) and LFS (lfsa_ugad) LMP expenditure by type of action (summary tables) [lmp_expsumm] Last update: 24 September 2013.

Labour market programme services cover the costs of providing services for jobseekers, together with all other expenditure of the public employment services (category 1). Arguably, it is very significant that there is very little spending upon active interventions to help the unemployed and other disadvantaged groups (categories 2–7). The negative consequences of this for disadvantaged groups are borne out by a recent enquiry into the Work Programme by the House of Commons Work and Pensions Select Committee. Moreover social investment in ALMPs by the current UK government has actually worsened the position for the most disadvantaged young people. The Coalition government has recently introduced the Work Programme welfare to work initiative, designed to support unemployed people in entering and sustaining a position within the labour market. Analysis of outcomes of the programme in the report of House of Commons Work and Pensions Select Committee (May 2013) revealed that the programme was 'giving least help to those people who were worst off'. In particular, the report revealed vulnerable groups such as people with disabilities and homeless people as being largely ignored by the Work Programme. The report also revealed that unemployment was continuing to rise in 'three quarters of Britain's poorest estates'. A central criticism of the Work Programme highlighted in the report was that it is a payment-by-results model based upon the specific benefit claimed, rather than being tailored to the individual needs of claimants, and is thus not responding adequately to the unique and multi-dimensional character of the barriers faced by vulnerable people within the labour market. Exacerbating this, the Coalition government reduced expenditure in further education by 25% in 2010. This underlines the stratification of societal risks as being the central issue relating to youth transitions in the UK. Differing forms and degrees of societal risks across European settings impact on the potential of young people to enter and sustain employment within distinct labour markets. In the UK there is substantive evidence demonstrating that the current education system in England is leading to underachievement among significant numbers of vulnerable children and young people (Goodman, Sibieta, and Washbrook, 2009; Platt, 2011; OECD, 2013). This in turn impacts upon the capacity of the British economy to compete within a global knowledge economy and, more importantly, condemns many young people to a life where they feel they have 'no future to risk'. A critical caveat is that education in the devolved nations of Scotland, Wales and Northern Ireland is governed separately. In Scotland, for example, a dedicated dual investment programme includes a guaranteed place in education or training for all 16- to 19-year-olds.

The provision of 26,000 apprenticeships is also embedded, alongside a range of multi-sectorial policies within the 'Solidarity Purpose' welfare framework, aimed at reducing inequality in Scotland: 'unlocking the economic potential of all individuals will support economic growth by increasing labour market participation and by removing the personal and social costs of poverty' (Scottish Government, 2012).This contrasts with the UK as a whole, where, for example, the number of young people aged between 16 and 25 without a job rose to 22.5%, the highest since records began in 1992.

In Scotland, economic growth is regarded as being contingent upon reducing income inequality and the improvement of access to employment opportunities, especially for those on lower incomes (Scottish Government, 2013). In contrast to the UK as a whole, Scotland has witnessed a significant reduction in the level of youth unemployment over the same period (Labour Force Study Data; ONS, 2013). Emphasising this trend, youth unemployment decreased significantly in Scotland, from 25.4% in December 2011 to 15.2% in April 2013.Whilst a significant number of jobs have been created in the private sector across the UK, a significant proportion of these jobs are part-time and temporary and are not conducive to increasing aggregate demand or strengthening labour market conditions for young people (Furlong and Cartmel, 2004; Lindsay, 2010; Macdonald and Shildrick, 2013). In the UK the Work Programme has failed to deliver for the most disadvantaged young people. Similar findings in Greece reinforce the need to assess the operation and outcomes of ALMPs for the most vulnerable in society. Research by Dimoulas (2013), for example, found that the beneficiaries of ALMPs in Greece were not usually the most vulnerable or disadvantaged unemployed but the better-off who had contacts with political party leaders. In Greece the reduction of the minimum wage for young people aged between 18 and 25 has also accentuated levels of poverty and personal crises for vulnerable and disadvantaged young people and the ineffectiveness of ALMPs in Greece arises largely from their operation as a way of allocating social protection payments, whilst benefiting people who already have access to political networks.These findings from contrasting political economies that are both following austerity agendas bring urgency to the need to evaluate the appropriateness and effectiveness of ALMPs for young Europeans who are at the margins of European labour markets.This requires any evaluation of the implementation of ALMPs to be conducted within the context of austerity most particularly, as these measures have an impact upon wider socio-economic inequalities and the stratification of social risks.

The experience of young people at the margins within social investment-orientated/cooperative models of capitalism

In contrast to 'liberal competitive' labour market systems within more 'coordinated cooperative' models of capitalism such as Norway, the Netherlands, Germany, Sweden, Finland and Denmark, the scope, effectiveness and legitimacy of ALM programmes is pivotal to broader socio-economic intervention strategies. For example, the Nordic welfare state model is typified by a strong commitment to social democracy, equality and a focus on the well-being of citizens as workers, parents and individuals contributing to a transparent market and social economy (Djernaes, 2013). The long-term policy commitment of Nordic states to maintaining resilient and inclusive labour markets is illustrated by the Norwegian economy, which is characterised by an even income distribution, high rates of enrolment into higher education, a tax-financed advanced welfare state and a high level of labour participation (Kananen, 2012). Whilst the Norwegian economy was largely cushioned from the effects of the great recession of 2008 by large public surpluses generated by high oil prices, the private sector in Norway was more vulnerable to the effects of the global economic crises and some workers did become more vulnerable to redundancy. Offsetting this, increased investment in the labour market has ensured low levels of youth unemployment in recent years. The Norwegian coordinated economy links strong trade unions, high taxes and high degrees of equality with strong economic performance within a global knowledge economy. Levels of youth employment are relatively high across all four Nordic states (Eurostat, 2013) and the impact of the recent economic crises on youth transitions within Nordic states has been of growing concern. Norway and Denmark have achieved more positive outcomes for young people in the labour market than have Finland and Sweden. Within the group of Nordic states, Denmark and Norway have lower youth unemployment rates of 9% and 13%, whilst Sweden and Finland have rates of 20% and 25%, respectively (Eurostat, 2013). It is important to note that these differences are in part due to how youth unemployment rates are calculated within each state. In Sweden and Finland the figures include young people who are in full-time education whilst also looking for work.

Numbers of young people registered as NEET are relatively low across all Nordic states, with 0.8% in Norway, 1.7% in Denmark, 1.2% in Sweden and 1.6% in Finland (Figure 9.3). Crucially, these young people who are NEET face an uphill struggle in all European societies and, as previously evidenced, are susceptible to the long-term effects of unstable or negative transitional experiences between education and employment. Exemplifying this, recent evidence from Sweden reveals that some activation measures are based upon coercion and focus upon immediate entry into work placements. This approach limits the extent to which measures can be tailored to the individual needs of the young person by restricting access to educational and training opportunities and the ability of young people to shape or influence the way that the work experience is implemented (Olofsson and Wadensjo, 2012). These measures have a particularly detrimental impact upon young people from disadvantaged backgrounds, who may also have low levels of education. This is largely due to the negative impact on self-esteem and social and psychological well-being of being compelled to take a job with low status or a job for which they do not feel equipped. This form of compulsion in 'social investment' may actually damage a young person's long-term potential within the labour market (Lindsay, 2010; Olofsson and Wadensjo, 2012; Bell and Blanchflower, 2013; Work and Pensions Committee, 2013).

In contrast, the Danish government prioritises education over a 'work first' approach for young people with low levels of education. Early intervention measures include reintegration into the education system for benefit claimants who have not completed their education. In addition, public expenditure on ALMPs both generally and for special measures for disadvantaged young people is higher in Denmark than in any other OECD country (OECD, 2013). In common with Norway, these measures include a youth package in the form of follow-up education for young people up to the age of 20 who did not complete their secondary education. Vocational training in both Denmark and Norway is completed professional education, whereas in Sweden and Finland it is pre-training. The security of professional accreditation and a prospect of long-term financial security are of particular benefit to disadvantaged young people who may have been subjected to situational constraints created by poverty and social exclusion. In this way an integrated approach to investment that involves both employers and the state can significantly compensate young people who have suffered poverty and social exclusion during childhood. Importantly, as Table 9.2 reveals, Denmark also allocates far higher levels of expenditure to category 2–8 labour market programme measures, designated for active interventions to help unemployed and other disadvantaged groups. More vulnerable or disadvantaged young people benefit from an approach to youth transitions, such as that taken in Denmark, that prioritises education over a work-first approach for young benefit claimants who have not completed formal education. Early intervention strategies such as those adopted by Denmark and Norway, focusing upon reintegration into the education or training system for young people with low-level or no qualifications, is a form of social investment that directly addresses the stratification of social risks and prioritises the long-term future of disadvantaged or low-educated young people. This contrasts sharply with measures for young people in the UK, who enter the Work Programme after nine months of being unemployed and who are then placed, with little or no experience, into work placements under threat of removal of benefits. Recent evidence has shown that these placements can have a negative effect on the self-esteem of young people if they are not given adequate support or training to do the job.

In Germany, social investment in young people centres upon the dual training system which provides young people with the opportunity to gain employment experience with a company. Importantly also, Germany allocates a high level of expenditure to special measures for disadvantaged young people through a range of training schemes. In recognition of the challenges that young people face in making the transition between education and employment, a resilient dual apprenticeship system facilitating effective transitions between education and employment has been established. Figure 9.4 illustrates the significance of integrated dual labour market approaches. The youth unemployment rate has been falling in Germany since 2005, and this is due in large part to the integrative capacity of dual apprenticeships in protecting young people from economic recession. In particular, sustained public expenditure on large-scale, high-quality training is combined with a very high level of corporate involvement. Recognised professional qualifications are also combined with sustained levels of investment in research and development to create a dual apprenticeship system that is of long-term benefit to young people, the resilience of the German economy and social cohesion. This degree of integration between labour policy and education is mirrored by youth employment strategies in Norway and Denmark. Finally, in the Netherlands, whilst there are a large proportion of part-time flexible opportunities available for young people, in contrast to the UK, the Dutch government has instituted increased employment protection, rights to training and wage guarantees and has invested in supplementary pensions for young people within sub-standard employment to mitigate against the negative effects of such employment.

Figure 9.4: Youth transitions in Europe: structure of youth population by education and labour market status, Germany, Netherlands, Greece and the UK, 2012

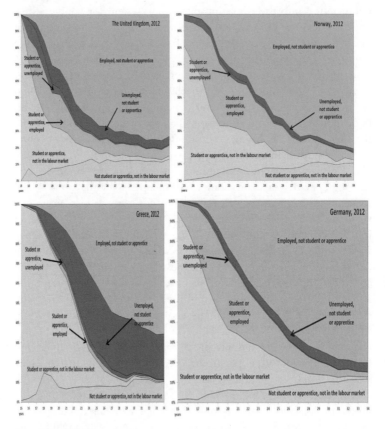

Source: Eurostat (2013)

Concluding discussion

Social investment in education, training, vocational and labour market policies for young people acts simultaneously to compensate for disadvantages created by inequality whilst contributing to more sustainable long-term social economies. In competitive economies such as the UK, very limited levels of public expenditure in labour market programmes have been directed at those who are most disadvantaged leading, to growing numbers of young people being trapped in a fragmented experience of work placements, insecure work and zero hours contracts and with no sense of future possibilities. In contrast, coordinated cooperative economies such as the Netherlands, Sweden and Norway have invested more in these areas, recognising both the personal implications for young people at the margins of society and the long-term sustainability of advanced welfare economies. Crucially, as Olofsson and Wadensjo (2012, p 1) argue, 'The demarcation between labour market policy and standard education should be re-examined. Distribution fairness and effectiveness motives speak for a more flexible use of the available labour market policy resources.' A more integrated and adaptable approach to education and labour market programmes facilitates more appropriate and tailored measures that take account of the long-term social, psychological, educational and training needs of young people. Importantly, messages emerging from both the UK and Sweden reveal that activation policies based upon coercion that is focused on immediate entry into work placements limit the extent to which measures can be tailored to the individual needs of the young person by restricting access to educational and training opportunities and the ability of young people to shape or influence the way in which the work experience is implemented (Olofsson, and Wadensjo, 2012; Bell and Blanchflower, 2013). This evidence is reinforced by the findings of the House of Commons Work and Pensions Select Committee in the UK (2013), which indicate that the Work Programme focusing upon placements under the threat of benefit sanctions was of little or no benefit for the most disadvantaged young people in the UK. Critically, the negative effects of social investment strategies intrinsically based upon coercion and a work-first approach are inextricably linked to widening social divisions within both the UK and Sweden. Whilst the problems suffered by disadvantaged youth in the UK are much more acute, it is very telling that income inequality in Sweden is also widening. The growth in levels of inequality in Sweden was larger than for any other OECD country between 1985 and 2009 as the distribution of market income became more unequal (OECD, 2013). In contrast, in Denmark's more balanced labour market, vocational and educational interventions operate within an integrated architecture of provision that provides tailored measures for young people as they make the transition between education and employment. The more fragmented nature of educational measures and labour market policy in Sweden is distinguished by strict demarcations between standard education and youth labour market programmes, the labour exchange and social service provision (Olofsson, and Wadensjo, 2012). Importantly also, Norway, Denmark and Finland do not set an upper time limit for completion of secondary school studies, with a broader range of educational opportunities. Denmark and Norway also offer widespread, well-funded apprenticeship schemes underpinned by employment rights and legally regulated by a system of trade licences. The broad scope and integrated architecture of labour market and educational programmes in Denmark and Norway have a positive impact on outcomes for disadvantaged young people, enabling them to benefit from well-funded tailored schemes with long-term value. Good-quality apprenticeships offering young people complete professional qualifications can be viewed as compensating for poverty and social exclusion by ensuring wage-earning opportunities for young people from disadvantaged backgrounds. In Germany, the integrative capacity of high-quality dual apprenticeships to protect young people from economic recession has been bolstered by continuing high levels of public and corporate expenditure. These schemes are strengthened by significant public expenditure in special schemes for more disadvantaged young people.

In contrast to austerity-driven social investment strategies, approaches within coordinated market economies emphasise long-term priorities for all young people and recognise the responsibility of the state and of employers within the labour market. Whilst conclusions relating to the efficacy of specific interventions and welfare models are limited by the complexity and specificity of economic and social variables within each setting, there is nevertheless growing evidence that policy frameworks and governance models that adopt a more integrated social investment approach, particularly in reducing societal risks, are developing more resilient labour markets whilst also adapting to the wider potential of a global knowledge economy. The reorientation of individual interventions from those based upon individual risk or pathology and towards a policy architecture that focuses upon what kinds of societies are inclusive and economically sustainable in times of crises offers a more rational, compassionate and sustainable economic and social future for all young people.

Note

[1] The research leading to these results has received funding from the European Community's Seventh Framework Programme under grant agreement no. 320121 (Project INSPIRES)

References

Arie, S. (2013) 'Has austerity brought Europe to the brink of a health disaster?', *BMJ*, 346: f3773.

Bell, D. and Blanchflower, D. (2013) 'Underemployment in the UK Revisited', *National Institute Economic Review*, 224: 8–22.

Bigos, M., Qaran, W., Fenger, M., Koster, F., Mascini, P. and Van der Veen, R. (2013) *Review essay on labour market resilience*, INSPIRES (FP7) European Research Project, EU.

Cantillon, B. and Van Lancker, W. (2013) 'Three shortcomings of the social investment perspective', in M. Fenger and M. Ellison (eds) '"New" welfare in practice: trends, challenges and dilemmas', *Social Policy and Society*, 12: 553–64.

Carlson, A. (2013) 'Young people on the periphery – Nordic policies against unemployment and exclusion', Oslo: Nordic Network for Adult Learning. Available at: www.infonet-ae.eu/articles-national-affairs/1285-young-people-on-the-periphery-nordic-policies-against-unemployment-and-exclusion

Chang, S., Stuckler, D., Yip, P. and Gunnell, D. (2013) 'Impact of 2008 global economic crisis on suicide: time trend study in 54 countries', *BMJ*, 347: f5239.

Council of the European Union (2013) *Council Conclusions on investing in education and training – a response to Rethinking Education: Investing in skills for better socio-economic outcomes and the 2013 Annual Growth Survey*, Education, Youth, Culture and Sport Council Meeting, Brussels: EU Publications.

Dearden, L., Fitzsimons, E. and Wyness, G. (2011) *The impact of tuition fees and support on university participation in the UK*, London: Institute for Fiscal Studies.

Dicken, P. (2007) *Global shift, mapping the changing contours of the world economy* (5th edn), London: Sage Publications.

Dimoulas, C. (2013) *Greece, financialization and the European Union; The political economy of debt and destruction*, Athens: Palgrave Macmillan.

Djernaes, L. (2013) 'A Nordic perspective on youth unemployment', *Life Long Learning in Europe*, (1).

Du Bois Reymond, M. and López Blasco, A. (2003) 'Young people and contradictions of inclusion: towards integrated transition policies for young adults in Europe', in A. López Blasco, W. McNeish and A. Walther (eds) *Yo-yo transitions and misleading trajectories*, Bristol: Policy Press, pp 19–42.

Ellison, M. and Fenger, M. (2013) Review article: 'Social investment, protection and inequality within the new economy and politics of welfare in Europe', *Social Policy and Society*, 12: 611–25, Cambridge: Cambridge University Press.

European Commission (2012) *Recommendation to Member States on introducing the Youth Guarantee*, Employment Social Affairs and Inclusion, Brussels: EU Publications.

European Commission(2010) *European Union 2020 Strategy Youth on the Move*, Employment Social Affairs and Inclusion, Brussels: EU Publications.

Eurostat (2013) *Central government expenditure on education*, Brussels: EU Publications.

Fahmy, E. (2007) 'Poverty and youth transitions in Europe: an analysis of the European Communities', in H. Colley, P. Boetzelen, B. Hoskins and T. Parveva (eds), *Social inclusion and young people: Breaking down the barriers*, Strasbourg: Council of Europe, pp 43–56.

Furlong, A. and Cartmel, F. (2004) *Vulerable young men in fragile labour markets*, York: Joseph Rowntree Foundation.

Goodman, A., Sibieta, L. and Washbrook, E. (2009) *Inequalities in educational outcomes among children aged 3 to 16: Final report for the National Equality Panel*, London: Institute for Fiscal Studies. Available at: http://sta.geo.useconnect.co.uk/pdf/Inequalities%20in%20education%20outcomes%20among%20children.pdf.

Grusky, D.B. and Kricheli-Katz, T. (2012) *The new gilded age: The critical inequality debates of our time*, Stanford, CA: Stanford University Press.

Hall, P. and Soskice, D. (2001) 'An introduction to varieties of capitalism', in P. Hall and D. Soskice (eds) *Varieties of capitalism.: The institutional foundations of competitive advantage*, Oxford: Oxford University Press.

Hay, C. (2005) 'Too important to leave to the economists? The political economy of welfare retrenchment', *Social Policy and Society*, 4(2): 197–205

Hogarth, T., Owen, D., Gambin, L., Hasluck, C., Lyonette, C. and Casey, B. (2009) *The equality impacts of the current recession*, Human Rights Commission, Warwick: Warwick Institute for Employment Research.

Hurley, J., Storrie D. and Jungblut J. (2011) *Shifts in the job structure in Europe during the great recession*, Luxemburg: European Foundation for the Improvement of Living and Working Conditions,.

ILO (International Labour Organisation) (2012) *World of Work report 2012: Better jobs for a better economy*, Geneva: International Institute of Labour Studies.

ILO (2013) *World of Work report 2013: Repairing the economic and social fabric*, Geneva: International Institute for Labour Studies.

International Labour Organisation (2013) *Global employment trends for youth 2013*, Geneva: ILO.

Kananen, J. (2012) 'Nordic paths from welfare to workfare: Danish, Swedish and Finnish labour market reforms in comparison', *Local Economy*, 27(5-6): 558–576.

Katikireddi, V., Niedzwiedz, C. L. and Popham, F. (2012) 'Trends in population mental health before and after the 2008 recession: a repeat cross-sectional analysis of the 1991–2010 Health Surveys of England', *British Medical Journal Open*, Oct 17; 2(5). pii: e001790.

Kersbergen, K. and Hemerijck, A. (2012) 'Two decades of change in Europe: the emergence of the social investment state', *Journal of Social Policy*, 41: 475–92.

Kitschelt, H., Lange, P., Marks, G. and Stephens, J. (2012) 'Convergence and divergence in advanced capitalist democracies', in H. Kitschelt, P. Lange, G. Marks and J. Stephens (eds) *Continuity and change in contemporary capitalism*, Cambridge: Cambridge Univerisity Press, pp 427–60.

Kompier, M., Ybema, J., Janssen, J. and Taris, T. (2009) 'Employment contracts; cross-sectional and longitudinal relations with quality of working life, health and well-being', *Journal of Occupational Health*, 51: 193–203.

Kousta, E. (2013) *Income and payment systems in Greece*, Athens: Labour Institute of Greek General Confederation of Labour (INE/GSEE).

Leventi, C., Levy, H., Matsaganis, M., Paulus, A. and Sutherland, H. (2010) 'Modelling the distributional effects of austerity measures. The challenges of a comparative method', Research note 8/2010, Social Situation Observatory, European Commission.

Lindsay, C. (2010) 'In a lonely place? Social networks, job seeking and the experience of long-term unemployment', *Social Policy and Society*, 9(1): 25–37.

Lynch, K. (2006) 'Neo-liberalism and marketisation: the implications for higher education', *European Educational Research Journal*, 5 (1): 1–17.

Macdonald, R. and Shildrick, T. (2013) 'Youth and well-being: experiencing bereavment and ill-health in marginalised young people's transitions', *The Sociology of Health and Illness*, 35(1): 147–61.

OECD (2013) *Crisis squeezes income and puts pressure on inequality and poverty*. Available at: www.oecd.org/els/soc/OECD2013-Inequality-and-Poverty-8p.pdf.

O'Higgins, N. (2010) *The impact of the economic and financial crisis on youth employment*, Geneva: International Labour Organisation.

Olofsson, J. and Wadensjod, E. (2012) 'Youth unemployment – conditions for young people in the Nordic countries', *Social Europe Journal*. Available at: http://www.social-europe.eu/2012/09/youth-unemployment-conditions-for-young-people-in-the-nordic-countries/.

ONS (Office for National Statistics) (2013) *Public sector finances, November 2013*, London: Office for National Statistics.

Paull, G. and Patel, T. (2012) *An international review of skills, jobs and poverty*, York: Joseph Rowntree Foundation.

Platt, L. (2011) *Understanding inequalities, stratification and difference*, Cambridge: Polity Press.

Schelkle, W. (2012) *Tackling the jobs crisis: The labour market and social policy response: Theme 2: Maintaining the activation stance during the crisis*, London: London School of Economics.

Scottish Government (2012) *Solidarity purpose*, Edinburgh: Scottish Government.

Scottish Government (2013) *Europe 2020, Scottish national reform programme*, Edinburgh: Scottish Government.

Shildrick, T., MacDonald, R., Webster, C. and Garthwaite, K. (2012) *Poverty and insecurity: Life in no-pay, low-pay Britain*, Bristol: Policy Press.

Sinfield, A. (2011) 'Credit crunch, inequality and social policy', in K. Farnsworth and Z. Irving (eds), *Social policy in challenging times: Economic crises and welfare systems*, Bristol: The Policy Press, pp 65–81.

Stuckler, D., Basu, S., Suhrcke, M., Coutts, A. and McKee, M. (2009) 'The public health effect of economic crises and alternative policy responses in Europe: an empirical analysis', *The Lancet*, 374: 315–23.

Taylor-Gooby, P. (2013) *The double crisis of the welfare state and what we can do about it*, London: Palgrave Macmillan.

The Prince's Trust (2010) *The cost of exclusion: Counting the cost of youth disadvantage in the UK*, London: The Prince's Trust.

The Prince's Trust Macquarie (2014) *Youth index 2014*, London: The Prince's Trust.

Vaitilingam, R. (2013) *Recession Britain: Findings from economic and social research*, Swindon: Economic and Social Research Council.

Whyman, P., Baimbridge, M. and Mullen, M. (2012) *The political economy of the European social model*, Routledge Studies in the European Economy, Abingdon: Routledge.

Work and Pensions Committee (2013) *Public Accounts Committee – Thirty-Third Report Department for Work and Pensions: Work Programme outcome statistics*, London: UK Parliament.

World Health Organisation (2011) *Impact of economic crises on mental health in Europe.* Copenhagen: WHO.

TEN

Aristotle on the front line

Emilie Whitaker

This chapter outlines how Aristotle's concept of phronesis has gained traction as an analytical concept for research in recent years, particularly in areas of social policy most concerned with the professions of social work, education and medicine. Firstly, the chapter will outline Aristotle's conception of the intellectual virtue he called 'phronesis', referred to in contemporary parlance as 'practical wisdom'. Explicated in the *Nicomachean Ethics*, phronesis brings together Aristotle's thought on virtue and eudaimonia within a social framework.

Following this, the chapter will turn to why research in the sociology of organisational life has found fruitful ground in the application of the concept of phronesis. The focus on organisational studies is twofold: firstly, because this is a field that has traditionally been rooted in modernist assumptions of progress, empiricism and the quest for universal rules or truths of organisational life. Thus, a turn to a more context-bound exploration of the practice of work marks a significant shift. Secondly, the collision of the so-called 'practice-turn' in sociology with a series of shocks and challenges to public sector organisations and their professionals will be explored as background for a neo-Aristotelian revival. Finally, the chapter uses the policy of personalisation as a lens through which to view phronesis within the context of social work practice where practical wisdom as a category for analysis can be identified as arising from the interactions of social workers implementing this policy. To explore phronesis as a cultural and professional decision-making asset, a vignette from a recent study into social work and personalisation is explored.

Aristotle's *phronesis*

In the *Nicomachean Ethics*, Aristotle (1999) outlines three classes of intellectual virtue: *episteme*, *techne* and *phronesis*. *Episteme* (scientific knowledge) can be likened to the concept of ethics based on rules and principles of how to act, most readily associated with the philosophical field of deontology. *Techne* (craft knowledge) is concerned with the skills and know-how of craft and production. Techne is concerned with knowledge that meets designated ends – so, the knowledge to create a table, for example, or the ways software is used to create a presentation. *Phronesis* is different from these first two intellectual virtues. Aristotle identifies phronesis as a form of knowledge that is capable, in the face of ambiguous or uncertain circumstances, to guide actions that will be good for others. Phronesis is a virtue closely aligned to ethical judgement, prudence and practical wisdom. Aristotle states that phronesis is 'concerned with action about things that are good or bad for a human being' (Aristotle, 1999, p 89). It is social in nature – concerned with how prudent action taken for the ethical good is supportive of the *polis*, or community.

Phronesis is the virtue that enables us to judge what it is we should do in any given situation. Phronesis is therefore about context-based, situated action, it places practice in the foreground, 'since [phronesis] is concerned with action and action is about particulars' (Aristotle, 1999, p 92). Using the example of how doctors need context-specific knowledge within which to undertake 'good' practice, Aristotle states:

> For what the doctor appears to consider is not even health [universally, let alone good universally], but human health, and presumably the health of this human being even more, since he [sic] treats one particular patient at a time. (Aristotle, 1999, p 7)

A good doctor knows how to treat each particular patient, based not only on general knowledge of medicine but, more importantly, on practical experience of actually treating individual patients. The same holds true for social workers, teachers, nurses or almost all of those working in human service organisations, where context is fluid and frequently uncertain. Consequently, ethics must focus on activities in a particular situation, since no patient, pupil or family is the same as another. The good action cannot be described independently of the situation in which it is performed, or generalised into universal laws or rules, since that would separate knowledge from actions and the rule from the contextual circumstances. Phronesis is about doing 'the right thing, in the right way, and at the right time' (Aristotle, 1999, p 94). The concept of practical wisdom is useful because it helps us to understand problems in ethical terms, as it deals with unpredictable, dynamic aspects of human social life, while also considering practical expediency (Statler and Roos, 2005).

Phronesis cannot be seen in isolation from the broader points Aristotle was seeking to make in the *Ethics*. At the heart of almost all Greek ethics, and certainly within Aristotle's thought, lies the elusive concept of *eudaimonia*. *Eudaimonia* is often translated as 'happiness', but is arguably better understood as 'flourishing', for, as Kant (1996, p 70) complained, 'the concept of happiness is such an indeterminate concept that, although every human being wishes to attain this, he can still never say determinately and consistently with himself what he really wishes and wills'. Flourishing has the advantage of being visible, which contrasts with contemporary discourses on happiness that describe it as an internalised and subjective state. Social discernibility is important, as Aristotle's vision for the exercising of the virtues and the development of phronesis is social in nature: being good is doing good for the *polis*. The greatest human calling is to flourish, and this flourishing is greater than the sum of all of our actions; *eudaimonia* for Aristotle is thus an individual quest and a collective ambition for all of humankind. Simply put, *eudaimonia* is human flourishing, the ends; virtues are both natural and habituated; *phronesis* is the means to realise the virtue on the path to social and individual *eudaimonia*. Thus, practical wisdom does not tell us what ends to pursue, but only how to pursue them; our ends themselves are set by our ethical characters as part of our telos to flourishing.

The episteme of organisational life

The formal study of organisations has traditionally sought to embed itself as part of the scientific rationalistic project. This is of little surprise, given that the birth of organisational studies occurred around the period of the Enlightenment, which focused on the scientific unearthing of universal laws and principles. The formal study of organisations as a discipline or 'science' is rooted in these modernist origins.

Early organisational theorists (Ure, 1835; Gergen and Thatchenkery, 1996) sought to conceive of their newly founded discipline as a science, thus being in tune with the spirit of the time. They believed a science of the organisation was possible because they felt that, while organisations are varied, at source there is an underlying order that can be captured by social scientists (Taylor, 1911). In addition, the Cartesian rational agency attributed to the self-conceptions of these organisational scientists helps to validate their role within organisations. This implicit claim to reason has provided the justification for the organisational theorist to pronounce on practical and theoretical matters – they are, by virtue of scientific training, better able to think clearly, objectively and profoundly than others and are therefore deserving of voice within the organisation. This expertise was premised on the importance of careful and considered observation undertaken by those with specific training. As such, burgeoning organisational science was underpinned by a logical empiricist philosophy – only observable, causal propositions capable of testing were candidates for a genuinely scientific endeavour (Ayer, 1940). The implication of such thought was that organisational reality had its own distinctive shape and ontology; organisations are capable of observation and measurement. Organisations must have an objective world, capable of empirical study similar to the plants and bodies of biology or the compounds of chemistry. These biological metaphors were themselves espoused by modernist organisational theorists. William Wolf (1958, p 14) spoke of the organisation as 'a living thing; it has a concrete social environment, a formal structure, recognized goals, and a variety of needs'. The presumption among these organisational scholars was that waiting to be observed were some innate, pure, intrinsic properties spanning organisations.

Historically, theorists have tried to construct lists of variables to observe and test across organisations in an attempt to generate some meta-theory of organisational life (Hage, 1963; Pugh et al, 1963). The quest to reveal and quantify organisational life was underpinned by the status afforded to empiricism, which began to pervade theories of the effective organisation (Simon, 1957). The emphasis on the observable, measurable and testable places an imperative upon organisations for systematically gathering information, facts or data for purposes of optimising decision making. This necessarily leads to research focusing on a search for regularities and patterns, to establish their validity and finally to codify them into rules or principles:

> As the science of business administration develops ... there will be more and more stress on stating rather precisely cause and effect relationships and on securing empirical data to substantiate or disprove these statements. Then the results of one investigation may be integrated with another until very substantial evidence is accumulated in support of a set of scientific principles. (Simonds, 1959, p 136)

In Aristotle's terms, research in organisations has a history of aligning itself with *episteme* – the scientific endeavour to establish universal laws to guide action and decision making. This alignment is captured in the subject/object metaphors that, while sustainable in the heyday of Taylorism and Fordism, become problematic as organisations are increasingly networked and fluid. With the rise of the large, complex, bureaucratic structures of 20th-century welfare states these universals are unable to offer a template for understanding organisational life. However, the deployment of universal rules continues to serve useful sense-making purposes, as they enable practitioners to filter, organise and impose order on complexity. They can make work 'do-able' in the face of competing imperatives and pressures (Lipsky, 1980). Systems-level solutions based on such logic have abounded with the advent of formalised information technologies – benchmarking practices, digitalised flowcharts and checklist-based assessment databases. This rationalising approach to knowledge tends to produce abstract, often decontextualised information about organisational life and professional practice, for example school league tables or child-protection referral data. However, such an approach to knowledge offers professionals a method to manage-out complexity; an adherence to rules enables bureaucracies to contend with large demands by sifting people into manageable categories (Lipsky, 1980). Alternatively, the imposition of performance management and targets can constrain professional decision making by refuting the situational awareness needed to deploy discretion usefully, by directing professional attention to meeting targets (Wastell et al, 2010).

If the net result of this form of knowledge leads to managerial 'how to' guides, it often leads to an increased focus on standardising and quantifying the practices of employees. In the 1980s this modernist intellectual quest for universals collided with the new public management reforms, which were preoccupied with guaranteeing the three 'Es' – economy, efficiency, effectiveness. To ensure value for money, a degree of consistency and improvement in 'organisational ends', be they profit, child attainment or social work case processing, had to be assured. In addition, concerns were being raised at the time about the (in)adequacies of practice across social care and education. The remedy for such a diagnosis within a value-for-money framework was of a technical-procedural kind. The ascendancy of this form of instrumental knowledge can be found in approaches to certain professions and public services. In particular, since the 1980s, social work (and health and welfare more generally) has seen the rise of managerialism and a proliferation of technical, procedural and bureaucratic devices for the regulation and monitoring of professional practice (Newman and Clarke, 1994).

Social work is an area where technical rationality has firmly rooted itself in recent times as part of this broader managerialist framework. We can see this through the assumption that social work learning is about acquiring technical competencies and expertise on task-based activities (Howe, 1994; Parton, 2008). Other instances of this rationalist preoccupation can be found in the introduction and expansion of pro formas and schedules to guide the processes of assessment, case recording and report writing, now ingrained through the use of information technologies and techniques of data capture (Wastell et al, 2010; Taylor and White, 2001). The justification for such intrusions into professional practice is commonly the benchmarking and setting of standards in the attempt to achieve greater consistency among practitioners. The proliferation of performance indicators and timescales for 'processing cases' in social work concern themselves with forcing practice towards the ends of 'efficiency' and 'effectiveness'. Howe (1994, p 529) describes modern-day social work as

> task-orientated and performance related, quantifiable and measurable, product-minded and subject to quality controls. Procedure manuals and lists of competences define more and more what social workers should do and how they must do it. Professional discretion disappears under a growing mountain of departmentally generated policy and formulae.

This concern with the collection of information, the evidencing of practice in data rather than narrative form and attempts to standardise practice across disparate contexts has led some to characterise social work knowledge as moving from the 'social to the informational' (Parton, 2008). Wastell et al (2010) explored this epistemological move in their study on the use of information technologies in social work. They found that 'references to percentages are commonplace, exercising team managers in referral and assessment teams particularly. Statistics on the number of assessments completed to timescale are used to measure efficiency and effectiveness' (Wastell et al, 2010, p 314). Social work performance is one demonstrated through managing cases, processing tasks and being driven by time constraints.

This disciplining of contextual knowledge seeks to filter out or deny the messy ambiguities of everyday organisational life (Howe, 1996). In short, it buries the contingent, the context-dependent, the specific and the particular. 'Coherent causal accounts which attempted to provide a picture of the subject in their social context was of declining importance, for the key purpose of the social worker was to gather information in order to classify clients for the purpose of judging the nature and level of risk and for allocating resources' (Parton, 2008, p 260). This abstracting of information seeks to discipline variable factors like the agency of social actors within an organisation. The human experience of being part of an organisation is deemed under this rationalistic framework as adding muddle and mess to the scientific pursuit of naturalistic laws. People – their experiences, interpretations and social activities – are managed out or, at best, formalised into new principles.

The turn to Aristotle: scandals and character in professional life

In addition to the practice-related weaknesses of a scientific organisational discipline, public sector organisations have been hit by a series of shocks and changes that challenge the conception of organisations as stable, machine-like entities. In public services, recent reforms across many welfare systems have added new sources of instability to organisational life. Markets are playing a greater role in service delivery (Tritter et al, 2010); users are being given more choice and control (Glasby and Dickinson, 2009); traditional professional roles are being supplemented by support staff (Newman and Clarke, 2009). In response to new forms of instability and challenge, scholars have looked to the subjective aspects of organisational life (Weick, 1995; Fu-Lai Yu, 2003) as organisational studies took a discursive turn. The universal, abstract and theoretical organisational science struggled to answer these more profound questions of ontology (*what are modern organisations?*), epistemology (*what knowledge do practitioners use and need?*) and praxis (*what modes of action do practitioners adopt in these changing times?*).

Within the context of public sector organisations, the turn to Aristotle can be seen as a response to a series of evolutions and shocks that the sector has experienced in recent memory. Managerial reorganisations, market creation in health and social care, individualising welfare provision, the decommissioning of services and the impact of budget cuts are a few profound changes that public sector organisations are contending with. These moves of course have their own antecedents and trajectories and are not isolated events; however, attempts to understand these developments have diversified. In tandem with the focus on praxis offered by the practice turn (Bourdieu, 1990; Schatzki et al, 2000), the contemporary study of phronesis explores virtue within and across professional settings. While notions of practice are interpreted in various ways, the common thread is an appreciation of the skill by which people manage to creatively use the formal and informal resources they have in their everyday lives (de Certeau, 1984) to get the work of the performance done. The intellectual orientation to the practice turn is itself Aristotelian, primarily interested in the practical wisdom that makes work achievable and manageable within the scopic regimes of detached truths and theories of conventional science (Tsoukas and Cummings, 1997).

The scandals in health and social care in the UK since 2012 may also be driving a broader re-evaluation of the place of character and virtue within professional practice. Such events include the abuse of patients at Winterbourne View, the failings at Stafford Hospital and, most recently, the child deaths of Daniel Pelka in Coventry and Hamzah Khan in Bradford. Inquiries examining these events and others have alluded to a failure of care, more broadly attributed to a failure to instil and sustain moral practice within professional settings. Investigations into such events revealed not only doubts about the professional competency of those involved, but also about their values or character. For example, the Francis Inquiry into Mid Staffordshire NHS Foundation Trust found shortcomings in the 'care, compassion and humanity' shown by staff, that staff showed a lack of 'respect for patients' dignity', showed a 'callous indifference to suffering' and demonstrated 'a lack of candour in reporting poor standards of care' (Francis, 2013). The Serious Case Review for Daniel Pelka, which brought into doubt the actions of multiagency professionals, indicated that professionals had not cared enough:

> Despite arriving at school with facial injuries on at least two, or more likely, three occasions in late 2011/early 2012, no arrangements were made to speak with him directly or formally about these in relation to any child protection concerns. Without proactive or consistent action by any professional to engage with him via an interpreter, then his lack of language and low confidence would likely have made it almost impossible for him to reveal the abuse he was suffering at home. (Coventry LSCB, 2013, p 32)

The inquiries into and reviews of such scandals attribute failings to a lack of care, compassion and curiosity on the part of professionals involved – they point to a moral failing. But they also explore how professional and organisational cultures instil or fail to prepare individuals for undertaking ethically good practice. In responding to these professional scandals, conventional policy remedies are advocated – increased monitoring and changed accountability regimes – but an emphasis is also placed on the importance of culture and education on ethical practice. The ministerial statement in the Winterbourne View review stated:

> while stronger regulation and inspection, quality information and clearer accountability are vital, so too is developing a supportive, open and positive culture in our care system. I want staff to feel able to speak out when they see poor care taking place as well as getting the training and support they need to deal with the complex and challenging dilemmas they often face. (Department of Health, 2012, p 5)

As public debates about care and character intensify, so the need for a language and examination of virtue in action increases. This may explain the decidedly upward trajectory of studies into and about phronesis in contemporary professional and academic discourse (Carr and Steutel, 1999; Farrely and Solum, 2007).

These upheavals, compounded by the increasingly contested nature of managerial and expert knowledge (Beck, 2000), have offered scope to explore organisational life from an Aristotelian perspective, drawing particular attention to how phronesis can be cultivated within complex organisations to meet public demands and organisational imperatives. A wide array of authors working across numerous organisational contexts have highlighted problems with reductionist approaches to both knowledge and professional practice (Weick and Browning, 1986; Orr, 1990, Good, 1994; Nonaka, 1994; Tsoukas, 1997). Researchers working in health, education and social care have found fruitful ground in exploring how practical wisdom is developed by professionals and how this contextualised form of decision making operates in action. In medicine Pellegrino and Thomasma (1993) and Kaldjian (2010) emphasise phronesis as a cornerstone for both medical practice and medical education. In education phronesis has been wielded as a defence against hypo-deductive approaches to professional knowledge. Smith (1999) puts forward a concept of practical wisdom against what he views as the prevailing technicism in education. He argues that 'The distinctive nature of practical judgement is that it is ... characterised by attentiveness ... a sensitive attunement to what we usually think of as the object of apprehension, rather than the more dominating kind of "grasp" which instrumental or technical reason practises' (Smith, 1999, p 330).

Within social work research, authors are more forthright in outlining practical wisdom in social work as something crucial to practise and a hallmark of the profession's capability (Chu and Tsui, 2008). Such authors also note the problematic history that the profession has with regard to knowledge claims for expertise and how the hermeneutic tradition of understanding and interpretation offers greater insight than formalised theoretical knowledge for contemporary social work (Chu and Tsui, 2008). Hudson (1997) outlines how phronesis is strength to the profession, despite practice wisdom being offered a lower status of truth-value than propositional knowledge derived from scientific research. The common theme running through these studies is that to be competent in practice demands more than adherence to abstract laws. It involves the enacting of phronesis or practical wisdom supported by localised tacit and experiential knowledge. This is the very contextualised, specific and particular form of knowledge that the traditional scientific approach sought to discredit (MacIntyre, 1985).

Personalisation

In looking at shocks and challenges to organisations, social care in the UK is one such area undergoing a fundamental strategic change driven by the demand to give more choice and control to service users. 'Personalisation' – the policy narrative guiding these changes – redefines the role of both service user and professional (Needham, 2011). Within this narrative, service users are no longer conceptualised as passive recipients of services and professional expertise, but as participants and experts in creating their own support. Professionals no longer direct clients or control resources, but are expected to facilitate and advise service users to establish and reach their own aspirations and goals. Two premises are inherent in these descriptions. Firstly, that service users are active, assertive and well informed (Kelly et al, 2002; Greener and Mannion, 2009). Secondly, that state actors (particularly social workers) must cede claims to expert professional knowledge and reform their performance to reflect the primacy of service-user voice, expertise and right to self-determination (Angus and Gillian, 2002; Needham, 2003). The front-line encounter is thus reconceived as a facilitative resource, where professionals guide, advise and navigate with the service user on their journey to self-actualisation.

Drawing on calls from the disability user movement, alongside broader shifts in thinking about welfare that premise concepts of citizenship, consumerism and the introduction of markets into social care, personalisation formally entered the government lexicon under New Labour (HM Government, 2007). Since then, the Coalition government has furthered personalisation as an agenda into education, health and children's social care. Despite continuing political commitment to personalisation, commentators across the field have recognised its ambiguity, its lack of clear definition and guidance for action on the front line (Cutler et al, 2007; Ferguson, 2007; Beresford, 2008; Duffy, 2010). Social work has been identified in particular as struggling with the contradictions and uncertainties that personalisation brings to the front line (Lymbery and Postle, 2010; Lymbery, 2012).

Phronesis in the field

Using an ethnographic case study of a children's disability social work team, the empirical research discussed in this chapter concerns the ways in which social workers make sense of personalisation within an organisational context of change and ambiguity. The study explores these areas of ambiguity and uncertainty to build a sociological picture of how personalisation is currently being implemented in children's services. It is concerned to explore the dilemmas of contemporary social work with families through the lens of personalisation. Importantly, the study takes an agent-focused orientation, exploring what personalisation means to those front-line social workers tasked with its implementation.

The case study focused on a team that had been recently created as part of a large restructuring of children's services within an English local authority. The team comprised six social workers and two business support officers. Each social worker worked with 35 families, many of whom were met for the first time since the team was formed. Before the team members were interviewed, observations in the office and at team meetings were undertaken in order to understand how work is organised, talked about and experienced in daily life. It is within these observations that Aristotle's concept of phronesis began to take shape as an analytical category for exploring decision making within the context of social work. In order to illustrate how elements of phronesis can be argued to be present within the resolving of these dilemmas, a brief exchange between two team members will be analysed.

Emily is a newly qualified social worker who has been working with Grace and her family for three months. Sophie is an experienced social worker who had previously worked with the family in supporting their eldest child, who had learning difficulties.

Emily: "I'm working on the Grace case at the moment. I think the best thing for Grace is if we get her a support worker. She'd be able to get out more, go swimming which she loves and generally do more 'kid' things."

Sophie: "What about mum though? I know she's done a really good job of meeting Grace's needs and you know how she feels about long-term outside support."

Emily: "This is what I'm worried about. Technically in this new system the personal budget belongs to Grace and I do think a support worker would be good for her. Grace has said she wants to go out more. Mum hasn't got the time to do the swimming stuff. But I don't want to make mum feel like she isn't doing a good job, because she is. I think I'll go back to mum and speak to her about other avenues so we can make this work."

A few days later ...

Sophie: "So how did it go with Grace?"

Emily: "I remembered that mum had mentioned a friend of hers who Grace loves after I spoke to you. So when I went round there [Grace's home] mum and I spoke about Sue [the friend]. Mum was really enthusiastic about Sue helping them out, so when I said, 'maybe she could do some swimming with Grace?' mum jumped at the chance and said she'd call Sue straight away."

Sophie: "Result! Well done, I knew you'd find a way."

Phronesis alerts us to the importance of case knowledge. Case knowledge as championed by Aristotle and denigrated by Plato and Socrates is premised upon attentiveness and is pre-eminently flexible in outlook. *Aisthesis*, the Aristotelian term capturing this attribute of attentiveness, implies a mind open to further experience and the possibility of modifying an original judgement, just as Emily does in this example. This attribute has been identified by Weick as 'mindfulness', a skill fostered within certain organisational cultures by developing within their members a commitment to resilience and reluctance to simplify interpretations of events (Weick et al, 1999). MacIntyre (1985) interprets this as a reflexive ability to see things anew from within a specific setting, while others have written of the creative aspects of practical wisdom within professional life (Wall, 2003).

Phronesis is most valued and important at times of competing moral objectives, some enshrined in the particulars of the case, others with the overall direction of a policy, as in this instance, or with an organisational imperative. It is in the balance that phronesis as wisdom proves itself. In the conversation above Emily has worked out the need to balance the moral imperative of being child focused against undermining the parent, and navigates a middle course. She has the pressure of trying to deliver to both the ethical standards of her profession and to the moral demands of ambiguous personalisation policy that places a high value on self-determination. In navigating a path through these considerations she enacts 'a persistent awareness of balance epitomized by the occupation of a middle way' (Holt, 2006, p 1663). Emily's moral action is not thus bound either absolutely to abstract moral principles of a deontological ilk, or totally to informal tacit knowledge based on the contingent factors of the case. Emily's phronesis is tied up in the recognition that the meaning of moral rules and considerations is not carried in definitions but arises from a practical awareness of the conditions in which they might be useful (Williams, 1981).

Emily's approach to decision making may seem as little more than an exercise in everyday reasoning and judgement. It shares similarities with the reasoning of ordinary life, but it is informed by her professional education, training and experience – she had established a good working relationship with the family and had already ruled out any impediments to the course of action proposed. Moreover, her decision to return to her initial assumptions was supported by the resources of the occupational and organisational culture in which she is a part. Aristotle makes the point that virtues themselves are simultaneously innate and habituated; cultural and social conditions thus can inhibit or support their development.

All professionals must work with imperfect information in time-constrained circumstances. Practical wisdom can be useful in such circumstances, enabling workarounds to get the job done based on tacit knowledge or prior experience, rather than drawing upon a formalised knowledge base. Decisions supported by the informal logics of phronesis are relatively free to deliver useful and persuasive judgements in the fleeting time available. This contrasts with the ways in which deductive logic tends to operate. The importance of time and temporal decision making is thus a significant component in the decision-making schemata of social workers. As Bourdieu notes of ordinary social interaction, it 'unfolds in time', as contrasted to scientific analysis, which, he notes, is always retrospective and detached from the immediacy of practice where it is offered the 'privilege of totalization' (Bourdieu, 1990).

Conclusion

This chapter tentatively opens up a discursive space to consider how alternate forms of professional knowledge are used and justified by utilising Aristotle's conception of phronesis as a path to explore professional practice and decision making. In doing so it has sought to explore how phronesis as a creative attribute linking social good with private virtue offers scope to understand professional decision making beyond the technical-rational frame. Using recent research findings, the chapter found that the way social workers deploy justifications for decision making reflects both the complexity of the work and the need to find a balance between the extremities of scientistic claims to a metaphysical 'view from nowhere' and provocative postmodern relativisms. In practice, this balance reveals itself as lying between the rationalising and often constricting boundaries of flow charts and databases and the experiential and tacit skills more commonly associated with phronesis. Too much emphasis on the informal and tacit, and decision making may begin to look like a glorification of improvisation. Too much reliance on the *episteme* of decontextualised rules, and professionals are open to being levelled as rationing bureaucrats not attuned to the needs of particular families. While the tacit reasoning of the time-bound professional offers situated insight, it is rarely sufficient in isolation. The time demands of professional practice and the real consequences of professional decision making mean that all practices are infused by stories, formulae and procedures that provide a lifeline for the agent when the present reality is rife with complexity and difficult to comprehend (Hunter, 1996).

References

Angus, L. and Gillian, H. (2002) 'Political exhortation, patient expectation and professional execution: perspectives on the consumerization of health care', *British Journal of Management*, 13: 173–88.

Aristotle (1999) *Nicomachean ethics*, London: Dover.

Ayer, A.J. (1940) *The foundation of empirical knowledge*, New York: Macmillan.

Beck, U. (2000) *The brave new world of work*, Cambridge: Polity Press.

Beresford, P. (2008) 'Whose personalisation?' *Soundings*, 40 (Winter): 8–17.

Bourdieu, P. (1990) *The logic of practice*, Cambridge: Polity Press.

Carr, D. and Steutel, J. (1999) *Virtue ethics and moral education*, London: Routledge.

Chu, W. and Tsui, M. (2008) 'The nature of practice wisdom in social work revisited', *International Journal of Social Work*, 51(1): 47–54.

Coventry LSCB (Local Safeguarding Children Board) (2013) 'Serious case review re Daniel Pelka overview report', Coventry: Coventry LSCB.

Cutler, T., Waine, B. and Brehony, K. (2007) 'A new epoch of individualization? Problems with the "personalization" of public sector services', *Public Administration*, 85(3): 847–55.

de Certeau, M. (1984) *The practice of everyday life*, Berkeley, CA: University of California Press.

Department of Health (2012) *Transforming care: A national response to Winterbourne View Hospital Department of Health Review: final report*, London: Department of Health.

Duffy, S. (2010) *The future of personalisation: Implications for welfare reform*, Sheffield: Centre for Welfare Reform.

Farrely, C. and Solum, L. (2007) *Virtue jurisprudence*, New York: Palgrave Macmillan.

Ferguson, I. (2007) 'Increasing user choice or privatizing risk: the antimonies of personalization', *British Journal of Social Work*, 37: 387–403.

Francis, R. (2013) *The Mid Staffordshire Foundation Trust Enquiry*, London: The Stationery Office.

Fu-Lai Yu, T. (2003) 'A subjectivist approach to strategic management', *Managerial and Decision Economics*, 24: 335–45.

Gergen, K.J. and Thatchenkery, T.J. (1996) 'Organization science as social construction: postmodern potentials', *Journal of Applied Behavioural Science*, 32: 356–77.

Glasby, J. and Dickinson, H. (eds) (2009) *International perspectives on health and social care*, Oxford: Wiley-Blackwell.

Good, B.J. (1994) *Medicine, rationality, and experience*, Cambridge: Cambridge University Press.

Greener, I. and Mannion, R. (2009) 'Patient choice in the NHS: what is the effect of choice policies on patients and relationships in health economies?', *Public Money and Management*, 29: 95–100.

Hage, M. (1963) 'An axiomatic theory of organisations', *Administrative Science Quarterly*, 10: 289–20.

HM Government (2007) *Putting people first: A shared vision and commitment to the transformation of adult social care*, London: The Stationery Office.

Holt, R. (2006) 'Principals and practice: rhetoric and the moral character of managers', *Human Relations*, 59: 1659–80.

Howe, D. (1994) 'Modernity, post modernity and social work', *British Journal of Social Work*, 24: 513–32.

Howe, D. (1996) 'Surface and depth in social work practice', in N. Parton (ed), *Social work theory, social change and social work*, London: Routledge.

Hudson, J.D. (1997) 'A model of professional knowledge for social work practice', *Australian Social Work*, 50(3): 35–44.

Hunter, K. (1996) '"Don't think zebras": uncertainty, interpretation, and the place of paradox in clinical education', *Theoretical Medicine*, 17(3): 225–41.

Kaldjian, L.C. (2010) 'Teaching practical wisdom in medicine through clinical judgement, goals of care, and ethical reasoning', *Journal of Medical Ethics*, 36: 558–62.

Kant, I. (1996) *The Cambridge edition of the works of Immanuel Kant: Practical philosophy*, ed and trans Mary J. Gregor, Cambridge: Cambridge University Press.

Kelly, G., Mulgan, G. and Muers, S. (2002) *Creating public value: An analytic framework for public service reform*, London: Cabinet Office Strategy Unit.

Lipsky, M. (1980) *Street-level bureaucracy: Dilemmas of the individual in public services*, New York, NY: Russell Sage Foundation.

Lymbery, M. (2012) 'Critical commentary: social work and personalisation', *British Journal of Social Work*, 42(2): 783–92.

Lymbery, M. and Postle, K. (2010) 'Social work in the context of adult social care in England and the resultant implications for social work education', *British Journal of Social Work*, 40(8): 2502–22.

MacIntyre, A. (1985) *After virtue* (2nd edn), London: Duckworth.

Needham, C. (2003) *Citizen-consumers: New Labour's marketplace democracy*, London: Catalyst.

Needham, C. (2011) 'Personalisation: from story-line to practice', *Social Policy and Administration*, 45(1): 54–68.

Newman, J. and Clarke, P. (1994) 'Going about our business? The managerialization of public services', in J. Clarke, A. Cochrane and E. McLaughlin (eds) *Managing social policy*, London: Sage.

Newman, J. and Clarke, J. (2009) *Public, politics and power: Remaking the public in public services*, London: Sage.

Nonaka, I. (1994) 'A dynamic theory of organizational knowledge creation', *Organization Science*, 5: 14–37.

Orr, J.E. (1990) 'Sharing knowledge, celebrating identity: community memory in a service culture', in. D. Middleton and D. Edwards (eds) *Collective remembering*, London: Sage.

Parton, N. (2008) 'Changes in the form of knowledge in social work: from the "social" to the "informational"?' *British Journal of Social Work*, 38: 253–69.

Pellegrino, E. and Thomasma, D. (1993) *The virtues in medical practice*, Oxford: Oxford University Press.

Pugh, D.S., Hickson, D.J., Hinings, C.R., MacDonald, K.M., Turner, C. and Lupton, T. (1963) 'A conceptual scheme for organizational analysis', *Administrative Science Quarterly*, 8: 283–315.

Schatzki, T., Knorr-Cetina, K. and von Savigny, E. (2000) *The practice turn in contemporary theory*, London: Routledge.

Simon, H. (1957) *Administrative behaviour* (2nd edn), New York: Macmillan.

Simonds, R.H. (1959) 'Towards a science of business administration', *The Journal of the Academy of Management*, 2: 135–138

Smith, R. (1999) 'Paths of judgment: the revival of practical wisdom', *Educational Philosophy and Theory*, 31(3): 327–40.

Statler, M., and Roos, J. (2005) *Everyday strategic preparedness: The role of practical wisdom in organizations*, London: Palgrave Macmillan.

Taylor, C. and White, S. (2001) 'Knowledge, truth and reflexivity: the problem of judgement in social work', *Journal of Social Work*, 1(1): 37–59.

Taylor, F.W. (1911) *Principles of scientific management*, New York: Free Press.

Tritter, J., Koivusalo, M., Ollila, E. and Dorfman, P. (2010) *Globalisation, markets and healthcare policy: Redrawing the patient as consumer*, London: Routledge.

Tsoukas, H. (1997) 'Forms of knowledge and forms of life in organized contexts', in R. Chia (ed) *In the realm of organization*, London: Routledge.

Tsoukas, H. and Cummings, S. (1997) 'Marginalization and recovery: the emergence of Aristotelian themes in organization studies', *Organization Studies* 18(4): 655–83.

Ure, A. (1835) *The philosophy of manufactures*, London: Charles Knight.

Wall, J. (2003) 'Phronesis, poetics, and moral creativity', *Ethical Theory and Moral Practice*, 6: 317–41.

Wastell, D., Broadhurst, K., Hall, C., Peckover, S., Pithouse, A. and White, S. (2010) 'Children's services in the iron cage of performance management: street level bureaucracy and the spectre of Švejkism', *International Journal of Social Welfare*, 19: 310–20.

Weick, K. (1995) *Sensemaking in organizations*, London: Sage.

Weick, K, and Browning, L. (1986) 'Argument and narration in organizational communication', *Journal of Management*, 12: 243–259.

Weick, K., Sutcliffe, M. and Obstfeld, D. (1999) 'Organizing for high reliability: processes of collective mindfulness', in B. Staw and R. Sutton (eds), *Research in Organizational Behaviour*, 1, Greenwich: JAI: 81–123.

Williams, B. (1981) *Persons, character and morality in moral luck*, Cambridge: Cambridge University Press.

Wolf, W. (1958) 'Organisational constructs: an approach to understanding organisations', *Academy of Management Journal*, 1: 7–15.

Part Three

Towards integrated services?
The integration of social policies
and other policy domains

Integration of social and labour market policy institutions: towards more control and responsiveness?

Cyrielle Champion and Giuliano Bonoli[1]

Introduction

Integration of social and employment policies has been a highly topical issue over past decades in Europe. Faced with the complex task of facilitating the return to employment of jobless people with multiple barriers to work, several countries have developed integrated structures for delivering labour market and social support. 'One stop-shops', 'integrated jobcenters' and 'interagency collaboration' are some of the tools that are being developed in this context (Askim et al, 2011). These initiatives have taken different shapes in different countries. In some countries, such as in the UK, 'one-stop' jobcentres integrate the tasks of benefit payment and employment services, while in others, like in Denmark, the focus has been limited to activation and job-related services.

In spite of these differences, there are striking similarities in the motivations put forward by governments for these reforms. In many European countries the search for integrated services has been part of a broader trend towards the coordination of the public sector. The integration of social and employment policies clearly shares many of the goals of public sector coordination. Among these can be cited the aims to make better use of money by pooling resources and competences, to create more efficient services and to simplify clients' access to services (Pollitt, 2003).

In the field of the welfare state, coordination has also emerged in close relationship with the turn to activation and the new emphasis on labour market integration (van Berkel et al, 2011). In this context, the initial goal was generally to widen access to employment-related services to all categories of benefit claimants, including those on social assistance and incapacity-related benefits, and to offer support based on individuals' needs rather than on benefit entitlement (Newman, 2007; van Berkel et al, 2011). Further, in countries where responsibilities for benefits and employment services were traditionally divided among a number of separate actors, a second frequent motivation was to limit a sort of 'institutional egoism' that led actors to prioritise their own interests over the overall goal of labour market integration.

Against this background, this article examines the capacity of reforms geared towards the integration of social and employment policies to effectively deliver their multiple objectives. Its focus is primarily on two goals that were central in most reforms: increasing responsiveness to individual needs and strengthening central control. Based on a comparison of experiences in Germany, Denmark and Switzerland, this chapter shows that, although there has been some progress, none of the three countries managed to gain clear-cut achievements on these two goals. It is argued that one reason for the mixed results lies in the tensions and contradictions inherent in the simultaneous pursuit of these two goals. The chapter starts by examining the two goals of responsiveness and control and the tensions that can emerge in their pursuit within the context of active welfare states. It then discusses reforms undertaken in Germany, Denmark and Switzerland from the perspective of their effects on responsiveness and control. The chapter concludes by discussing the extent to which efforts to promote more responsiveness and more control have been successful in the three countries.

Integrated services in active welfare states: towards greater responsiveness and control?

Achieving greater responsiveness and central control in the provision of employment-related support have been two core objectives at the heart of recent organisational reforms. Depending on the country, they were often accompanied by other objectives (like user-friendliness, efficiency and reduction of social expenditures) and their respective importance sometimes varied. However, in all cases the two goals were closely linked to the reorientation of welfare states towards labour market integration and to the difficulties of fragmented welfare states to sustain this reorientation effectively.

Coordination and responsiveness

The need for greater responsiveness is perhaps the first and most obvious goal found in political and academic debates about the coordination of social and employment policies in the active welfare state. However, it is worth noting that this goal has not been unique to coordination reforms and has been a general concern of new public management reforms. At a general level, it denotes an intention to make public services more flexible and tailored to citizens' needs and demands. In this context, not only coordination efforts but also decentralisation and contractualisation have often been motivated in the name of a greater responsiveness of public services (Clarke and Newman, 1997).

In the case of active welfare states, the search for greater responsiveness has usually been synonymous with building 'personalised', 'individualised' employment-related support (Goerne, 2011). In all countries, this objective has figured very prominently in the political rhetoric and has tended to be associated with two elements of change. The first element was a wish to abolish the existence of separate activation systems for the unemployed and other jobless benefit claimants previously deemed as inactive, and to open access to the services offered by public employment services (PES) that were formerly reserved for the short-term unemployed. Concretely, this meant a need to pool the various portfolios of active labour market programmes and make them available to all benefit claimants, irrespective of their benefit status (Goerne, 2011). The second element of change often emphasised by governments was greater involvement of case-workers and local agencies so as to guarantee that active labour market programmes are implemented in accordance with local labour markets and that employment support addresses all individual needs (Berthet and Bourgeois, 2012)

Coordination and central control

Besides the goal of achieving greater responsiveness on the part of employment services, another important motive behind the creation of integrated services has been the desire to strengthen central control over the implementation of active labour market policy (ALMP).

The provision of income protection and employment services in a majority of European countries has traditionally been characterised by a division of responsibilities and tasks between central and regional/local government and between the state and other, non-state actors like social partners. In federal states and in the Nordic countries social assistance has traditionally been the responsibility of local authorities (or other, lower tiers of government), thereby granting them much autonomy in developing their own systems of activation. Social partners have also played an important role in many countries. In Denmark and Germany, for instance, social partners have long had a say in the definition of priorities in active labour market programmes through their presence on labour market boards at national or regional level.

Historically, this division of responsibilities made some sense as long as the main goal of welfare states was to passively protect against income losses. However, with the turn to active welfare states and the emergence of labour market integration as an overarching goal of social and employment policies, this division began to be seen as a major problem by many national governments, for a number of reasons. First, the turn towards activation highlighted large variations existing across local/regional authorities in their efforts to help the recipients of social assistance to get back into work. Second, the division of labour among several schemes resulted in redundancies between the activation systems developed to deal with different categories of benefit claimants. Third, and perhaps most importantly, in federal countries like Germany and Switzerland, the multi-tiered structure of the welfare state provided a formidable incentive for all the relevant actors to engage in the cost-shifting game. Instead of promoting labour market participation, in many cases an easier way to reduce the case load was to shift clients onto other schemes controlled by a different jurisdiction. In fact these problems constituted the multiple facets of the same problem: the lack of general macro-control over the performance of ALMP (Wilkins, 2002).

Tensions and contradictions in the implementation process

Responsiveness and control refer to totally different dimensions of public policy. We argue that there are some relationships between them and that the simultaneous pursuit of both objectives may result in trade-offs and contradictions. Some degree of central control is certainly necessary to ensure that all categories of jobless people receive the help they need, irrespective of their benefit entitlement. However, there are at least two ways in which increasing central control over policy may be in contradiction with the objective of promoting more responsiveness.

First, whether in a fragmented or in an integrated system, the jobless are a highly diverse group of people. As a result, imposing a single institutional framework on the whole of the non-working client population requires the establishment of some sort of internal subdivisions, which are usually operated by means of profiling tools. In theory, profiling should promote individualisation. In practice, it tends to result in a renewed segmentation of jobless people on the basis of their distance from the labour market (Berthet and Bourgeois, 2012), which may run counter to aspirations for individualised support when the different categories of jobseekers are offered different forms of support.

In fact, in the context of scarce resources, profiling and segmentation risk being turned into 'rationing' tools that allow the prioritisation of available means to some jobless people (often the job-ready) at the expense of other categories of clients (often those who are more distant from the labour market). In this way, the context of limited resources limits the scope of responsiveness.

Second, the introduction of control and performance management procedures that are meant to strengthen local and street-level compliance in the implementation of ALMP may also largely contradict ambitions for more responsive systems. Whereas responsive support requires large room for professional discretion for front-line staff to decide on appropriate individual integration strategies, control and performance management techniques, in contrast, tend to foster standardised approaches and to prioritise efforts on those people who are closest to the labour market – the so-called creaming effect (Newman, 2007, Caswell et al, 2010).

Increasing responsiveness and central control over social and employment policies are admittedly difficult objectives in their own right. We argue that these difficulties are compounded by the fact that, especially under currently prevailing circumstances (limited resources), these objectives are likely to be contradictory. Next, in the empirical part of the chapter, we present three case studies exploring the extent to which different integration efforts have attained these two goals, with a particular focus on the tensions and dilemmas that have arisen from their simultaneous pursuit. Methodologically, the case studies are based on an analysis of secondary sources of information and a re-examination of 26 semi-structured interviews conducted in the context of previous research on the politics of coordination reforms.

Germany: the Hartz IV reform

In 2005, Germany introduced the so-called 'Hartz IV' reform, which replaced two benefits for the long-term unemployed with a single benefit scheme for all able-bodied claimants (Unemployment Benefit II – UB II), and established a new agency dedicated to administering benefit payment and employment services for its beneficiaries. Prior to 2005, in addition to unemployment insurance (UI), Germany had two co-existing benefit schemes for the long-term unemployed: unemployment assistance and the last-resort social assistance scheme.

Following steady increases in benefit case loads, the idea of integration first emerged in political debate in the late 1990s. From the outset, the idea encompassed two general objectives. The first was to reinforce the focus on work and improve access to activation policies, especially for social assistance recipients, as municipal employment efforts varied greatly and access to the services of the PES was sporadic. The second was to tackle the co-existence of two schemes targeting similar clienteles and that had been criticised for generating important overlaps and cost-shifting problems between the federal state – which tightened unemployment assistance benefits – and the municipalities – which developed subsidised temporary jobs to shift their clients back onto unemployment insurance (Hassel and Schiller, 2010).

Hence, in Germany achieving greater responsiveness and clearer lines of responsibility for the long-term unemployed were two driving motives for the integration of unemployment assistance and social assistance.[2] They remained central in 2003 when the red-green Schröder government unveiled its proposal for the Hartz IV reform (Bundestag, 2003). According to the proposal, the integration should aim to provide more intensive support to help jobseekers return to the labour market. To do this, all active labour market instruments should be made available to any jobseeker, and more resources should be released so as to improve the workload of front-line staff and achieve the ideal ratio of one case-worker to 75 jobseekers. Then, to increase transparency and eliminate cost-shifting games between the federal state and local authorities, it was proposed to give full responsibility for the new integrated unemployment benefit to the federal state (Bundestag, 2003). This choice also reflected a long-standing preference within the Social-Democratic Party for labour market policy as a federal task (Projektgruppen 'AFG-Reform' und 'Sozialhilfe', 1998).

From initial ambitions to effective implementation

Politically, the reform proved very contentious, especially in respect of the issue of responsibility. Following tough negotiations, the initial plan of the Schröder government was severely compromised. Organisationally, rather than setting up a single jobcentre in charge of both jobseekers on UI and those on UB II, a separate agency was established to administer

UB II at the local level. Then, instead of a full federal competence, negotiations produced two different organisational models for the jobcentres. Besides the dominant model in which local PES agencies have to cooperate with local authorities, a second model allows local authorities to take over full responsibility for administering UB II. In 2013, 106 out of 416 local jobcentres were run according to this second model (http://statistik.arbeitsagentur.de/, accessed 14 November 2013).

Hence, the government's aspirations for centralised control over unemployment policy have barely been realised. Local authorities still have important responsibilities, over which the responsible Federal Ministry of Employment and Social Affairs has only limited supervisory authority (Jantz and Jann, 2013, p 239). Admittedly, the reform has successfully abolished 'institutional' opportunities to shift costs onto another level, notably through a complete reorganisation of financial responsibilities (Clasen and Goerne, 2011). However, conflicts of interest still exist, although they seem to be confined to the local level, in the daily management of jobcentres. This is visible in the definition of local activation strategies. Our interviews with jobcentre managers suggest that PES representatives tend to prioritise a rapid return into paid work, whereas local authorities, which cover housing and heating costs, are more concerned with jobseekers' long-term financial autonomy.

In terms of responsiveness, it can be argued that the creation of a separate agency for UB II constitutes an advantage. Compared to Schröder's initial plan to have a single jobcentre for all unemployed people, the creation of separate jobcentres considerably limits the risk of creaming effects between UI and UB II recipients. At the same time, they do not prevent UB II recipients from having access to the core labour market programmes provided by the PES. This latter aspect can be considered an important achievement of the Hartz IV reform. With the reform, the portfolios of ALMPs have been merged and extended, and UB II recipients now have the right to participate in a large array of labour market programmes, including training and wage subsidies (Clasen and Goerne, 2011). However, it should be noted that some differences still persist between UI and UB II recipients. Hence, UB II recipients remain legally excluded from a few labour market programmes available to UI recipients, such as start-up allowances or job creation schemes (*Arbeitsbeschäftigungsmaßnahmen*). What is more, they are still largely overrepresented in social integration-oriented programmes. For these clients, public employment still constitutes the most frequent active measure (Bonoli and Champion, 2013b).

Ambitions for more intensive individual support have been mitigated. Partly because of an unexpected rapid increase in new benefit claims on the introduction of the Hartz IV reform, many jobcentres quickly found themselves overburdened. As a result, the ratio of one case-worker for 75 jobseekers has never been achieved. Compared to the situation prior to 2005, where PES case-workers had to deal with 400 to 800 long-term unemployed on average, the Hartz IV reform has nevertheless brought about significant improvements (Knuth 2010). Yet, genuine individualised support is still far from being realised. Part of the explanation lies in high workloads, but another part lies in a more systematised use of instruments such as profiling and individual integration agreements, which turned out to limit individual case-workers' room for manoeuvre (Schütz et al, 2011).

In sum, in Germany the Hartz IV reform has produced mixed results in terms of both responsiveness and centralised control. The government's choice to engage in a radical integration of two benefits systems at both the organisational and benefit levels was certainly successful in tackling institutional incentives to shift costs between the federal and local levels. It significantly extended the range of ALMPs provided to the long-term unemployed. However, this radical solution has also had some negative consequences, notably in terms of responsiveness. Jobcentres are now responsible for integrating the vast majority of jobseekers in Germany, which has generated a need for a re-categorisation of benefit clients and rights. Finally, due to the jobcentres' chronic work overload since 2005, the reform has not managed to implement the aim of providing more intensive support.

Denmark and the establishment of municipal jobcentres

In Denmark, integration efforts have concentrated on gathering employment support under a single roof. Until the mid-2000s, Denmark had a dual activation system based on unemployment status (Hendeliowitz and Woollhead, 2005). Governed according to separate legislation, the insured and non-insured unemployed were subject to different rights and obligations and were dealt with by separate organisations. People entitled to unemployment insurance received employment support from the state-run PES. For this category of unemployed, there existed a large variety of ALMPs, especially in education and training, and participation rates were high, due to the decision in the 1990s to make activation mandatory after some time in unemployment (Goul Andersen and Pedersen, 2007).

In contrast, jobless people not entitled to unemployment insurance – the non-insured unemployed, according to the Danish terminology – had to rely on social assistance administered by local authorities. In the 1990s, several reforms extended the requirements for local authorities to provide a sufficient choice of labour market programmes and to activate social assistance recipients considered fit for work. However, because of the autonomy enjoyed by local authorities, employment efforts remained subject to large variations and were often restricted to subsidised public employment programmes (Rosdahl and Weise, 2001).

In 2007, this two-tiered activation system was brought to an end under the framework of an ambitious local government reform, the so-called 'Structural reform'. In each local authority jobcentres were established that gathered employment services for all jobless benefit claimants, including the non-insured unemployed and sick and disabled people, under one roof. The task of benefit payment was deliberately kept separate from the jobcentres, both because the government wanted a clear focus on labour market integration and because abolition of the unemployment insurance funds (close to the trade unions) was perceived to be politically unfeasible.

As regards the organisational model, the 2007 jobcentre reform deviated significantly from the initial plan of the Liberal-Conservative government, which was to abolish the state-run PES and give political and operational responsibility for employment services to local authorities. As in Germany, two organisational models were instead introduced, one in which the PES and municipalities worked side by side, and one pilot model for which a few local authorities had full responsibility. It was only in 2009 that the government eventually managed to impose its initial plan for fully municipalised jobcentres, which also meant the transfer of political responsibility for the labour market integration of insured unemployed to local authorities (Bredgaard, 2011).

Simultaneous pursuit of responsiveness and central control through jobcentres

In Denmark, the creation of integrated jobcentres very quickly emerged as a reform that would allow the government to pursue simultaneously the two goals of responsiveness and central control. In terms of responsiveness, two goals in particular were pursued. The first was to guarantee *equal treatment of the insured and non-insured unemployed* by harmonising rules and allowing the non-insured unemployed to have access to the same services and programmes offered to the insured unemployed (Carstensen, 2010). The second was to build a *more flexible provision of active measures*, in response to the allegedly overly bureaucratic activation system that had developed for the insured unemployed as a consequence of the introduction of mandatory periods of activation (Goul Andersen and Pedersen, 2007).

The reform aimed also to increase central control (Bredgaard, 2011). From this perspective, the municipalisation of employment services offered two advantages. The first was the possibility of weakening the influence of social partners in regional labour market councils. The second concerned the high level of municipal autonomy and street-level discretion, which was rapidly seen by the government as contributing to important implementation gaps in the activation of the non-insured unemployed. In this context, municipal jobcentres offered an opportunity not only to secure sufficient local flexibility in the definition of the portfolios of ALMPs, but also to strengthen local compliance with national legislation. Hence, through the jobcentre reform, municipalities were given the ability to adapt the content of ALMPs to the needs of local labour markets (albeit within the limits of the law) and to develop additional programmes for specific target groups (Mploy, 2011, p 35). At the same time, this autonomy was compensated for by the introduction of a sophisticated monitoring and performance management system and stricter steering of front-line case workers' practices (Bredgaard 2011).

In terms of street-level practices, changes that accompanied the establishment of jobcentres included the categorisation of jobseekers into three categories on the basis of a detailed profiling questionnaire, as well as the determination of minimum requirements for the conduct of job interviews and the provision labour market programmes. For instance, since 2012 jobcentres have been obliged to conduct job interviews at least every three months, with the first interview to be carried out within four weeks for young people below the age of 30. As to ALMPs, the first is to be provided after nine months of unemployment at the latest, and subsequent ones every six months.[3] The capacity of local jobcentres to deliver job interviews and activation programmes on time now counts for a good part of their performance evaluation and funding (Jantz and Jann, 2013).

A procedure-oriented implementation of jobcentres

Despite the focus in the government's rhetoric on the need to improve the responsiveness of the Danish active labour market policy, in the implementation of jobcentres the goal of strengthening central control largely took precedence over the goal of responsiveness. On the positive side, the establishment of integrated jobcentres admittedly removed inequalities that formerly existed between the insured and non-insured unemployed as regards access to ALMPs. The non-insured unemployed now legally have access to the same job-search support and array of ALMPs as do the insured unemployed. Currently, the activation rate is even higher among the non-insured unemployed (35–40%, as against about 20% for the insured unemployed, Svarer, 2013). In addition, the determination of minimum requirements for both the insured and non-insured unemployed guarantees that jobcentres do not cream off job-ready unemployed and keep other unemployed people further from the labour market on passive income support (Mploy, 2011, p 38).

However, beyond these improvements, it is worth noting that some distinctions between the insured and non-insured unemployed still persist (notably as regards to job availability criteria), while new distinctions have been created. Following the new profiling system, jobseekers are divided into three match groups, which are offered different types of employment support. In this context, only those deemed as not immediately job ready can be directed to ALMPs. Support for those immediately job ready concentrates on intensive job-search counselling, while for the last category – those temporarily on passive support – support is restricted to on-going contact (Mploy, 2011). For this clientele, local authorities have the possibility to set up specific active programmes. However, partly because of the injunctions for timely minimum requirements, and partly because of the financial crisis, local jobcentres have so far rarely made use of this possibility. As a result, in 2010 a majority of jobcentres reported that they were incapable of offering active programmes adapted to the needs of the most vulnerable groups of unemployed (Mploy, 2011, p 56–7).

In sum, in Denmark, the establishment of integrated jobcentres has created the necessary conditions for equal treatment of insured and non-insured unemployed focused on labour market integration, especially for the non-insured unemployed. Moreover, through the changes made in the governance structure of employment services, national authorities have gained considerable control over employment efforts for both the insured and non-insured unemployed. However, attempts to strengthen central control have also clearly hampered the initial aim to establish more flexible provision of ALMPs based on individual needs.

Switzerland: collaboration in a fragmented system

The Swiss welfare state is a highly fragmented, multi-tiered welfare state. While the big-spending programmes (unemployment insurance, old-age and invalidity pensions and health insurance) are controlled at the federal level, others such as social assistance are almost entirely the responsibility of the cantons (Bonoli and Häusermann, 2011). With regard to employment support, fragmentation is also high, as three different delivery agencies share this task for the three largest benefit schemes catering for jobless people, namely unemployment insurance, social assistance and disability insurance.

The issue of coordinating the various components of the welfare state came onto the agenda in the early 2000s as a result of a massive case-load increase in unemployment insurance, social assistance and invalidity benefits. The early responses to the crisis of the early 1990s had been rather un-coordinated and based on cost shifting. Unemployment insurance reforms shifted more and more unemployed people onto social assistance, whereas the cantons, responsible for social assistance, were trying to pass clients back to the federal level, either to unemployment or disability insurance.

In many cantons this was achieved by job creation programmes. These were meant to provide employment to the unemployed who could not find a job during the 18 months covered by unemployment insurance and would, as a result, have to rely on social assistance. Typically, clients would receive a contribution-paying job in the public or the non-profit sector lasting 12 months, just long enough to re-establish entitlement to unemployment insurance. These interventions had various objectives: to reduce the hardship experienced by the long-term unemployed and allow them to avoid the stigma of social assistance, but also to shift costs upwards to the federal level (Bonoli and Champion, 2013a). In addition, jobless people were encouraged to apply for (federal) invalidity benefit (Bütler and Gentinetta, 2007).

At the same time, and also in subsequent years, federal authorities were busy restricting access to federal social insurance programmes. So, for example, in 1995 an overall time limit of two years was imposed on the receipt of unemployment insurance benefits, and in 2003 a stricter procedure for the medical assessment of disability was introduced. There was a widespread perception among the social assistance authorities that these developments were contributing to the rise in the numbers of social assistance clients from the mid-1990s.

The overall impression of the response to the rise in case loads from the late 1990s to early 2000s is one of a nearly total absence of coordination and control, with the result that clients were shifted between programmes without necessarily having access to the labour market services they needed. In fact, the authorities in charge of the various schemes seemed mostly concerned with the preservation of their own budgets, and much less with increasing their jobless clients' chances of re-entering the labour market.

The response to these developments in Switzerland was the development of inter-agency collaboration. One idea behind this concept was to make available to the clients of each benefit scheme the same tools and capabilities for promoting access to employment that were available to clients of other programmes. Initially, inter-agency cooperation was strongly supported by all the relevant actors. The federal government saw in it an opportunity to improve the system without having to interfere with cantonal sovereignty. The cantons saw it as an opportunity to reduce expenditure on social assistance and as a first step towards a bigger reform (CDEP and CDAS, 2001).

From the very beginning, however, inter-agency cooperation was conceived as a minimalistic and pragmatic form of coordination (Gächter, 2006). The intention was to tackle the fragmentation of social security by developing a somewhat informal type of cooperation at the delivery level among case-workers. In the background, there was a clear imperative behind these early initiatives: to modify the existing system as little as possible. In addition, given the absence of a federal competence in the field of social assistance, the cantons had to be free to decide whether and how to develop inter-agency collaboration (Gächter, 2006).

A slightly more ambitious collaboration initiative was launched in 2005 under the name of MAMAC (Medizinisch-Arbeitsmarktliche Assessments mit Case Management). Its key elements were the development of a cooperation framework targeted at beneficiaries with health problems and based on early detection, a joint assessment and definition of a reintegration plan that was mandatory for the different agencies' three delivery agencies (Champion, 2008). The MAMAC pilot generated high expectations with regard to its capacity to deliver a real improvement in terms of activating social security claimants.

MAMAC was presented as a means of opening labour market programmes available to one scheme to clients of other schemes. In reality, however, access to labour market programmes offered by other schemes remained contingent upon eligibility rules as defined in legislation. This meant that access to labour market programmes of other schemes depended above all on the capacity of tripartite teams of case workers to play with the rules and revise their eligibility assessments. Yet, in spite of this, social assistance clients were almost systematically excluded from the more costly programmes such as full vocational training, which under certain conditions are available to recipients of unemployment and disability insurance. Moreover, from the beginning, the MAMAC project was conceived as a niche programme, targeted at only a small minority of benefit claimants confronted by multiple problems. As a result, between 2006 and 2010, only about 1,000 claimants across the entire country were directed to the project (Egger et al, 2010). For all these reasons, the MAMAC largely failed to improve the overall responsiveness of the system in terms of access to ALMPs. An evaluation of the MAMAC pilot was published in 2010. It showed that expectations had been too high. The evaluation came to the main conclusion that, despite a good assessment by the clients and case workers, CII-MAMAC did not lead to higher employment rates, nor did it reduce welfare expenditure. Moreover, from an administrative point of view, the evaluation concluded that collaboration procedures were too complex (Egger et al, 2010). Surprisingly, despite these disappointing results, the federal government decided to go down the road of inter-agency cooperation and develop it further.

While officially both the federal government and the cantons continued to support inter-agency collaboration, those in charge of social assistance became increasingly dissatisfied with the overall strategy. They felt that the federal government was continuing to pursue an ambiguous strategy. On the one hand, it promoted collaboration, while on the other hand it adopted reforms that restricted access to federal programmes and thereby continued to play the cost-shifting game, in spite of emphasis on collaboration (Darioli, 2006).

The Swiss story sheds light on the trade-off between responsiveness and control in a new way. First, the increase in central control has been very limited, in the sense that the federal government has not acquired new powers and the collaboration initiatives it has sponsored have never affected the governance structure that is in place. Second, the federal government has attempted to contain the cost of fragmentation and free-riding practices by closing down some access routes to federal benefits. However, by reducing access to federal benefits the government has also reduced the accessibility of the high-quality labour market programmes (for example, long-term training).

Discussion and conclusion

The accounts presented in the three case studies suggest that the extent to which integration efforts have managed to strengthen responsiveness and control is limited. Advances can certainly be seen on both dimensions, but at the same time results may have fallen short of the ambitions of those who initiated the reforms. In some cases the unwanted effects of reform, often due to the general context of limited resources, mean that actual responsiveness may have been curtailed.

Overall, we can identify different difficulties on the road to more responsiveness and control. First, there has been substantial resistance to attempts at centralisation. The German case study illustrates this well. The Hartz IV reform included an attempt at strengthening control over the activation of non-working benefit recipients. In the end, resistance from the municipalities and the Länder severely limited the extent to which a truly unified system could be developed. In Denmark too, social partners and opposition parties vigorously resisted plans for centralisation. Their resistance temporarily led to a complex organisational arrangement similar to that in Germany. However, the government was eventually able to bypass this opposition. The jobcentre reform dramatically reduced the influence of social partners in the whole system of activation, and in 2009 the dual organisational arrangement was terminated in favour of a fully municipal structure.

Second, goals in terms of responsiveness were often frustrated by the fact that the ideals behind the reform, such as making a full portfolio of labour market services available to all jobless claimants, would have been extremely costly. In addition, responsiveness implies favourable staff–client ratios, which, as we saw, were not so easy to achieve in the real world. Third, access to labour market services seems to remain linked to eligibility for a given programme, in spite of all the integration efforts put in place over the last 10–15 years. This is most clearly the case in Switzerland, where the most expensive training programmes are generally not available to social assistance clients.

Ultimately, the case studies illustrate that control and responsiveness can be contradictory objectives. If increased responsiveness needs some degree of centralisation, as proved in the Swiss case, aims for greater central control can also come at the expense of responsive programmes and support. Perhaps the clearest case is Denmark, where the wish of the liberal-conservative government to introduce more direct control over performance management and procedures de facto limited what room for manoeuvre was left to municipalities and case workers.

Such contradictions between the goals of responsiveness and central control in fact illustrate a long-standing concern about the coordination of public services. Whereas the idea of coordination can easily be viewed as a remedy to numerous problems, it remains very difficult to accomplish in reality. As some authors have regularly pointed out over several decades, this is particularly true for the ability to provide holistic responses to the complex needs of clients. Although it has focused on two specific objectives, control and responsiveness, this chapter further confirms that establishing coordinated services that are able to meet individual needs is probably one of the most challenging tasks in the provision of human services.

Notes

[1] This article is based on research funded by the Swiss national science foundation (Project 'Redefining the internal boundaries of European welfare states', No. 100017_126528). The paper was written up in the context of related project funded by the European Community's Seventh Framework Programme under grant agreement no. 320121 (Project INSPIRES). We are grateful to Menno Fenger, project coordinator, for comments on an earlier version of this article.

[2] Of course, they were not the only objectives. Financial concerns related to the costs of unemployment assistance and the municipal financial crisis were also important, and contributed much to the attractiveness of the integration option (Hassel and Schiller, 2010).

[3] Source: www.Jobindsats.ch (consulted on 11.09.2013)

References

Askim, J., Fimreite, A.L., Moseley, A. and Pedersen, L.H. (2011) 'One-stop shops for social welfare: the adaptation of an organizational form in three countries', *Public Administration*, Early View: 1–18.

Berthet, T. and Bourgeois, C. (2012) 'A European comparison of change in the national governance of integrated social cohesion policy', Project report for the EU LOCALISE research programme 'Local worlds of social cohesion', Bordeaux: Université de Bordeaux.

Bonoli, G. and Champion, C. (2013a) 'Federalism and welfare to work in Switzerland: the development of active social policies in a fragmented welfare state', Unpublished manuscript, Lausanne: IDHEAP.

Bonoli, G. and Champion, C. (2013b) 'La réinsertion professionnelle des bénéficiaires de l'aide sociale en Suisse et en Allemagne', *Cahier de l'IDHEAP*, Lausanne: IDHEAP.

Bonoli, G. and Häusermann, S. (2011) 'Swiss welfare reforms in a comparative European perspective: between retrenchment and activation', in C. Trampusch and A. Mach (eds) *Switzerland in Europe: Continuity and change in the Swiss political economy*, London: Routledge, pp 186–204.

Bredgaard, T. (2011) 'When the government governs: closing compliance gaps in Danish employment policies', *International Journal of Public Administration*, 34(12): 764–74.

Bundestag (2003) *Gesetzentwurf eines Vierten Gesetzes für moderne Dienstleistungen am Arbeitsmarkt*, Drucksache 14/1516, 05.09.2003, Deutscher Bundestag.

Bütler, M. and Gentinetta, K. (2007) *Die IV: Eine Krankengeschichte*, Zürich: NZZ Libro.

Carstensen, M.B. (2010) 'The nature of ideas, and why political scientists should care: analysin/g the Danish jobcentre reform from an ideational perspective', *Political Studies*, 58(5): 847–865.

Caswell, D., Marston, G. and Larsen, J.E. (2010) 'Unemployed citizen or "at risk" client? Classification systems and employment services in Denmark and Australia', *Critical Social Policy*, 30(3): 384–404.

CDEP and CDAS (2001) *Recommendation de la CDEP et de la CDAS concernant l'encouragement de la collaboration interinstitutionnelle (CII)*, Soleure et Berne: CDEP et CDAS.

Champion, C. (2008) *La collaboration interinstitutionnelle: prémices d'une réforme de la sécurité sociale suisse*, Working Paper de l'IDHEAP.

Clarke, J. and Newman, J. (1997) *The managerial state: Power, politics and ideology in the remaking of social welfare*, London: Sage.

Clasen, J. and Goerne, A. (2011) 'Exit Bismarck, enter dualism? Assessing contemporary German labour market policy', *Journal of Social Policy*, 40(4): 795–810.

Darioli, S. (2006) 'Positions et revendications de l'aide sociale à la CII', Rencontre nationale de la CSIAS *5e révision de la LAI et la Collaboration Interinstitutionnelle (CII): Chances et risques pour l'aide sociale*, Fribourg: 23 March.

Egger, M., Merckx, V. and Wüthrich, A. (2010) *Evaluation du projet national CII-MAMAC*, Aspects de la sécurité sociale, No 9/10. Berne: OFAS.

Gächter, T. (2006) 'Rechtliche Grundlagen der Interinstitutionellen Zusammenarbeit (IIZ)', *Schweizerische Zeitschrift für Sozialverischerung und berufliche Vorsorge*, 50: 593–618.

Goerne, A. (2011) 'Towards greater personalisation of active labour market policy? Britain and Germany compared', PhD dissertation, Edinburgh: University of Edinburgh.

Goul Andersen, J. and Pedersen, J.J. (2007) *Continuity and change in Danish active labour market policy (1990–2007): The battlefield between activation and workfare*, CCWS Working Paper No 2007-54, Aalborg University: Centre for Comparative Welfare Studies.

Hassel, A. and Schiller, C. (2010) *Der Fall Hartz IV: Wie es zur Agenda 2010 kam und wie es weitergeht*, Frankfurt am Main: Campus Verlag.

Hendeliowitz, J. and Woollhead, C.B. (2005) 'Employment policy in Denmark: high levels of employment, flexibility and welfare security', in G. Sylvain (ed) *Local governance for promoting employment: Comparing the performance of Japan and seven countries*, Tokyo: The Japan Institute for Labour Policy and Training, pp 121–38.

Jantz, B. and Jann, W. (2013) 'Mapping accountability changes in labour market administrations: from concentrated to shared accountability?' *International Review of Administrative Sciences*, 79(2): 227–48.

Knuth, M. (2010) 'Fünf Jahre Hartz IV: Zwischenbilanz und Reformbedarf', *Orientierungen zur Wirtschafts- und Geselschaftspolitik*, März: 14–23.

Mploy (2011) *Building flexibility and accountability into local employment services: Country report for Denmark*, OECD Local Economic and Employment Development (LEED) Working Papers, 2011/12, Paris: OECD Publishing.

Newman, J. (2007) 'The "double dynamics" of activation: institutions, citizens and the remaking of welfare governance', *International Journal of Sociology and Social Policy*, 27(9–10): 364–75.

Pollitt, C. (2003) 'Joined-up government: a survey', *Political Studies Review*, 1(1): 34.

Projektgruppen 'AFG-Reform' und 'Sozialhilfe' (1998) *Arbeitslosenhilfe und Sozialhilfe: Gemeinsames Positionspapier der Projektgruppen 'AFG-Reform' und 'Sozialhilfe'*, Düsseldorf: Unpublished report from SPD-led *Länder*.

Rosdahl, A. and Weise, H. (2001) 'When all must be active: workfare in Denmark', in I. Lødemel and H. Trickey (eds) *An offer you can't refuse: Workfare in international perspective*, Bristol: The Policy Press, pp 159–80.

Schütz, H., Steinwede, J., Schröder, H., Kaltenborn, B., Wielage, N., Christe, G. and Kupka, P. (2011) *Vermittlung und Beratung in der Praxis: Eine Analyse von Dienstleistungsprozessen am Arbeitsmarkt*, Nürnberg et Bielefeld: IAB und Bertelsmann Verlag.

Svarer, M. (2013) 'Labour market policies in Denmark: A story of structural reforms and evidence-based policy', CBS *Conference on Reform Capacity and Macroeconomic Performance*, 12 September.

van Berkel, R., de Graaf, W. and Sirovátka, T. (2011) 'The governance of active welfare states', in R. van Berkel, W. de Graaf and T. Sirovátka (eds) *The governance of active welfare states in Europe*, Basingstoke: Palgrave Macmillan, pp 1–21.

Wilkins, P. (2002) 'Accountability and joined-up government', *Australian Journal of Public Administration*, 61(1): 114–19.

TWELVE

Decentralised integration of social policy domains

Duco Bannink

In the Netherlands, political conflict on the most effective and most legitimate location of social policy formation and implementation is more than a century old. In social assistance and social care, different conceptions of the nature of the policies have gone hand in hand with different preferences for the location of the legal capacity of policy formation and implementation. For instance, during debate on the formation of the 1965 Social Assistance Act, the Ministry of Culture, Recreation and Social Support held an integrated concept of social assistance and social care. In this concept, the municipality was the primary actor in integrated policy formation and implementation. The Ministry of Social Affairs, on the other hand, considered social assistance to be an element of unemployment compensation policy, of which the social insurance arrangements also formed a part. In this conception, the ministry and social partners were considered to be the primary actors in policy formation, while implementation was decentralised to the municipality (Rigter et al, 1995). The conception of the Ministry of Social Affairs won, leading to the development of two sub-domains of social policy: social assistance and social care. However, the functioning of each of these sub-domains and their interaction has never been absent from political debate.

In the 1990s a new wave of debate commenced. The New Social Assistance Act (nAbw) of 1996 partially decentralised budgetary responsibilities to the municipalities. At the aim here was the introduction of performance incentives into the municipalities. The nAbw was followed by the further decentralisation of social assistance arrangements by means of the Work and Social Assistance Act (WWB) of 2004. Budgetary responsibilities were now fully decentralised: the financial risk of policy failure was transferred from national government to the municipalities. In the case of social assistance, the design of the budget forces municipalities to define policy success in terms of re-employment, by providing a budget for benefit disbursal to the municipalities in advance and allowing the municipalities to keep the surplus when re-employing benefit recipients, but to supplement the budget when the number of beneficiaries rises.

The WWB was considered to be successful. The 2007 evaluation (Bosselaar et al, 2007) stated that the quantitative objective of the Act was attained. Following social assistance, decentralisation was subsequently implemented in the domain of social care. The Social Support Act (WMO) of 2007 also transferred budgets to municipalities. The WWB and the WMO, however, differ in the type of decentralisation that was implemented (Bannink and Ossewaarde, 2012). The decentralisation of both social assistance and social care was intended to allow municipalities to integrate policies and policy implementation in these two fields. The main subject of this chapter concerns the question of whether the decentralisation of both sub-domains of social policy has supported municipalities in actually integrating these fields in practice.

The first section of this chapter presents a theoretical framework in which modes of multilevel governance are outlined that differ in two dimensions. The following section discusses the regulatory context of decentralised integration of Dutch social policy, focusing on two pieces of legislation, the Work and Social Assistance Act of 2004 and the Social Support Act of 2007. In the third section, the outcomes of decentralised integration in these social policy domains are considered. It is argued that the differences in the regulatory framework explain difficulties with regard to social policy integration, and the opportunities and risks of decentralised integration in the Dutch case are further considered. These findings are also important for other cases of social policy decentralisation because they illustrate how differing regulatory and financial frameworks interact at the level of local policy formation and implementation.

Theoretical framework: modes of centred and decentred governance

Bannink and Ossewaarde (2012) presented a model of four modes of governance. Decentralisation, they argue, takes place 'in response to policy capacities partially existing at the central and partially at the decentralized level of governance systems' (p 597). Where social problems become complex, control functions might still be located at the centred level, but expertise and case knowledge is increasingly located at the decentred level, allowing decentred levels of governance to de facto evade central control. Shifts in governance can be understood as a response to this.

Bannink and Ossewaarde define a policy as being comprised of policy content and policy resources, referring to a well-known Dutch (Hoogerwerf, 2003) definition. A mode of governance is defined by the allocation of policy resources and substantial capacities between the 'centred' and 'decentred' levels of governance. Content and resources can both be located at the centred and decentred levels, as set out in Table 12.1.

Table 12.1: Modes of centred and decentred governance and associated side-effects

Policy resource risks → Policy content ↓	Centred	Decentred
Centred	Capacity *Control paradox*	Accountability *Performance paradox*
Decentred	Task *Self-regulation paradox*	Virtue *Decentralisation paradox*

Source: Derived from Bannink and Ossewaarde, 2012, p 605

Different modes of governance support different types of administrative responsibility (Bovens, 1998). A system of centred policy content and centred policy resources constitutes 'government', a mode of governance in which capacities are located at the centred level. This governance mode presumes that 'capacity' (Bovens, 1998) to effectuate central policy objectives is indeed available at the centred level of the system. If not, a control paradox occurs. Capacity is insufficient (or the policy problem too complex) to actually control policy implementation and decentred policy implementation might evade centred control ambitions. In response, decentralisation of either policy resources or policy content or both may be expected.

Where policy resources are allocated at the decentred level but policy content is allocated at the centred level, responsibility as 'accountability' (Bovens 1998) is supported. The allocation of policy resources to the decentred level implies that decentred levels of governance bear the resource risks of policy failure and success, and are accountable to the centred governance level for the attainment of centred policy objectives. A market relation between centred and decentred levels of governance is constructed, in which the centred level obtains policy performance from the decentred level. A negative side-effect of such modes of governance is 'performance paradox' (Van Thiel and Leeuw, 2002, p 269), supporting 'an emphasis on phenomena that are quantified in the performance measurement scheme at the expense of unquantified aspects of performance', and 'an emphasis on measures of success rather than the underlying objective'. Where policy content is allocated at the decentred level, but policy resources are allocated at the centred level, responsibility as 'task' (Bovens, 1998) is supported. The allocation of policy content capacities to the decentred level implies that centred government seeks the cooperation of decentred policy actors in order to insert decentred expertise and local knowledge into the system that is lacking at the centred level. Centred government defines and enforces the role obligations of decentralised governance actors. Héritier and Eckert (2008) argue that self-regulation often implies 'weak control.' Under weak control, decentred actors show rent-seeking behaviour (Olson, 1971) and apply the available funds to strengthen their own organisational capacity (Bannink, 2004; Moe, 2005) or pursue 'closure' strategies (Ackroyd, 1996). A negative side-effect of this mode of governance therefore is a 'self-regulation paradox'. The allocation of policy content capacities to the decentred level is intended to increase the policy-making and implementation capacity of the governance system in which the centred actor is capable of only weak control. However, it also empowers decentred actors, allowing them to pursue decentred policy objectives.

Decentralisation of either policy resources or policy content may give rise to paradoxes. A performance paradox may occur where centred control of the policy objective does not lead to increased performance but to an instrumental emphasis on the performance that is rewarded in the definition of policy failure and success of the arrangement. A self-regulation paradox may occur where the weakening of centred control does not lead to the increased insertion of decentred knowledge into the system but to uncontrollable decentred policy action and associated costs.

In the fourth mode of governance, decentred 'virtue' is pursued. Both policy resources and content are decentralised. This might form an adequate response to the performance and self-regulation paradoxes of the decentralisation of either resources or content. But we cannot be sure that this is indeed the case. A virtue arrangement seems to address a 'double governance challenge' and pursue two objectives at once (cf. Bannink, 2013). Can the orientation towards decentred policy objectives of a task arrangement (self-regulation paradox) be repaired by decentralising policy-resource risks? Can – at the same time – the narrow orientation towards centrally rewarded policy objectives of an accountability arrangement (performance paradox) be repaired by decentralising policy-content capacities? Theoretically, in a 'virtue' arrangement decentred actors indeed cannot pursue decentred objectives funded by centrally provided means, because the budget is decentred. Neither can they adjust their policy implementation to centrally rewarded policy aims, because policy aims are defined at the decentred level. In practice, however, the attainment of decentred virtue is built upon the presumption that policy objectives are most feasibly addressed at the local level and that no relevant supra-local or intra-local interdependencies are included in the issue that need to be addressed at the centred level. A decentralisation paradox may occur: virtue is not attained, but the replacement of central-level policy conflicts, coordination problems and lack of resources and knowledge is displaced to the decentred level.

With this model in mind, the discussion in the next section focuses upon the decentralisations in the sub-domains of social assistance and social care. The section explores which modes of governance are implemented, how the governance modes in the two sub-domains interact and whether this interaction supports the actual integration of local policy formation and implementation.

Regulatory context: decentralised integration of Dutch social policy

In the Netherlands, various decentralisation operations have occurred in the social policy domain. The most prominent of these were arguably the decentralisation of social assistance arrangements by means of the Work and Social Assistance Act (*Wet Werk en Bijstand*, WWB) of 2004 and the decentralisation of social care and social participation policies by means of the Social Support Act (WMO) of 2007. A process indicated by the government as the 'three' or even 'four decentralisations' continues on the path of the previous decentralisations.[1] In this process, budgets for the implementation of participation-enhancing policies are being integrated in the social policy sub-domains of labour participation and income policies, social care and participation policies, youth care policies and education of vulnerable groups.

The WWB and the WMO demonstrate different modes of governance. As is argued below, the WWB might best be described as an accountability arrangement of 'decentred policy resource risks and centred policy content capacities'. The WMO, on the other hand, might be understood as a virtue arrangement of 'decentred policy resources and policy content objectives'. We first discuss the governance arrangement of the WWB and the WMO in their current state and then outline the further integration of regulations and budgets announced in various central government documents.

The policy and governance arrangement of the WWB

In 2004, a new WWB was introduced that replaced the New Social Assistance Act (*nieuwe Algemene bijstandswet*, nAbw) of 1996. The WWB made decentralised policy implementation actors (municipalities) increasingly responsible for the financial results of implementation, while national regulation was reduced.

The main objective of the Act was client activation (TK 28870, no 3, pp 3–4). In order to achieve this the WWB contains two main elements: a new main policy objective and a new governance arrangement for the implementation of the objective (Explanatory Notes to the Work and Social Assistance Bill, TK 28870, no 3).

'Work precedes income'

The main policy objective of the Act was that 'work precedes income'.[2] The new legislation shifted the emphasis from income support to recipient activation and the prevention of benefit dependency, through re-employment and the prevention of benefit claims, while maintaining the minimum income guarantee (TK 28870, no 3, pp 5–6). The obligatory nature of the new legislation is increased by the imposition upon recipients of an obligation to work towards re-employment. This recipient obligation is supported by an obligation imposed upon municipalities to offer support to clients in their re-employment efforts (WWB, art 7; TK 28870, no 3, p 36) and an individual obligation to utilise the offered support (WWB, arts 9 and 10; TK 28870, no 3, p 38). The recipient's obligation to seek re-employment is further supported by the competency of municipalities to 'adjust' the level of the benefit 'to the level of responsibility the recipient has shown' (TK 28870, no 3, pp 47–8).

The 'three Ds'

A system of 'three Ds' (TK 28870, no 3, p 2) formed the new governance arrangement.

The first 'D' was 'decentralisation'. This implied the further transfer of the financial risks and resources for social assistance disbursal to the municipalities. Municipalities are to 'experience positive financial results when people are re-employed into labour as quickly as possible. Active policy implementation is rewarded'. The financial risks of policy failure and success are being shifted to municipalities through the introduction of a decentralised 'macro budget for social assistance' (TK 28870, no 3, pp 15 ff). The complete budget for disbursed benefits is shifted to municipalities as they experience the full cost of increased numbers of disbursed benefits, or the full profit of a decrease. This, it is argued here, establishes an 'accountability' mode of governance.

The second 'D' concerned 'deregulation' and pointed to the decrease in the amount and complexity of rules, which is aimed at the reinforcement of municipalities' discretionary policy implementation capacities. In itself, this suggests a 'task' mode of governance, but the Act limits municipal discretion at the same time: the municipal re-employment regulation is required to show an explicitly 'balanced' approach and to address the needs of benefit recipients, non-benefit recipient citizens seeking re-employment support, and the combination of work and care and various target groups like ethnic minorities, disabled persons, younger people and citizens with weaker links to the labour market (TK 28870, no 3, p 40).

The third 'D' was the decrease of reporting obligations: bureaucratic obligations are reduced. The national government aims to reduce reporting obligations so that bureaucracy is reduced 'over the full breadth of the social assistance policy' in order to reinforce 'problem-solving capacities at municipal level' (TK 28600–XV, no 4, p 1–2).

After several years of experience, the rather uneasy solution of an incentive-based governance mechanism (which requires a high level of discretion for the decentralised actors) and additional regulation (which stands in the way of decentralised actors devising an optimal response to incentives) resulted in the central-level control effort becoming weakened. After the initial reluctance to fully decentralise decision-making capacities to local government that was apparent in the additional regulations, the governance of the WWB evolved and came to include 'softer', discursive arrangements, like the regular inventory and publication of municipal best practices rather than central regulation.

In December 2007 a 'Participation Budget' was announced in which the budgets for various work and non-work activation trajectories for citizens, including education, social integration and work rehabilitation, were integrated (TK 29674, no 25, p 7). The Participation Budget gives municipalities more discretion, as it concerns the application of the budgets related to the WWB and WMO and the adjustment of complementary services. Surpluses of re-employment provision may be applied to social integration provision. Additionally, the Dutch Association of Municipalities (VNG) and the Ministry of Social Affairs and Employment drafted a Plan of Work on Re-employment (TK 28719, no 60), in which it is agreed that municipalities are allowed to make a more selective use of re-employment instruments. Municipalities are now allowed to selectively allocate re-employment resources to those groups of clients who can, in their view, gainfully use these resources.

In this next phase of WWB development a different combination of deregulation and decentralisation was tried, to offer both increased input of local expertise and increased localisation of the risks and resources of policy implementation. That is, the expected 'performance paradox' is now no longer discouraged through regulation, but instead is accepted, while the efficacy of policy implementation is supported through discursive means. The WWB governance arrangement now more strongly than before supports the application of local discretion and knowledge in order to achieve the objectives implied in the incentive of the WWB budget system.

In terms of the theoretical model presented earlier, the WWB established an 'accountability' mode of governance. The arrangement is aimed at the strengthening of incentives for the achievement of the nationally defined policy goal that 'work precedes income'. The achievement of nationally defined policy objectives is pursued by the displacement of the resource risks of policy failure and success to the municipal government. We now turn to the domain of social care and argue that the Social Support Act that was put into effect in that domain established a 'virtue' mode of governance.

The policy and governance arrangement of the WMO

Van der Veer (2013b) makes a distinction between the general philosophy, the governance and the policy substance of the Social Support Act (WMO). While the governance arrangement and the policy substance of the WMO differ from that of the WWB, the general philosophies of the WMO and the WWB show similarities. As for the WWB, the general philosophy of the WMO emphasises 'participation' or 'joining in' (Explanatory notes to the WMO Bill, TK 30131, no 3, p 7; Van der Veer, 2013b, p 26). Citizens have an individual responsibility to participate in society, be it in relation to matters of work (as in the WWB) or to matters of social care (WMO).

Van der Veer (2013b, p 20) depicts this new central principle as a shift away from a 'servicing model'. In 2000, an interdepartmental committee started working on the integration at municipal level of care provision for disabled and other vulnerable citizens. The further development of ideas was increasingly informed by the larger societal and social-scientific debate on activation and social participation, as the Minister and State-Secretary of Health argued in the 2004 note on the contours of a new WMO (TK 29538, no 1, p 1). As a result, the name of the Bill was changed, from Social Care Act (in a previous letter in 2003, TK 26631, no 56) to Social Support Act. This change underscored the activating character of the Bill. The Bill no longer emphasises only the integration of social care provisions at municipal level, but also the objective of citizen participation in care provision.

In order to achieve the objective of increased citizen participation, the Cabinet opted for a 'three steps' system (TK 29538, no 1, p 2), in which a distinction is made between three levels of increasing severity of care requirements and three corresponding levels of decreasing opportunities to participate.

In the first step, 'people who are able to do so are required to invent solutions in their own social environment'. In the second step, the municipality has to offer support to citizens who 'are not adequately able – in some situations – to realise solutions themselves or together with others'. It is for this step that the new WMO will be introduced. The central government, in the third step, guarantees a provision arrangement that 'insures what it is meant to do: heavy and continuous care that entails large financial risks for individuals that cannot be privately insured' (TK 29538, no 1, p 2).

The main substantial policy principle of the WMO is the so-called 'compensation principle' (Van der Veer, 2013b, p 24). The compensation principle on the one hand protects the municipal discretion of substantial policy formation, while on the other hand it guarantees a minimum level of social support to needy citizens. The principle states: 'to compensate for limitations of a person […], the municipality makes available provisions in the field of social support that allow the person to: (a) maintain a household; (b) move in and around the home; (c) move locally in a means of transportation; (d) meet fellow citizens and engage in social connections' (WMO, Art 4-1). The subsequent section (WMO, Art 4-2) states that the municipality is required to take into account the personal characteristics and needs of the claimant and his capacity to provide for his needs himself. Van der Veer (2013b, p 25) argues that the compensation principle was a compromise between those political parties that supported increased local policy-making discretion and those that opposed local discretion for reasons of legal equality. The Act refrained from directly defining municipal provision, but instead obliged municipalities to offer provision to the extent and of such a nature that the citizen is supported to engage in social participation. The four 'aspects of self-efficacy and social participation' of WMO Art 4-1, as Van der Veer calls them (2013b, p 25), define the substance of municipal policy.

The reluctant attitude of the national government in regard to the actual definition of policy substance is also reflected in the main governance arrangement of the WMO. The definition of the main governance principle of the new WMO in 2004 (TK 29538, no 7, p 1) underscored the importance of municipal discretion: 'the formation of the WMO policy needs to take place at the local level in the municipal democracy. Therefore, it is required that municipalities have sufficient freedom and an adequate set of instruments.' With this, the WMO establishes a different governance mechanism than the WWB. Instead of the introduction of incentives in the WWB that were to encourage municipalities to minimise the number of beneficiaries, the WMO broadly defines a number of domains of responsibility of the municipality, without a budgeting design that encourages a specific outcome.

The financial arrangement of the WMO offers relatively broad freedom for municipalities to implement the Act. The financial resources for policy implementation are offered as an integrated part of the general allowance to municipalities. As such, the displacement of the budget to municipalities does encourage efficiency in care provision, but the budgeting system does not prescribe a specific outcome. Instead, nine domains of responsibility are defined. A broad budget is transferred to municipalities, and municipalities need to define how the deployment of this budget contributes to the performance in these nine domains.

This broad financial arrangement is coupled with a new arrangement of responsibility relations. A vertical national–local arrangement of responsibility relations is replaced by a horizontal intra-local system. In this new system the national government bears 'system responsibility' (TK 30131, no 3, p 9). The Minister is responsible for the design and adjustment of a system of regulation that permits societal objectives to be achieved. Apart from system responsibility, the national government's tasks are limited. Within the municipality, a 'horizontal' system of responsibility relations is implemented in which the municipality is obliged to consult with citizens and local organisations about the implementation of the performance domains defined in the Act, before submitting the local WMO policy to the municipal council. The arrangement defines a number of obligations: the municipality has to guarantee local policy formation, including recurrent research into citizen satisfaction, the obligation to consult with citizens and organisations and to support this by the provision of relevant policy information, and the obligation to request advice from local organisations on the intended policies and discuss the way the advice is addressed in the policy proposals before submission to the municipal council (WMO, Art 9-12).

In contrast to the WWB, the governance arrangement of the WMO established a 'virtue' mode of governance. In the WWB, the governance arrangement displaced the resource risk of policy success to the municipality, while the meaning of policy success (limitation of the number of beneficiaries) is defined in the budgeting arrangement. The WMO, on the other hand, contains an outline of domains where the municipality is responsible for 'performance', while the budgeting arrangement does not define performance itself. Additionally, the WMO imposes a number of regulations that are not related to the substance of local social support policies, but instead oblige the municipality to engage local actors in local policy-formation processes. The governance arrangement is thus aimed at supporting the local formation of policy substance, while at the same time transferring the resource risks of policy implementation to the municipal government. As such, it can be regarded as a virtue mode of governance.

Different modes of governance cause different responses

In this section, the local responses to the modes of governance of the WMO and WWB are considered. In researching the WWB and WMO, one question was whether the 'accountability' arrangement of the WWB would support similar processes of 'local welfare crafting' to the 'virtue' arrangement of the WMO (Bannink, Bosselaar and Van der Veer, 2013). The main finding was that it did not, as will be discussed below. In this finding there are important implications for our main subject of decentralised integration of sub-domains of social policy. These are discussed in the final section of the chapter.

Similarities between the WMO and the WWB concern the main policy objective of active citizenship and citizen responsibility, the enabling role of policy and the reduced role of national government in policy making and the related national control arrangement that is targeted at policy outcomes, not local policy input. However, Bannink et al (2013, pp 142 ff) argue that the similarities are accompanied by two main differences in the governance arrangements of the WWB and WMO. These differences concern the substantial content and breadth of municipal policy formation capacities and the substantial content and breadth of the budgeting mechanism. In the WWB, municipal policy-formation capacities are limited to re-employment, and the national government control effort is aimed at a substantive policy objective (re-employment) through budgeting. In the WMO, municipal policy-formation capacities concern the entire field of social support, and the national government control effort is aimed at a non-substantive policy objective (efficiency) through budgeting and a procedural objective (participation of citizens and organisation in policy formation) through regulation.

Both the WMO and the WWB include a residual conception (Gilbert, 2002) of public support, but the definition of the residual provision differs. In social assistance, the primary alternative for residual public income support is self-sufficiency of income. Policy intervention therefore is primarily oriented towards re-employment and the ending or prevention of benefit dependency (Van der Veer et al, 2013). In social support, on the other hand, there are a range of alternatives for residual public social care (the promotion of social participation and the self-organisation of care, personal budgets for market-based care, family care, community care), so that policy interventions are directed to a broader set of objectives, accordingly. The WMO establishes a communitarian vision of society in which neighbours, communal services and informal care enable the social participation of citizens in need of care. The role of government is to find a proper balance between encouraging people to take care of themselves, creating the conditions for a vital civil society and helping citizens in need of professional care (Timmermans et al 2010; Van der Veer et al, 2013, p 100).

Thus, while the resource risk of policy failure and success in the WWB is mainly related to the objective of re-employment, the cost of the WMO can be controlled in a variety of ways: provision can be withheld, local organisations can be supported to provide support, an individual's peers and family may be required to provide care and so on. As a result, the WMO's budgeting model offers a broad instead of a highly specific definition of policy objectives and the corresponding risk of policy failure and success: the connection between the substantial content of municipal policies and its budgetary outcomes is weaker.

The difference in governance, primarily budgeting, strongly affected the local response to the Act. The financial incentive of the WWB induced immediate local 'focus' (Bannink et al, 2013). After the introduction of the Act, processes of 'local welfare crafting' unfolded in response to the new challenges that the regulation posed. The WWB gave the processes of local welfare crafting a flying start in its early years. In response to the specific objective implied in the budgeting arrangement, these localised crafting processes were oriented towards the objective of reducing the number of beneficiaries. It is remarkable to observe that a specific set of local actors in the sub-domain quickly turned to the development of new measures and implementation procedures: local politicians are often absent from the process of crafting in the domain of work and social assistance. Given the nature of the budgeting arrangement, there is no strong need for local policy formation. Locally, it is sufficient to optimise policy implementation, oriented towards the nationally defined objective implied in the budgeting arrangement. Therefore, the WWB functioned as a 'manager's act' (Bosselaar et al, 2007). The managers of social services, some of them reluctantly, others proactively (Bannink, 2013), jumped into the political vacuum that had emerged. Localised crafting processes did actually occur, but social service managers took centre stage and a managerial, performance-driven approach to work and social assistance emerged. The governance arrangement of the WWB operated as a recentralisation of policy objectives in disguise rather than the localisation of the work and social assistance domain. The budgeting method hindered the building of localised welfare landscapes. Localised crafting processes built a nationally defined landscape strongly oriented to re-employment.

Since the WMO budgeting method did not imply a specific substantial focus, it took more time for local processes of local welfare crafting to commence. Be this as it may, localised processes did show a broader range of substantial objectives and the processes are still evolving. Next to municipal managers, other types of entrepreneurs (local politicians, but also care providers, client organisations, interest groups) also engaged in the crafting process, relying on their position and expertise in the local community. As a result, crafting processes in the social support domain led not only to the emergence of localised processes of welfare crafting, but indeed to the emergence of localised welfare landscapes. While in morphological form municipalities showed similar solutions to the challenges of local social support provision (demand clarification, the one-stop shop, Timmermans et al, 2010, pp 278 ff), the actual policy substance implemented through these forms proves to be built upon local social support traditions. In her research on WMO implementation in three middle-sized Dutch cities, Van der Veer shows that policy implementation follows the local socio-cultural institutions (the 'couleur locale'), leading to 'integrated care in Almere, cooperative welfare in Dordrecht, and social investments in Enschede' (Van der Veer 2013a, p 137).

While the arrangement of the WWB appeared to support the emergence of local welfare-crafting processes, it did not support the emergence of local welfare landscapes. Policy-making processes were increasingly locally determined, but the outcomes of these processes remained strongly bound to the nationally defined policy objective of re-employment. The arrangement of the WMO, on the other hand, appeared to support the emergence of local welfare-crafting processes that effectively created local welfare landscapes in which care policies reflect the 'couleur locale'. Policy making was increasingly locally determined, while also actually creating locally determined solutions.

The concluding section of this chapter discusses the implication of these differences for the processes of decentralised integration of social policies.

Conclusions: further decentralised integration of social policy domains

In the Netherlands, social assistance and social support budgets are currently being integrated, while at the same time budget cuts are being implemented. The findings reported above point to a risk for the further decentralised integration of social policy domains. The findings show, after all, that the 'accountability governance arrangement' of the WWB results in nationally defined objectives overruling local policy preferences and support a system that is not fully responsive to local conditions. The accountability governance mechanism creates a 'performance paradox' (Bannink and Ossewaarde, 2012) in which local actors mechanistically respond to the financial incentives included in the arrangement.

It is to be expected that the 'virtue governance arrangement' of the WMO cannot cope with the pressure of accountability. Previously, the decentralisation of both policy resource risks and policy content capacities has given rise to a landscape of local welfare systems that are built upon locally institutionalised policy traditions. The recent further integration of budgets, however, creates the risk that the local welfare landscapes of the WMO that have emerged will come to conform to the nationally defined welfare landscape of the WWB. This implies that local social care arrangements will increasingly be evaluated on the basis of their contribution to re-employment objectives.

This Dutch finding shows that the decentralised integration of social policy sub-domains is a challenging issue. On the one hand, decentralised integration of social policies forms a response to the multi-dimensional and integrated nature of social problems. Health, income and participation appear strongly related. The main argumentation of the Dutch Cabinet for the decentralised integration of social policy sub-domains is that a decentralised, case-based approach supports the mutual adjustment of sub-domain solutions and the integration of sub-domain policies. In the problem-driven new public governance approach (Osborne, 2006; 2010), the integration and mutual adjustment of sub-fields of policy making and implementation is presented as a strong alternative to the fragmentation of service implementation in the performance-driven new public management approach.

The Dutch case shows that the decentralised integration of sub-domains of social policy might, however, be intrinsically difficult. The various sub-domains of social policy address social problems that differ in nature; to be more precise, they differ in specificity. While the social problem of care, social support and active citizen participation is multi-dimensional in nature and calls for a variety of solutions, work and income is a uni-dimensional social problem that calls for a single solution. We might phrase it as follows: while the main objective in the sub-domain of social support is a social problem, the main objective in the sub-domain of work and income is performance. A social problem can be understood as a broadly defined set of issues that need be addressed, while the actual response is not defined. Performance, on the other hand, can be understood as a specifically defined output that need be achieved.

The difference of the main objective to a large extent determines the mode of governance that is applied in these sub-domains. The broad definition of the issue in the sub-domain of social care makes it difficult to implement an accountability mode of governance. Since performance is not defined, the governance arrangement leaves substantial policy formation to the decentred actor: a virtue mode of governance. At the same time, the specificity of the required performance in the sub-domain of work and income in fact supports a governance arrangement that encourages decentred actors to contribute to the centrally defined objective: an accountability mode of governance.

This difference stands in the way of an easy integration of sub-domains because the integration of sub-domains causes governance modes to *interact*. While a theory of the interaction of governance modes is as yet lacking, we observe that it creates the danger that policy implementation in the less strongly specified field of social care is forced to come up to the more strongly specified policy objective of the field of social assistance. To put it bluntly: while budget surpluses in social assistance can be achieved through investment in re-employment measures, investments in social care merely invoke costs. Municipal investments in the social care field therefore need be informed by re-employment considerations. Local social care policies then tend to increasingly include (additional) objectives related to the re-employment of citizens in need of social care.

Notes

[1] www.invoeringwmo.nl/bibliotheek/gemeenschappelijke-taal-het-sociale-domein, accessed 9 October 2013.
[2] All Dutch-language legislative and government texts translated by author.

References

Ackroyd, S. (1996) 'Organization contra organizations: professions and organizational change in the United Kingdom', *Organization Studies*, 17(4): 599–621.

Bannink, D. (2004) *The reform of Dutch disability insurance. A confrontation of a policy learning and a policy feedback approach to policy change*, Enschede: Universiteit Twente.

Bannink, D. (2013) 'Het managen van activering: een dubbele uitdaging', in H. Bosselaar and G. Vonk (eds) *Bouwplaats lokale verzorgingsstaat. Wetenschappelijke reflecties op de decentralisaties in de sociale zekerheid en zorg*, Den Haag: Boom Juridische uitgevers, pp 89–100.

Bannink, D., and Ossewaarde, R. (2012) 'Decentralisation. New modes of governance and administrative responsibility', *Administration & Society*, 44(5): 595–624.

Bannink, D., Bosselaar, H. and Trommel, W. (eds) (2013) *Crafting local welfare landscapes*, The Hague: Eleven.

Bannink, D., Bosselaar, H. and Van der Veer, J. (2013) 'Local welfare and activation in the Netherlands. Introduction to part II', in D. Bannink, H. Bosselaar and W. Trommel (eds) *Crafting local welfare landscapes*, The Hague: Eleven, pp 97–104.

Bosselaar, H., Bannink, D., Van Deursen, C. and Trommel, W. (2007) *Werkt de WWB? Resultaten van de ontwikkeling van nieuwe verhoudingen tussen Rijk en gemeenten*, Den Haag: Ministerie van SZW.

Bovens, M. (1998) *The quest for responsibility: Accountability and citizenship in complex organizations*, Cambridge: Cambridge University Press.

Gilbert, N. (2002) *Transformation of the welfare state: The silent surrender of public responsibility*, Oxford: Oxford University Press.

Héritier, A. and Eckert, S. (2008) 'New modes of governance in the shadow of hierarchy. Self-regulation by industry in Europe', *Journal of Public Policy*, 28(1): 113–38.

Hoogerwerf, A. (2003) 'Beleid, processen en effecten', in A. Hoogerwerf and M. Herweijer (eds) *Overheidsbeleid. Een inleiding in de beleidswetenschap*, Alphen aan den Rijn: Kluwer, pp 17–36.

Moe, T. (2005) 'Political control and the power of the agent', *The Journal of Law, Economics, & Organization*, 22(1): 1–29.

Olson, M. (1971) *The logic of collective action: Public goods and the theory of groups*, Cambridge, MA: Harvard University Press.

Osborne, S. (2006) 'The new public governance?' *Public Management Review*, 8(3): 377–87.

Osborne, S. (ed) (2010) *The new public governance? Emerging perspectives on the theory and practice of public governance*, New York: Routledge.

Rigter, D., Van den Bosch, E., Van der Veen, R. and Hemerijck, A. (1995) *Tussen sociale wil en werkelijkheid. Een geschiedenis van het beleid van het ministerie van Sociale Zaken*, 's-Gravenhage: VUGA Uitgeverij.

Timmermans, J., Gilsing, R. and De Klerk, M. (2010) *Op weg met de Wmo. Evaluatie van de Wet Maatschappelijke Ondersteuning 2007–2009*, The Hague: Sociaal en Cultureel Planbureau.

TK 26631, no 56 (2002–2003) *Zorg en maatschappelijke ondersteuning. Brief van de Minister en de Staatssecretaris van Volksgezondheid, Welzijn en Sport.* [Ministerial Note on the Social Care Act], The Hague: Documents Second Chamber of Dutch Parliament.

TK 28870, no 3 (2002–2003) *Vaststelling van een wet inzake ondersteuning bij arbeidsinschakeling en verlening van bijstand door gemeenten (Wet werk en bijstand). Memorie van Toelichting.* [Explanatory Notes to the Work and Social Assistance Bill]. The Hague: Documents Second Chamber of Dutch Parliament.

TK 29538, no 1 (2003–2004) *Zorg en maatschappelijke ondersteuning. Brief van de Minister en de Staatssecretaris van Volksgezondheid, Welzijn en Sport.* [Ministerial Note on the Contours of a new WMO]. The Hague: Documents Second Chamber of Dutch Parliament.

TK 29674, no 25 (2007–2008) *Evaluatie Wet Werk en Bijstand. Verslag van een algemeen overleg.* [Evaluation Work and Social Assistance Act. Report on a parliamentary debate]. The Hague: Documents Second Chamber of Dutch Parliament.

TK 30131, no 2 (2004–2005) *Nieuwe regels betreffende maatschappelijke ondersteuning (Wet maatschappelijke ondersteuning). Voorstel van Wet*. [WMO Bill]. The Hague: Documents Second Chamber of Dutch Parliament.

TK 30131, no 3 (2004–2005) *Nieuwe regels betreffende maatschappelijke ondersteuning (Wet maatschappelijke ondersteuning). Memorie van Toelichting.* [Explanatory notes to the WMO Bill]. The Hague: Documents Second Chamber of Dutch Parliament.

Van der Veer, J. (2013a). 'Local welfare landscapes. The case of social care in the Netherlands', in D. Bannink, H. Bosselaar and W. Trommel (eds) *Crafting local welfare landscapes*, The Hague: Eleven, pp 121–40.

Van der Veer, J. (2013b) *Weg uit het verleden. Een institutionele analyse van de gemeentelijke uitwerking van de Wet maatschappelijke ondersteuning (Wmo)*. Amsterdam: VU University Press

Van der Veer, J., Bannink, D. and Bosselaar, H. (2013) 'Do local landscapes emerge? Reflecting on local welfare crafting in the Netherlands', in D. Bannink, H. Bosselaar and W. Trommel (eds) *Crafting local welfare landscapes*, The Hague: Eleven, pp 79–94.

Van Thiel, S. and Leeuw, F. (2002) 'The performance paradox in the public sector', *Public Productivity and Management Review*, 25(3): 267–81.

THIRTEEN

Rescaling inequality? Welfare reform and local variation in social assistance payments

Renate Minas, Olof Bäckman, Vibeke Jakobsen, Tomas Korpi, Thomas Lorentzen and Timo Kauppinen[1]

Welfare reform and benefit inequality

Social assistance schemes generally comprise the last resort in countries' social protection systems, guaranteeing citizens help when they cannot support themselves and have exhausted other alternatives. The benefit's means-tested character implies that variation in social assistance payments is foreseen by law, a normal and intended result of applicants' different needs and circumstances. However, variation in assessments and payments can also be generated by local government discretion in implementing national legislation. Thus, depending on where they live, persons with the same circumstances and needs may face different eligibility criteria and/or receive different benefit amounts.

Local discretion is believed to have increased in many countries following reforms in the 1990s, yet little is known regarding the impact of changes in vertical divisions of power on variation in benefits. The distribution of responsibility between central and local government has also been an issue in the Nordic countries. The Nordic countries are interesting here since they often are classified as a distinct type of welfare state (for example, encompassing or social democratic), a classification that tends, however, to overlook substantial differences within the cluster. Social assistance is a case in point. There are notable differences in the extent and character of local discretion, and the countries have also seen a variety of reforms in the areas of standardisation and institutional integration.

The aim of this chapter is to examine the relationship between shifting divisions of power and the degree of variation in social assistance payments in Denmark, Finland, Norway and Sweden. Specifically, the reforms that we examine relate to changes in local autonomy such as, for example, limiting or extending local responsibility with regard to activation policies, processes of standardisation, and institutional integration of social assistance systems with labour market policy. Somewhat simplified, the assumption is that the more detailed the regulation, the less variation is possible, and vice versa.

We use individual-level national register data that in Finland and Norway pertain to the whole population and in Denmark and Sweden to very large samples thereof. The data spans roughly the period 1990 to 2010. To examine the impact of the reforms on variation in social assistance payments we employ multilevel modelling, controlling for both individual and municipal characteristics. In the next section we review the literature on power shifts and inequality, before in the following section briefly discussing the Nordic reforms. Subsequent sections present the data and the method used in the analysis, the results and the conclusions.

Reform trends and local variation

In recent decades, reforms in developed welfare states have addressed the institutional structure of income protection and activation services. Throughout Europe sub-national levels of government have become responsible for delivery of services, and also for regulation and financing (van Berkel et al, 2011; Minas et al, 2012). However, there were also reforms in the opposite direction, limiting local autonomy and transferring power back to the national level (Minas et al, 2012). To this can be added reforms addressing responsibilities at a particular level, for example through integration of separate benefit systems. Such institutional reforms were also central components of reforms in social assistance systems in both Canada and the US.

Empirical analyses of the relationship between shifts of power and various welfare outcomes have often used fairly crude indicators such as variation in public spending and economic growth along vertical or horizontal dimensions. Nonetheless, there are studies focusing explicitly on legislative changes, and among them a few that examine changes in social assistance legislation and local variation in social assistance payments. These include studies by Meyers and Gornick (for example 2005), who examined changes in benefit inequality following welfare reforms in the US in 1996. They found a somewhat mixed pattern, yet overall their results indicated that inter-state variation in means-tested cash and in-kind benefit levels as well as in take-up rates often increased following decentralising reforms. The relationship between local autonomy and benefit variation was also examined in two Nordic studies, although these focused on centralisation rather than decentralisation. Bergmark (2001) studied inter-municipal variation in social assistance expenditures in Sweden following the introduction of a national benefit standard in 1998. This appeared to have had no impact on variations in expenditure, as the variation in benefit expenditures increased continuously throughout the 1990s.

These studies used the coefficient of variation in municipal expenditures as their outcome measure. In their analysis of the introduction of governmental guidelines for social assistance benefits in Norway in 2001 (similar to the Swedish standard but formulated more loosely), Brandtzæg et al (2006) instead examined the deviation of local benefit amounts from the national guidelines, as well as the deviation of local benefit expenditures from the national average. In contrast to the other studies, they were also able to control for a number of structural differences between municipalities, such as differences in population structure (and, in some models, also introduced municipal fixed effects). Their results showed a slight decrease in the average difference between local benefit amounts and the guideline rate after the introduction of guidelines, and this relatively weak effect was attenuated further when they turned to expenditures where no clear impact of the reform was found. This difference between the impact on set amounts and actual payments was seen as being related to the discretion retained by case workers and administrators in the assessment of benefit needs.

In sum, although the pattern was somewhat mixed, the US analyses tended to show a reduction in expenditure variation following the devolutionary reforms in the 1990s. In contrast, the Nordic studies examining centralising reforms around the turn of the millennium found only a weak or no reduction in variation. One interpretation of these mixed results is that there may be differences in the legislation not captured in the analyses that are generating the differences in the results. Reforms do not always fall along a decentralisation–centralisation continuum but can involve a concomitant expansion and limitation of local autonomy (decentralised centralisation). In addition, different reforms with contradictory implications for local autonomy can be carried out simultaneously. Other differences between the studies may of course also be important; for instance, only the Norwegian study controlled for structural differences across localities. In other words, there is a need for analyses that pay close attention to the particulars of the reforms while examining their impact using longitudinal data from representative samples controlling for confounding factors.

De- and recentralisation of social assistance policies in Nordic countries

All Nordic countries have means-tested social assistance schemes where the right to support is stated in national legislation outlining the legislators' general intentions while at the same time giving local government varying degrees of autonomy in implementation. When discussing the reforms in the four countries it is essential to take the starting point into consideration, as decentralised systems undergoing further decentralisation may be less likely to see an increased variation than centralised systems undergoing the same change. Comparing the countries in the early 1990s, Gough et al (1997) placed Finland, Denmark and Sweden in the 'citizenship-based but residual assistance' category, whereas social assistance in Norway was categorised as 'decentralized, discretionary relief'. Norway would accordingly appear to have been somewhat less centralised than the other three.

Denmark

Social assistance in Denmark was originally an entirely discretionary benefit that has gradually been turned into a standardised allowance (Heikkilä et al, 2001). This process started in the 1970s, when ceilings for social assistance were established, and continued in 1987, when nationally fixed rates for the basic benefit were introduced.

The recession in the 1990s, combined with perceived welfare state passivity, triggered a series of activation reforms. Denmark's first mandatory activation programme, the Youth Allowance Scheme for 18- to 19-year-old recipients, was introduced in 1990. In 1991 municipalities received the right to act as an employment service for especially vulnerable individuals in all age groups. Activation efforts were then gradually expanded, in 1992 including the unemployed under the age of 25 on social assistance benefits and in 1996 those under 30. The benefit was turned into taxable income (1994) and discretionary supplements were almost entirely abolished (Heikkilä et al, 2001). The Law on Municipal Activation (1994) expanded the target group for activation to also include social assistance recipients over 25 years, and also persons considered to have other problems in addition to unemployment. However, in 1996 this municipal obligation changed to municipal discretion, as local authorities now could decide to formulate action plans if deemed necessary in individual cases (Bredgaard, 2001). With the Law on Active Social Policy (1998), the obligation to participate in activation programmes was extended to social assistance claimants between the ages of 25 and 30 (Rosdahl and Weise, 2000). Local authorities were required to offer activation programmes, but were allowed discretion regarding the form of activation. Moreover, while municipalities previously could sanction noncompliance with discretionary reductions in benefits within narrow bands, new acts (1998, 2000) standardised benefit reductions in such cases (Kvist and Meier Jæger, 2004).

Subsequently, the reform 'Bringing More People into Work' (2002–03) introduced a social assistance ceiling and reduced assistance in a number of situations so as to force people into employment.[2] In addition, the law on immigration (2002) drastically limited immigrants' access to social assistance, introducing a seven-year qualifying period for full benefits during which immigrants could receive only a lower integration allowance (Goul Andersen, 2007). In 2006 another programme, 'A New Chance for Everyone', primarily targeted at immigrants and their offspring who were not subject to the integration programme, made cash assistance for people aged between 18 and 25 conditional on participation in education activities (Liebig, 2007). Standardisation also increased as central rules and manuals were introduced to control local actors and measures encouraged/obliged municipalities to contribute more actively to the inclusion of the unemployed (UWT, 2007).

In sum, although the development after 1990 was characterised by increasing local responsibility for activating social assistance recipients, this remained under central control. The latter was evident in a continuous standardisation of the benefit, obligations implying harder sanctions and lower benefit levels, as well as extensions of the target group for activation. Organisationally there has been an attempt to establish closer links between social and labour market policy (integration).

Finland

A gradual standardisation of the benefit level has also occurred in Finland, and municipal discretionary power has been successively reduced. For instance, a national monetary standard was introduced in 1989. However, recent reforms contained elements of decentralisation. First was the VALTAVA reform (1992), implying a shift of regulatory power from central and provincial government to municipalities, which obtained the right to distribute government grants and also greater leeway in deciding how to organise services. The Social Assistance Act (1998) gave social workers the power to reduce social assistance in cases of refusal of work or training, although sanctions were regulated nationally. The Act on Rehabilitating Work Experience (2001) authorised municipalities to organise active labour market programmes or to purchase programmes from non-state actors.

The 2001 Act also promoted closer integration of activation measures carried out by local employment and social welfare offices. The key element in the reform was the activation plan that officers from the Public Employment Service (PES) and local authorities were obliged to prepare together with the unemployed recipients of social assistance. Institutional integration of activation services was further enhanced in 2002 and 2003, when services provided by employment offices, municipalities and the social insurance institution were brought together in so-called Joint Service Centres (JOIS) on an experimental basis at the local level. These were in 2004 divided into joint municipal–state Labour Force Service Centres (LAFOS) for the unemployed with multiple problems and Job Search Centres for the job-ready unemployed. LAFOS were established after voluntary agreements at the local level and thus do not exist everywhere. They include PES, social and healthcare services and the services of the national social insurance agency, as well as other experts if needed (Minas, forthcoming).

A mixed vertical shift occurred in 2006 when the financing responsibilities of central and local government were changed to increase the incentives for municipalities to organise activation programmes for the long-term unemployed. Municipalities now had to co-finance 50% of the benefit, while the state covered activation costs.

Summarising these developments, it is possible to talk of a tendency towards standardisation of the benefit, but also increased local autonomy within the centralised framework and a strong trend towards integration of various services directed at recipients with more serious problems who are far from the labour market.

Norway

Extensive local discretion is a main feature of the Norwegian social assistance scheme. No national monetary standard exists, instead assessment of benefit levels is up to social workers at the municipal level. Since 1991, municipalities have the right to condition social assistance benefits on work or retraining activities, yet without specification regarding the target group, sectors in which work can take place, duration and so on (Lødemel and Trickey, 2000). Municipalities have maintained their prerogatives with regard to benefit rates following the introduction of governmental guidelines on social assistance (no legally binding standards) in 2001.

Large differences in municipal activation efforts created demands for better linkages between municipal social policies, health-related services and central government's labour market policies (Øverbye 2010). Increased emphasis on welfare-to-work policies and aims to modernise the welfare state resulted in the Action Plan to Combat Poverty in 2002. The plan contained a broad spectrum of rehabilitation and activation measures to be implemented over the following years, targeted at young social assistance recipients (aged 20–24), single parents, long-term recipients, immigrants and people who receive drug substitution treatment (Rønsen and Skarðhamar, 2009). The Action Plan emphasised closer cooperation between the PES and social welfare system. Intensified cooperation was also a goal in the amendment to the Act on Social Services in 2004. Social assistance recipients were granted the right to an 'individual plan' worked out between the social worker, the client and other relevant actors. A programme for newly arrived immigrants lacking basic qualifications was introduced, simultaneously entitling and obliging them to partake in individually planned training programmes. This so-called introduction programme was initially a voluntary programme for the municipalities in 2003, becoming compulsory in 2004. Participants were entitled to an introductory benefit financed directly by the state, not by local councils.[3]

In summarising the development in Norway, two features can be emphasised. First the high degree of local discretion, and second the increasing efforts to integrate labour market and social welfare systems in recent years.

Sweden

Sweden did not see as many reforms as the other countries. From the beginning of the 1990s Swedish municipalities increasingly required the participation of social assistance recipients in activation programmes. This accelerated in 1994 when government declared that every unemployed person under the age of 25 who was unable to find work within three months should be offered placement in labour market programmes (Bergmark, 2001). Responsibility for labour market measures for unemployed youths under the age of 20 was transferred to the municipalities (1995) and later expanded to young people between the ages of 20 and 24 (1998). The revision of the Social Service Act (1998) also gave municipalities the option of making participation in activation programmes obligatory for recipients of social assistance between 20 and 24 years of age, and to refuse or lower benefits for individuals not participating in assigned programmes. Thus, local autonomy increased. However the revision also introduced a national monetary standard aimed at reducing local variation in social assistance payments, implying a simultaneous reduction of local autonomy. The impact of this reform is nevertheless unclear, as the standard stipulated only minimum amounts for certain core items, leaving it to municipalities to decide on additional items and greater amounts.

The development in Sweden can be summarised as a decentralisation trend in the 1990s, with increasing conditionality for the receipt of social assistance among youth. After 1998 the picture is more mixed, although there may be some centralisation. In contrast to the other countries, we see an increased central steering of activation policies through a concentration of responsibilities to the PES.

Expectations regarding variation in social assistance payments

What does this imply for local variation? Based on the reform patterns in the different countries, we would expect the following.

- *Denmark*: decreasing variation among young recipients in the 1990s and after 2002; also among recipients with an immigrant background.
- *Finland*: increasing variation in the 1990s, while it is difficult to form an expectation regarding the development after 2001 as institutional cooperation builds upon voluntarism.
- *Norway*: unchanged variation in the 1990s, decreasing variation towards the end of the period because of extensive coordination efforts and increasing activation demands towards young recipients of social assistance, single parents, immigrants and long-term recipients.
- *Sweden*: increasing variation among young recipients during the 1990s, unchanged thereafter since national monetary standard implies decentralised centralisation.

Data and method

To isolate the effects of the legislative changes we need to eliminate other potential sources of variation such as individual differences or business cycle variations and for this purpose we employ multilevel modelling. In the case of individuals embedded, or clustered, in a geographical unit multilevel models decompose the total variance in the dependent variable into individual level (level 1) variance and variance at the geographical level (level 2). Formally the regression model we estimate can be expressed as:

(1) $Y_{ij} = \beta_0 + \boldsymbol{\beta_1}\mathbf{x}_{ij} + u_{0j} + e_{0ij}$,

where Y_{ij} is the annual social assistance benefits received by individual i in municipality j, β_0 is the intercept, $\boldsymbol{\beta_1}$ is a vector of regression coefficients and $\mathbf{x}_{ij}$ represents its corresponding vector of covariates. Covariates can be measured on both levels.

However, our main interest is not the effects of covariates but the remaining random part of the equation where u_{0j} is the error term at level 2 and e_{0ij} is the error term at level 1. These capture variation in the dependent variable not captured by the rest of the model, and in this chapter we focus on variance unexplained at the municipal level 2. This consists of two components; one related to the composition of individuals within the second level and another 'real' contextual component that goes beyond the sheer composition effect. By including explanatory factors at both levels we reduce the impact of compositional effects on municipal variation and are therefore more likely to detect the impact of legislative change on the inter-municipal variance.

The parameters to be estimated in the random part of the model are the variances of the error terms, σ_{u0}^2 and σ_{e0}^2 respectively, indicating inter- and intra-municipal variation. We concentrate on changes in the unexplained variance at level 2 as a proportion of the total variation, the so-called variance partition coefficient (VPC). Then, the VPC = $\sigma_{u0}^2/(\sigma_{u0}^2+\sigma_{e0}^2)$. The evolution of the VPC in other words indicates changes in inter-municipal variation in social assistance payments not related to changes in covariates, which, with an appropriate selection of covariates, will indicate the effect of the legislative changes. This model has then been estimated separately for each country, year and demographic group.

The data that has been used consists of national register data for each country covering a time period from the beginning of the 1990s until late 2000s. More specifically, the Danish data spans the period 1990 to

2007, the Finnish data the period 1993 to 2010, Norwegian data the period 1993 to 2007 and the Swedish data the period 1990 to 2007.

In all four cases, the data consists of administrative data collected in connection with the payment of transfers and collection of taxes. The Finnish and Norwegian data covers all social assistance recipients, the Swedish a 50% random sample thereof, while the Danish covers a 10% sample of the population born in Denmark as well as all immigrants. We examine recipients between ages 18 and 64. The dependent variable refers to total annual individual social assistance payments, in Denmark *kontanthjælp*, in Norway to *sosialstøtte*, in Finland *toimeentulotuki* and in Sweden *socialbidrag*. Social assistance has been measured in local currencies and inflation adjusted to 2006 prices.

The independent variables included in the analyses have been chosen to capture both individual- and municipal-level variation in the likelihood of social assistance receipt. The individual-level variables that have been used are age, born abroad, recent immigration (<= 5 years), educational level (5 levels), children under the age of 18 in the household, whether the individual lived alone, received any sick pay during the year and had been unemployed without receiving any form of unemployment compensation. The municipal-level variables include population size, the proportion of the population of working age that were aged 18–19, 20–24 and 25–64, the proportion of immigrants in the population, of sick pay recipients and of unemployed without unemployment compensation, as well as the average employment earnings in the municipality.[4] The variation in space and time in these variables is intended to capture differences in benefit receipt not related to the reforms.

The analyses have been conducted separately for the different groups that have been the target group for the various reforms, for example immigrants or 20- to 24-year-olds. The development of the VPC for these groups is then compared with the variation among 25- to 64-year-olds. This group, the 25- to 64-year-old recipients, will generally act as 'comparison group' as most reforms were directed at other groups of recipients. A reform is considered to have had an effect if there are changes in variation in the expected direction for the affected group without there being simultaneous similar changes for the comparison group of 25- to 64-year-olds. An exception is of course reforms affecting all recipients, such as the Finnish reforms, for which we can look only at the overall development. The structure of the analyses is thus akin to a so-called difference-in-difference model in which changes in the treatment group are compared to changes in a control group.

Nevertheless, the analysis of institutional reforms is often complex. Many reforms have been initiated in each country, implying shifts of power in various directions. Some were enacted late in the period examined here and it may therefore be too early to identify their effects; some reforms were directly followed by others strengthening, counteracting or neutralising the effects of the original reform. Implementation research has furthermore shown that reforms do not necessarily develop as intended by legislators. Moreover, the political discussion prior to a reform may in itself change the behaviour of social welfare agencies and social workers, and in some cases new legislation may merely turn already existing practices in law. Identifying a 'reform effect' may therefore be quite difficult. For these reasons we will not take the date of legislation as the exact date of a reform but, rather, look at a 'window' around the enactment date. Likewise, the focus will not necessarily be solely on individual reforms but also on packages of reforms that may increase or decrease local autonomy with regard to social assistance policies.

Results

The VPCs from models with all covariates included are presented in graphs showing their evolution for each country and group. Vertical bars in the graphs indicate reform years. After the inclusion of the control variables, municipal variation in all countries lies roughly around 10% of the total variation. Empty models without covariates are not shown, but VPCs are in all cases around 5 percentage points higher in the empty models than in those presented.

Denmark

Starting with Denmark, as shown in Figure 13.1 inter-municipal variation among 25- to 64-year-olds is roughly halved during the 1990s and remains at a lower level during most of the 2000s despite notable annual fluctuations. Falling VPCs are also evident among youths and immigrants.[5] Among youths the change in inter-municipal variation roughly parallels that among 25- to 64-year-olds, although it seems to have reached its lowest level already in 1997, whereas the comparison group bottoms out in 2000. The fall in the VPC is, however, particularly dramatic among immigrants. Inter-municipal differences in social assistance payments among immigrants were originally twice as large as among 25- to 64-year-olds, yet by the end of the period they had fallen by two-thirds, to about the same level. It is also obvious that the immigrant VPC displays greater fluctuations than the others, presumably related to the changing composition of the immigrant group. Although we distinguish between recent and earlier immigrants we do not, for instance, differentiate based on country of origin.

Figure 13.1: Inter-municipal variation in social assistance payments in Denmark. Variance partition coefficient from multi-level analyses, by recipient group and year

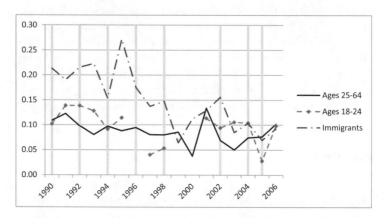

However, this general reduction in the VPC does not seem to be related to the reforms. Recall that, although many of the reforms contained elements of standardisation, most of the early reforms (1992, 1996, 1998) were directed at youths and, despite not being targeted, the development of the VPC among the 25- to 64-year-olds is largely similar. Likewise, immigrants first became the target of reforms after the turn of the millennium (2002, 2005), that is, after their VPC had approached that of the other groups. However, it does seem likely that the drop in the immigrant VPC after 2002 was at least partly caused by the reforms: recall that they included the introduction of a new standardised benefit that in many cases replaced discretionary social assistance. Apart from this it seems fairly clear that the changes in the VPC were not related to the reforms.

Finland

For Finland only one VPC curve is presented, as reforms did not target any specific group of benefit recipients. Figure 13.2 shows that, with regard to inter-municipal variation, 2003 is a turning point. Specifically, there is a decade-long slide in the VPC between 1993 and 2003, a slide followed by an almost uninterrupted rise between 2003 and 2010. The initial reduction is relatively small (about a third), and the same may be said of the subsequent increase.

Figure 13.2: Inter-municipal variation in social assistance payments in Finland. Variance partition coefficient from multi-level analyses, by recipient group and year

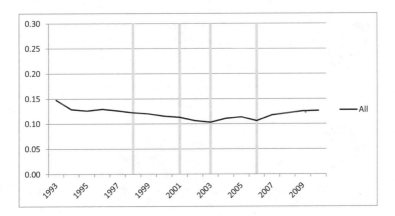

Regarding the reforms, the period of decline was actually a period of increasing local responsibility. In contrast, the integration reforms in the latter half of the period were basically expected to produce a standardisation across municipalities and thus decreasing variation. However, as noted above, the type of integration chosen in Finland has so far built upon local decisions regarding whether to introduce joint cooperation centres (in 2010 LAFOS existed in only around 40% of the municipalities) and who is referred to LAFOS, and is furthermore characterised by weak national steering and aimed at a difficult target group (those 'far from the labour market'). These are all aspects that might explain the slightly rising variation from 2003 onwards.

Norway

Turning next to Norway, as is evident in Figure 13.3, there is very little fluctuation in the VPC in the comparison group of 25- to 64-year-olds as well as among youths. Among single parents the VPC drops slightly during the 1990s, only to trend upward after the turn of the millennium. The fluctuations are, however, fairly limited and the ups and downs furthermore basically cancel out, leaving the VPC for this group at the end of the period at the same level as in the beginning. The greatest variation is instead, again, evident among immigrants were the VPC oscillates noticeably. An initial rise is thus reversed in 1995, with the reduction continuing until 1998. Another increase then ensues, culminating in 2003, and is in turn followed by a final drop.

Figure 13.3: Inter-municipal variation in social assistance payments in Norway. Variance partition coefficient from multi-level analyses, by recipient group and year

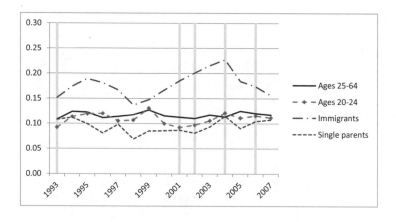

That local variation for the most part would remain unchanged during the 1990s was expected. The only reform during this period, the sanctioning rights introduced in 1993, did not generate an increase in variation, presumably due to the local reluctance in implementing the reform documented elsewhere (Lødemel, 1997). The same applies to the guidelines introduced in 2001. Here we would expect a decreased VPC, yet no such tendencies are evident and the reason may again be an implementation deficit (Brandtzæg et al, 2006). The 2002 Action Plan against Poverty, the organisational reforms in 2004 and the introduction programme were also expected to lead to a decreased VPC. There is actually a drop in the VPC among youths and single parents in 2005, yet this seems unlikely to be reform-related as it is quickly reversed. The pronounced drop in the VPC for immigrants might be a result of the joint efforts towards activation, but even more likely is the launch of the introduction allowance. Although this benefit here is not counted as social assistance, in contrast to our Danish analyses, its inception implies that many immigrant social assistance recipients were transferred to another scheme, leaving a more homogenous recipient group with less variation.

Sweden

The results for Sweden are shown in Figure 13.4. The VPC among adults displays an initial rise and subsequent stabilisation, albeit with some short-term fluctuations. Among both youths and teenagers we see a somewhat similar pattern, although with greater annual oscillations. It may be noted that Sweden is the only country where there has been an increase in variation, and that among all groups.

Figure 13.4: Inter-municipal variation in social assistance payments in Sweden. Variance partition coefficient from multi-level analyses, by recipient group and year

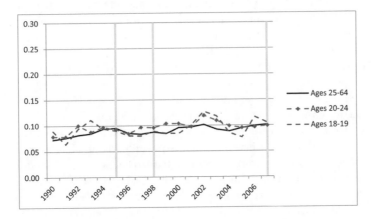

Relating these developments to the various Swedish reforms suggests that they have had no effects. There is thus little indication that increased local responsibilities in 1995 affected local variation; the weak signs of rising VPCs occur prior to the reforms and are more clearly evident among groups not targeted. Nor do the reforms in 1998 affecting youths seem to have an effect. The effects of the other reforms introduced in 1998 also appear rather limited: if anything it seems that the sanctioning rights and the right to decide on social assistance items have more than countered the introduction of the national norm, as there are signs of a rising VPC in the comparison group.

Discussion

The reforms in Denmark, Finland, Norway and Sweden over the past two decades have clearly impacted on the administrative distribution of power. This was in turn conjectured to effect the variation in social assistance payments, for example, through the processes of standardisation and institutional integration of social assistance systems with labour market policy. Generally speaking, decentralisation was expected to increase variation in benefit payments across jurisdictions, and centralisation vice versa. The results can be loosely grouped into three categories: instances suggesting an impact of the reforms, instances where the lack of an expected effect can be explained by either the character or implementation of the reforms and instances where an expected effect is missing yet no plausible explanation is available.

In the first category we find the two standardisations of benefits available for immigrants in Denmark and Norway. Not surprisingly, partial replacement of discretionary social assistance with a centrally determined introduction benefit appears to have decreased variation, either by standardising the benefit itself (Denmark) or by homogenising the recipient group (Norway). In the second group we find the decentralisation of sanctioning rights in Norway, the standardisations of benefits through the introduction of national guidelines in Norway and Sweden as well as the institutional integration in Finland. The Norwegian reforms both seem to have been undermined by the implementation process in which case-workers acted contrary to intentions. The Swedish and Finnish reforms instead appear to fall short because of the way the reforms where designed. Despite the guidelines, Swedish municipalities retained substantial discretion over the benefits, thereby negating the attempt at standardisation. (The Norwegian and Swedish guidelines also illustrate that not all reforms directly related to benefit structure need affect benefit inequality.) The Finnish service centres were voluntary and allowed substantial leeway in other respects as well. In these cases, the absence of the predicted effect does not appear surprising.

The final category is made up of reforms where no explanation for the absence of expected effects was readily apparent. This group is for obvious reasons difficult to interpret. However, it is notable that it mainly consists of the different activation reforms in the four countries, often directed at specific groups such as youth. The decentralisation involved in these cases may for different reasons have been more apparent than real. Although these are only conjectures, it may for instance be the case that municipalities failed to make use of opportunities given to them, or that they introduced different activation measures, yet without changing the benefit. Many of these reforms were also enacted during recessions, and another possibility is that sanctions against groups initially far from the labour market may then appear unreasonable. While no definite explanation for the lack of the expected effect can be provided here, it seems as if activation reforms differ from the rest.

At a more general level, reform effects appear to depend on the often complex *nature of the reforms* as well as the *reform process* itself and the *context* they are embedded in. With regard to the former, a specific reform may be difficult to characterise as a de- or recentralising reform, instead reforms often contain aspects of both de- and recentralisation. Although the national standard in Sweden aimed to reduce local autonomy and variation, the remaining municipal discretion still counteracted the reform. Governance reforms such as integrated services that bridge several policy domains located at different territorial levels display an especially complex interplay between responsibility for service regulation, administration, delivery and financing.

Moreover, the reform process is not static, and decentralising reforms may be followed by centralising ones and vice versa. As a particular reform may be implemented with some delay a series of reforms and counter-reforms may leave only a limited imprint. As discussed above, actual implementation may also deviate from intended.

When it comes to the context, the political and administrative settings have to be taken into account. In general, the Nordic countries present similar contexts (unitary states, strong municipalities, framework legislation) even if they differ regarding local autonomy. However, decentralisation in highly decentralised countries (such as Italy) may differ from reforms in more centralised countries (such as France). Thus, similar reforms (for instance, the recent integrated services) are carried out in clearly different manners and contexts, potentially effecting standardisation and local variation. Reforms in neighbouring policy areas (mainly labour market policy and education) may also impact on attitudes and/or local policies, spilling over to social assistance payments.

Finally, this study has examined the link between the Nordic reforms and benefit inequality, and has not assessed the appropriateness of variation in social assistance payments. However, the results indicate that, to the extent that inter-municipal benefit variation is deemed problematic, reducing benefit inequality may be difficult. Variation is fairly limited and, even in the models without controls for individual and structural differences, inter-municipal variation accounts for only around 15% of total variation. Introducing controls diminishes variation even further, suggesting that the possibility for reforms to affect benefit inequality is small. This may of course be due to the fact that this is a discretionary benefit and, short of replacing it with standardised benefits, reforms may be ineffectual. On the other hand, the fact that variation appears relatively limited suggests that the problem may be smaller than is sometimes believed.

Notes

[1] We would like to acknowledge funding from the Nordic Council of Ministers, and Bäckman, Korpi and Minas also acknowledge funding from Riksbankens Jubileumsfond. In addition, Korpi received funding from the Swedish Council for Working Life and Social Research. Any errors are our own.

[2] The reform also integrated the national PES and the municipal employment services, abolishing the distinction between municipal activities for social assistance recipients and the PES's activities for unemployment benefit recipients. This initiated a reform process resulting in the introduction of so-called jobcentres in each municipality (Minas, forthcoming), yet this occurred in 2007 and will therefore not be covered in our analyses.

[3] At this time the Norwegian parliament also began to consider combining the social service, the labour market and the social insurance agencies, which in 2006 resulted in the merger of the employment and national insurance services (Minas, forthcoming). As in the Danish case, this will not be covered in these analyses.

[4] The Finnish data differs slightly, as it lacks individual-level information on birthplace, immigration date, educational level and sick pay receipt. In addition, unemployment here measured long-term unemployment (>= 6 months), proportion immigrants measured the proportion with a foreign mother tongue, proportion unemployed measured

the unemployment rate, and average employment earnings in the municipality measured the average municipal earnings in 2010.
[5] Estimates for ages 20 to 24 are missing here for some years, as the models did not converge.

References

Bergmark, Å. (2001) 'Den lokala välfärdsstaten? Decentraliseringstrender under 1990-talet', in M. Szebehely (ed) *Välfärdstjänster i omvandling*, SOU 2001:52, Stockholm: Fritzes.

Brandtzæg, B., Flermoen, S., Lunder, T.E., Løyland, K., Møller, G. and Sannes, J. (2006) *Fastsetting av satser, utmåling av økonomisk sosialhjelp og vilkårsbruk i sosialtjensten*. Rapport nr 232. Telemarksforsking-Bø.

Bredgaard, T. (2001) 'A Danish job training miracle? Temporary subsidised employment in the public and non-profit sector', Working Paper no 5, Centre for Labour Market Research, Aalborg University.

Gough, I., Bradshaw, J., Ditch, J., Eardley, T. and Whiteford, P. (1997) 'Social assistance in OECD countries', *Journal of European Social Policy*, 7(1): 17–43.

Goul Andersen, J. (2007) 'Restricting access to social protection for immigrants in the Danish welfare state', *Benefits*, 15(3): 257–69.

Heikkilä, M., Fridberg, T. and Keskitalo, E. (2001) 'Guaranteed minimum income – recent trends and a socio-political discussion', in M. Heikkilä and E. Keskitalo (eds) *Social assistance in Europe*, Helsinki: STAKES/EU.

Kvist, J. and Meier Jæger, M. (2004) *Changing the social rights and obligations of social citizenship in Europe. The case of in unemployment compensation, social assistance and family benefits in the 1990s*, Copenhagen: Danish National Institute of Social Research, www.issa.int/pdf/initiative/reports/2Denmark.pdf.

Liebig, T. (2007) *The labour market integration of immigrants in Denmark*, OECD Social, Employment and Migration Working Papers no 50, DELSA/ELSA/WD/SEM(2007)5, Paris: OECD.

Lødemel, I. (1997) *The welfare paradox: Income maintenance and personal social services in Norway and Britain, 1946–1966*, Oslo and Stockholm: Scandinavian Universities Press.

Lødemel, I. and Trickey, H. (2000) *An offer you can't refuse: Workfare in international perspective*, Bristol: Policy Press.

Meyers, M.K. and Gornick, J.C. (2005) 'A devolution revolution? Change and continuity in U.S. state social policies in the 1990s', in B. Cantillon and I. Marx (eds) *International cooperation in social security: How to cope with globalization?* Amsterdam: Intersia.

Minas, R. (forthcoming) 'One-stop shops: increasing employability and overcoming welfare state fragmentation?', *International Journal of Social Welfare*.

Minas, R., Wright, S. and van Berkel, R. (2012) 'Decentralization and centralization: governing the activation of social assistance recipients in Europe', *International Journal of Sociology and Social Policy*, 32(5): 286–98.

Øverbye, E. (2010) *Activation and the coordination problem. Socialpolitik i förändring – utveckling mot flernivåstyrning i Europa*. Oslo: Högskolen i Oslo og Akershus.

Rønsen, M. and Skarðhamar, T. (2009) 'Do welfare-to-work initiatives work? Evidence from an activation programme targeted at social assistance recipients in Norway', *Journal of European Social Policy*, 19(1): 61–77.

Rosdahl, A. and Weise, H. (2000) 'When all must be active – workfare in Denmark', in I. Lødemel and H. Trickey (eds), *An offer you can't refuse. Workfare in international perspective*, Bristol: Policy Press.

UWT (2007) 'Denmark Country Report', Roskilde University, www.undocumentedmigrants.eu/library/s15990_3.pdf.

van Berkel, R., de Graaf, W. and Sirovátka, T. (2011) *The governance of active welfare states in Europe*, Basingstoke: Palgrave Macmillan.

FOURTEEN

The competition–collaboration dilemma: the perverse effects of mixed service integration policy approaches in Queensland

Robyn Keast

Introduction

Integration, the combining of parts so that they work together, has long been advanced as a core strategy for the more efficient and effective delivery of social services in Australia, as exemplified by the numerous experimentations in form and location that have taken place since the late 1800s (Tierney, 1970). Integration continues to remain high on the Australian social policy agenda and is evident in a range of recent policy statements (for example, Australian Government, 2008; 2013; Australian Public Service Commission, 2009) as well as in prime ministerial speeches on improved social service integration (for example, Rudd, 2009). In the search for integration a number of approaches have been utilised, including structural initiatives such as central government agencies, mega-departments and lead agency models as well as procedural directives, including funding regimes and operational mandates. Vertical integration arrangements work by organising the various parts of a system under one umbrella organisation or body (Powell, 1990) and have been supplemented by horizontal forms such as whole-of-government approaches, partnerships, networks and collaborative arrangements that act as the 'glue that binds' people and resources together for collective action (Powell, 1990, p 325).

While the *collaborative push* (O'Flynn, 2009) currently shapes much of the public rhetoric for social services integration, several other approaches are also in play. Some of these can be traced back to new public management and its use of competition policy to establish more efficient and economical connections between sectoral elements (Earles and Moon, 2000) and to support growing demands by government and other funding providers for higher levels of accountability for outcomes (Australian Productivity Commission, 2010). In a recent twist to the integration and accountability reform agenda, amalgamation and merger have reappeared as key mechanisms to link up 'like' departments and smaller not-for-profit organisations to achieve a greater level of consistency in service provision (Deloitte, 2009). Amalgamation is the combination of two or more organisations or units into a new agency or a subsidiary controlled by one of the constituent members (Craswell and Davis, 1993). The benefit of such an approach is reduction of duplication and overlaps, for example through shared administration, co-location and closer alignment of outcomes or merger (Deloitte, 2009). In this way, efficient scale and scope can be achieved and resources can be more effectively targeted toward persistent problems.

The global financial crisis of 2008 also provided an opportunity for many governments to review and revise the size and function of their public services, as well as the ways in which they are provided and delivered. Consequently, a range of policies generally couched in terms of economic austerity have been implemented to deliver widespread and deep cuts to public and community services around the globe (McDermott and Stone, 2013). In Queensland a Commission of Audit was established to review the state's finances, providing the government, as Quiggin (2012, p 3) notes, with 'the intellectual ammunition needed to justify an austerity program'.

Through an on-going programme of reform, a wide array of policies has been amassed to drive service delivery and its integration. It is argued that with this mix, the juxtaposition of competition and collaboration as opposing forms of integration has resulted in a complex policy and implementation environment, often leading to unfulfilled or, worse, unintended outcomes. While it has long been recognised that policy actions can generate counterproductive results (Merton, 1936), also referred to as perverse policy effects (Popper, 1974; Peters and Pierre, 2006), there has been limited examination of the effect of the dual competition–collaboration integration agenda. In order to more fully examine this policy problem, this chapter first provides an overview of integration models, including those defined broadly as competitive and collaborative, and outlines the policy context for the study cases under examination. The research approach and methodology employed to gather and analyse data are then set out. Finally, the findings are discussed, implications outlined and a conclusion is derived.

Integration frameworks

Integration refers to the bringing together of various parts into some form of cohesion. Integrated approaches can draw on either vertical or horizontal dimensions to achieve their purpose (Matheson, 2000; Ling, 2002). Reflecting this duality, they are often described as following 'top-down' or 'bottom-up' models (Martinson, 1999). Top-down or vertical integration refers to initiatives emanating from the authoritative core, usually the political or strategic leadership levels that flow down to management and service levels. Top-down initiatives are pursued principally for the objectives of efficiency and coherency (Ryan et al, 2008) and entail the use of mandate, incentives and other formalised integration mechanisms. By contrast, bottom-up integration describes initiatives emerging voluntarily from the service-delivery front, often driven by scarce resources, uncertainty in the organisational environment as well as a desire for enhanced service outcomes. Bottom-up methods draw more deeply upon the establishment of shared problem spaces and agreed solutions and point strongly to horizontal integration forms.

Horizontal integration is often used to indicate an ideal or end state, but it more accurately represents a continuum or scale of connection that extends from the complete autonomy of separate parts (fragmentation) at one end, through a series of graduated steps involving more intensive forms of linkage, to a fully integrated system (Konrad, 1996). Authors have used different categories to denote the levels of integration and the types of relationships that can occur between organisations. The terms most frequently used in this context are cooperation, coordination and collaboration (Himmelman, 1994), elsewhere referred to as the '3Cs' (Brown and Keast, 2003; Keast et al, 2007). While these terms are often used interchangeably in the literature and practice, increasingly they are considered to be analytically distinct (Winer and Ray, 1994; Konrad, 1996) and therefore located at different points on the continuum. Specifically, cooperation refers to low levels of connection based predominantly on shared information; coordination refers to the alignment of resources and effort; while collaboration is focused on achieving systems change through dense interdependent relationships (Keast et al, 2007). A fourth 'C', competition, has traditionally been considered to work against integration; however, there is a growing view that, if designed and implemented judiciously, it can facilitate integration outcomes (Ham, 2012). At the other end of the continuum, interest in amalgamation pushes the levels of connection past collaboration to tighter integrative models where participating bodies form single entities.

Aligned to the top-down and bottom-up modes, attention has also been directed to the levels at which integration occurs. Three levels of integration activity have been identified: the macro level of policy, strategic planning and financing decisions; the meso or middle level involving relationships among services in a region and integration at the managerial level; and the micro level, which concerns the direct relationships between practitioners and the people they assist (Walfogel, 1997; Kodner and Spreeuwenberg, 2002). Adopting a stratum approach provides greater detail on the practical tasks and tools at each level of integration activity. For example, from top to bottom these initiatives can range from funding and incentives to inter-sectoral planning, co-located services and joint training and case management. More recently, the breadth and depth of integration initiatives have come to be included in the formulation of inter-agency models (Glasby and Dickenson, 2008). In this conceptualisation, breadth equates to the types or strengths of integration arrangements that occur between agencies, linked to, for example, the 3Cs; while depth relates to the extent or degree to which initiatives are spread over a locale, region or state.

While proving useful in shaping the broad conceptual aspects and directions of joined-up processes, it has been argued that the largely singular dimension of each of these frameworks does not adequately reflect the complex and often layered approaches generally adopted by integration initiatives (6, 2004). In response, a number of authors, for example Fine (2001) and Keast (2011), have combined various elements to produce a multi-dimensional perspective of integration and joined-up arrangements. Figure 14.1 is a model of such an integrated framework, incorporating the elements discussed above.

The framework provides a more detailed picture of the complexity of integrative approaches and, in doing so, highlights the many junctures or points of vulnerability that can lead to and be affected by ill-conceived or poorly implemented policies, leading to unintended negative consequences of this purposeful effort for social change. Notably, through the inclusion of competition and amalgamation, the framework extends conventional integration typologies. On-going Queensland reform experimentations provide an excellent basis from which to examine the tensions between the integration policies of competition and collaboration and their impacts.

Institutional context: Queensland

Figure 14.1: Multi-dimensional integration framework

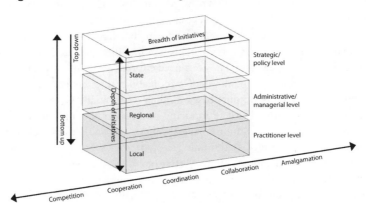

Throughout Queensland's history periodic efforts have been made by both the government and non-government sectors to integrate their work and resources. It has been argued that these integration efforts were largely transitory and superficial (Scott et al, 2001; McDonald and Zetlin, 2004), relying predominantly on government fiat or personal relationships, respectively. However, in the 1980s, worldwide fiscal constraints exposed Queensland's continued underinvestment in community and social infrastructure (Walsh, 1993) and set the scene over the next decades for a renewed interest in services integration, supported in part by Commonwealth of Australia funding allocations and stipulations. This was coupled with a growing realisation that the state alone could not provide the physical or social infrastructure necessary for continued prosperity and growth and would need to partner with the not-for-profit and private sectors. As a consequence, Queensland entered an unprecedented period of joined-up and whole-of-government policies and strategies. Many of these relied on the direct authority and mandate of the prime minister to better integrate policies and services across the state (O'Farrell, 2002) or lead-agency models to secure coherent policy implementation (Queensland Government, 2000). Others drew more extensively on the emerging concepts of networks, collaborations and partnerships, as key integration forms aimed at bringing together the expertise and resources of the multiple organisations located within the not-for-profit sector, to address intractable social problems and provide a range of social and physical services across geographically dispersed and isolated locations (Reddel, 2002; Queensland Government, 2000).

While Queensland social services had been largely been immune from many of the competition-based reforms imposed upon other sectors (House of Representatives Standing Committee on Family and Community Affairs, 1998), recent reform foci have placed stronger demands on the sector for greater accountability, productivity and efficiency in its operations. The concerted effort at both the national and state levels to embed higher levels of accountability into the sector is most evident in the shift to outputs-based funding (Queensland Government, 2010). It was reasoned that introducing output funding and reporting (coupled with amplified monitoring arrangements), rather than relying on grant or outcomes-based funding, would provide greater clarity on what is purchased and delivered (McBratney and McGregor-Lowndes, 2012). Business and other major donors, for example corporate entities, are increasingly demanding evidence of the effectiveness of not-for-profit (NFP) activities and have stated a funding preference for NFPs that can provide robust business cases for the investment they seek (Australian Productivity Commission, 2010).

This chapter draws on data generated from a suite of 19 integration initiatives conducted within and across the Queensland social services sector between 2000 and 2013. These initiatives, all broadly defined as having an integration objective, include: the Government Service Delivery Project; Service Integration Project; Chief Executive Officers' Forum; Reconnect Network; Child-Safety Partnerships; Homelessness Service Systems Integration Parts 1 (2008) and 2 (2011) (seven cases) and the Housing Services Collaboration (2013). The cases are located at different levels of operation: strategic, administrative/managerial and practice, allowing for variation in perspectives and experiences. Semi-focused interviews, focus groups and workshop sessions provided a rich data set from which to mine the perceptions of NFP and government respondents.

In particular, this chapter focuses primarily on two related themes distilled from the data analysis: (a) upsizing, which refers to both the perceived preference by governments towards the larger NFP organisations and the amalgamation of smaller NFPs (see Keast, Mandell and Waterhouse, 2011), and (b) more recent 'economic austerity' policies introduced by the Queensland government and their consequences (Quiggin, 2012).

Upsizing: bigger NFPs

Competition policies have been in place in national and state social sectors since the Himler Inquiry of 1993 (Commonwealth of Australia, 1993). There is solid evidence that competition has impacted negatively on the community sector in a number of ways, including, for example, the provision of greater government control of community sector operations through stricter service agreements (McBratney and McGregor-Lowndes, 2012); a greater emphasis on performance reporting at the expense of sectoral values and services (Wapner, 2002); as well as the loss of a service ethos (McDonald and Zetlin, 2004) and reduced service diversity and access (Hancock, 2004).

Also widely acknowledged have been the fragmenting effects of competition on a sector that has traditionally functioned with cooperative and collaborative relationships as the primary integrative tools (Lyons, 2003; Keast, 2011). Under the market model, instead of working together, organisations compete against each other to win tenders. As a result of the secrecy, turf protection and perceived positioning to secure 'competitive advantage', services are reporting greater, rather than less, fragmentation (Lyons, 2003). The folding of several long-standing homelessness service networks as a consequence of competitive tendering opportunities was a frequently mentioned example across several regions (Keast et al, 2011). Even where competition policy is encouraging the development of strategic partnerships, there remain problems in implementation as existing relationships have been strained by successive manoeuvrings for optimal partnership formations, as well as by what has been referred to as government manipulation of processes (Keast et al, 2011).

The cases point to a deepening of the view that competition and the related strategies of increased accountability and corporatisation favour large over small NFPs (Lyons, 2003; Phillips, 2007) and that this, in turn, impacts on collaborative integrative practice. This process has increased more recently as competition has become more entrenched within the sector. A common concern expressed by many smaller agencies was the growing prominence of for-profit and larger NFP agencies in the sector. Respondents noted that these organisations are able to draw on a wider pool of resources and capabilities than are smaller organisations and are brought into the mix because of their business-like functioning and capacity, and therefore more sophisticated accountability regimes. It was further stated that larger NFPs were better able to attract funding because they had the capacity to write 'beautiful applications', thus increasing their financial viability. The following quote from a managerial-level community respondent encapsulates this widely held view:

> Government prefers these big organisations, because they are structured the same as government; they operate the same way. The reasoning is that the bigger ones will meet the requirements for stronger corporate accountability and will have staff that can monitor these processes.

The perceived preference for larger NFP organisations has led to tensions in terms of service delivery and integration. Firstly, many smaller organisations considered the larger NFPs as hierarchical in their operation and that their participation in service activities, particularly network and coordination group meetings, results in an uneven sharing of information about funding and the types of services each is contracted to provide.

> When you are sitting around the table talking about things and planning actions, the small non-government agencies ... are very open ... they tell you everything about their organisation including the funding they get and then you get the larger organisations ... they can't necessarily be [open] ... [they] can't talk about the funding because they don't know or are not able to, so they can't actually participate to the same level.

Furthermore, the tendency for larger organisations to be headquartered in capital cities means that their personnel are often seen by the smaller, more localised service providers as unable to participate fully in local service-planning processes. This situation was thought to cause difficulties in terms of immediate decision making and resource allocation and was seen to be problematic to local level integration, and is explained by a managerial-level community respondent:

> To tell you the truth, I do have a problem when very big organisations come in ... because a lot of times they don't really have an understanding of the sector ... They are not connected and don't act as part of our network.

Additionally, and perhaps of main concern for the smaller, localised service providers, larger NFPs and for-profit entities were considered to be taking work away that could be done by existing providers. On this it was stated:

> I don't know that they [government] need to establish another agency; … there are existing service providers who are doing a good job and should be given the opportunity.

It was stated by many respondents that the inclusion of 'newer' as well as existing larger NFPs was squeezing smaller service providers out of operation and adding to, rather than decreasing, the fragmentation of the sector.

> Bringing in new players [to a sector that is already struggling], who have never been in the homelessness sector and that probably was one of the things that didn't help [area] to be able to respond appropriately to issues.

Exacerbating the sense fragmentation was the view that larger providers have not always demonstrated long-term commitment to regional areas; moreover, that they have sufficient organisational slack and spare resources to be able to withdraw from a region, if their initiative proves to be not financially viable. Examples were provided where this withdrawal has occurred, causing a loss of the service to the community and placing higher workloads on local service without financial recompense.

> And when they work out it is not economically viable they just pull out and leave us to pick up the pieces. And this is how relationships breakdown … because you really get frustrated and staff get annoyed … but they don't do what they have to do [other agencies] and you are the one that is supposed to be picking up all these things, and you can't do it and then the clients get angry at you and everyone is ringing up and getting annoyed for something that you are expected to do but are not funded to do it.

In this way it is argued that, as it is currently designed and implemented, competition policy has been largely detrimental to integration, especially collaboration-based integration models, with cleavages appearing between small and large operators, despite concerted effort to 'smooth these over'. Further, as is highlighted below, this situation has been exacerbated by the growing number of for-profit organisations entering the service space.

The rise of for-profit providers

It has been determined that the number of for-profit organisations operating within the sector increased by 36% between 1996 and 2000 (Australian Council of Social Services, 2006). As competition policies continue and new policy initiatives such as the National Disability Insurance Scheme roll out, it is likely that more for-profit providers will be attracted to the service arena. There is a growing concern that the continued rise of for-profits will lead to smaller NPFs folding, resulting in reduced diversity and a loss of the overall vibrancy of the sector, thus hampering its important role as a safety net. Ryan (1999), commenting on the US situation (but equally relevant to the current Australian context) has argued that the continued blurring of the distinctions between NFP and for-profit organisations will raise questions about whether NFP organisations can adapt to this more competitive operating environment without compromising the qualities that distinguish them from government and the private sector.

Integration requires effort on the part of all members in order to be successful. There was a mix of responses in terms of how well existing NFPs welcomed and enabled the newer or larger agencies to fit into local service systems. One network, although acknowledging a sense of 'slight resentment', nonetheless made significant efforts to link the newcomer to the partner services and provided administrative and service support until the newcomer was able to become fully operational. At the other end of the continuum, some new larger entrants noted that they were 'actively' closed out of the local service network, despite numerous attempts to engage, making it very difficult for the agency to fulfil its obligations. The tensions between the entities are encapsulated in the following:

> It takes about eighteen months for a new agency to settle down, you know to get everyone to know the system and how it works – by that time the rest of them are so stretched and strained that it immediately sours any working relationship.

A further factor identified as undermining the relationships between agencies, at least in two case sites, was the competition for funding that transpired between previously collaborative programmes, coupled with what were perceived as 'government manoeuvrings' in the selection and implementation processes. In these cases, several smaller long-term agencies had worked together to develop a collaborative programme, only to have the project and the funding transferred to another external provider, resulting in distrust between agencies and government, which spilled over to the emergent providers. It was stated that government's deeper reach into community services via stronger accountability requirements has given it a greater ability to intervene in areas that have traditionally been shaped by the sector.

It is clear that the greater inclusion of larger, more business-like service agencies has resulted in a shake-up in the social services sector. While, in part, this seems to be unintentional, there is some evidence of a strategic effort to deliberately unsettle what was seen by government as the 'entrenched thinking' of the traditional NFPs and thereby to open them to the growing demands for change (Government: practitioner-level respondent). This perspective has led to a growing disconnect between the sectors that has been manifested in some cases in the rise of a range of 'conspiracy theories' at the practice level that are acknowledged as being detrimental to current and future integration efforts. It was acknowledged on both sides (small and big organisations) that some effort to 'broker' or 'facilitate' their entry may have 'smoothed over' the initial hurdles of change.

Austerity measures

Adding to the growing disconnect within the sector is the impact of a more recent policy strategy arising from the economic austerity measures implemented in 2012 following the change of state government administration following a general election. Following a Commission of Audit into the state's finances, the government implemented a forced redundancy of up to 14,000 public servants in order to turn around a large public sector debt (Elthan, 2012). The consequence of this policy has been a high number of former senior government personnel moving into prominent positions within the larger NFPs. On the surface the transfer of high-level policy and administrative skills to the NFP sector appears to be a useful development, raising the capacity and capability and, thereby, proficiency of the sector, a long-held government desideratum, and more closely linking the sector into high-level decision making and influence via connections back into departments. However, it has been identified that something of a 'government block' has developed, with most of those transferring to the larger NFPs creating a stronger operational base for these groups. It has been argued by some respondents that this 'block' and its capacity to 'think and write' like government makes it much more attractive to government as a service. This issue was further explained:

There has been such as large number of people [from government] transferring across, the sector has previously absorbed and even assimilated smaller, natural flows … but the new flood are now forming their own network blocks … rather than adjust to the sector.

Thus, while the exchange has positive potential for capacity building within the sector and for the building of closer bridges between government and community, in the short term at least, it is likely that the economic austerity policies have added to the distrust that has long characterised government–community sector relations in Australia (Lyons, 2003); and, moreover, have created a growing chasm between smaller and larger NFPs. McDermott and Stone (2013) add that the government cuts were 'self-defeating', as they led to reduced productivity and other workforce capability issues, as well as the dismantling of good working relations.

From this it can be seen that the policies and strategies aimed at downsizing government and government services have led to a 'hollowing-out' of the state (Milward and Provan, 2000) and a greater reliance on the NFP sector as a 'shadow government' (Wolch, 1990). More worryingly, it has been argued that larger NFPs are becoming a shadow branch of government. Downsizing has also occasioned a growing preference for upsized services, in terms both of a preference for larger organisations and, as is highlighted below, of strategies aimed at more closely integrating smaller agencies through amalgamation and mergers.

Upsizing: amalgamation and mergers

The current diversity and broad scope of services has been presented as an ineffective system and, as such, both individual agency and government objectives can be compromised. In response there has been a move toward amalgamated and merged service sets. The rationale for this policy agenda is centred on the search for efficiency: bringing related services together makes them more cost-effective, more accessible and therefore more efficient (Queensland Government Department of Housing and Public Works, 2013). In this study, the benefits of upsizing the sector via amalgamation were acknowledged by some respondents; for example, sharing management committee members, participating in joint training and other potentially costly up-skilling activities. Conversely, the potential for dominant groups within amalgamations to control other, less powerful partners was also identified as a real concern. Craswell and Davis (1993) highlighted similar issues in relation to government departmental amalgamations in the 1990s, commenting that these negatively impacted on service flexibility and good decision making. It seems that community sector agencies are much more comfortable with adopting less 'intense levels of integration'. One respondent summarised the general feeling:

> Coming together through consortia and other forms is okay because we are not totally giving up our autonomy, but amalgamation and merger means we can lose our service identity.

Thus, there was concern expressed that the benefits of amalgamation would come at the cost of a diverse and vibrant sector, the very attributes that have made the NFP sector a viable 'alternative' and 'safety net' for government.

It is notable that several networks of agencies have sought to achieve integration and efficiency through the application of alternative strategies to amalgamation. The Reconnect and the Gold Coast Homelessness Networks, for example, both turned to incorporation as a substitute approach in response to government 'policy and funding pushes' for better integration. Reconnect became incorporated in 2004, following strong policy pressures from the Queensland state government for agencies to become 'more collaborative' (Ryan, 2003; Keast and Brown, 2006). Although seemingly falling in with the government agenda, it was explicitly stated by members of this network that they were adopting a collaborative approach despite the goals of government. Further, rather than being 'tools of government' and adopting government's model, they were going to develop a collaboration model that worked best for their situation.

> We moved to this new collaborative model, not because government required this and made it a condition of funding. We did it because it was the right thing to do. We also moved early, to make sure that we controlled what it looked like, how it worked and what it stood for.

The growing interest by governments in the merger of smaller NFPs has also resulted in a noticeable cleavage appearing at different levels of the integration framework, with personnel at the managerial/practitioner level pursuing a horizontal integration form through the formation of consortia or collaborations, while their governance boards (comprised mostly of corporate representatives) are exploring vertical integration via merger or amalgamation. This duality of strategies has caused considerable tension and distrust between previously aligned workers and organisations and has had the effect of further fragmenting the system, particularly at the service-delivery level. As one collaboration member noted:

> There are collaboration partners whose boards are simultaneously pursuing alternative approaches, like mergers. It is difficult to be truly collaborative when you can't fully trust your partners.

Together these findings highlight the disconnect between the two sectors in terms of preferred processes and mechanisms to meet mutual goals of integrated services. It also points to a lack of systems-wide understanding of the range and type of integration policies in place. Furthermore, ideologically driven policy or programmatic direction (Adams and Hess, 2001), rather than evidence-based approaches, often informs policy decisions, resulting in what Ham (2012, p 3) has described as 'the pendulum swing' between competition and integration.

Future directions and conclusions

Both government and community sectors consider integration to be the Holy Grail informing optimal social services. Numerous models and strategies have been employed, with competition and collaboration policies being the most recent and persistent. The findings of the study discussed here have highlighted a number of unintended outcomes of the pursuit of this dual integration approach. Most significant are the growing fragmentation of the sector and the intensifying divide between government and community sectors, particularly around the upsizing issue. Other impacts include the loss of productivity associated with turf protection and conspiracy theorising, the cost of relationship breakdowns, the social costs of distracted or discontinued service delivery and the lack of certainty in employment for many workers in this sector. The cumulative effect of all these is that the defining feature of the sector – its autonomy, diversity, social justice ethos and advocacy role – are under threat and, in some cases, may have already been undermined.

Both competitive and collaborative integration policy approaches have merit and application. However, as they are currently conceived and implemented, there are inherent difficulties. Problems occur when policies push too far in each direction, without checks and balances, leading to opposing effects. It is therefore important that policy makers understand and support the different types of integration form that are available to be applied, rather than oscillating between or creating contested policy domains. Further, there is a need for a more holistic or systems-wide mapping of policies, highlighting their layers of influence and points of overlap or disjuncture, and better enabling the management of these policy interfaces. As Ham (2012, p 2) notes in relation to healthcare: 'A bundle of policy initiatives is needed to support the evolution of an integrated system … The wrong kind of integration may emerge unless policy-makers think two or three steps ahead.' The upsizing combinations present as a genuine challenge to the on-going viability of the NFP sector in its current form. There is no doubt that the social services sector, including smaller bodies, should not be immune to review and reform. However, such an undertaking should occur jointly, through shared planning, co-design and negotiated agreements. As a start, a communication strategy, in the form of genuine dialogue, has been presented as one means to bridge the competition–integration divide. Further, as public spending continues to contract, and austerity measures and the mixed economy become more embedded, capacity building support will be required so as to assist NFPs to more easily transition to more self-reliant business models – for example, the diversification of funding sources and the exploration of innovative service and business practices, including competition. At the same time their collaborative capacity needs to be retained and nurtured so as to continue to bind multiple interests and agencies into a coherent, collective force.

To conclude, the need for integration is likely to intensify rather than decrease, demanding access to the full suite of available integration policies and strategies. By crafting a set of policies that promote the right mix of competition and collaboration for the scale, pace and level of integration needed, the present clashes between competition and collaborative integration, and their often perverse effects, can be overcome.

References

6, P. (2004) 'Joined-up government in the western-world in comparative perspective: a preliminary literature review and exploration', *Journal of Public Administration Research and Theory*, 14(1): 103–38.

Adams, D. and Hess, M. (2001) 'Community in public policy: fad or foundation', *Australian Journal of Public Administration*, 60(2): 13–23.

Australian Council of Social Services (2006) *Australian community sector survey 2006*, Redfern, Australia: Australian Council of Social Services.

Australian Government (2008) *Which way home? A new approach to homelessness*, Canberra: ACT.

Australian Government (2013) *Transforming Service Delivery Report,* , Canberra: AGPS, Department of Human Services.

Australian Productivity Commission (2010) *Contribution of the not-for-profit sector, research report*, Canberra: Australian Productivity Commission.

Australian Public Service Commission (2009) *Delivering performance and accountability*, Sydney: Commonwealth of Australia, Australian Government Printing Service (AGPS).

Brown, K. and Keast, R. (2003) 'Citizen–government engagement: community connection through networked arrangements', *Asian Journal of Public Administration*, 25(1): 107–132.

Commonwealth of Australia (1993) *National competition policy* (Himler Report), Canberra: AGPS.

Craswell, E. and Davis, G. (1993) 'Does the amalgamation of government agencies produce better policy coordination', in P. Weller, J. Forester and G. Davis (eds) *Reforming the public service: Lessons from recent experience*, Macmillan Education Australia: Melbourne, pp 180–207.

Deloitte (2009) *New South Wales government service delivery: Agency amalgamation: our point of view*, August, Sydney, NSW: Deloitte.

Earles, W. and Moon, J. (2000) 'Pathways to the enabling state: changing models of social provision in Western Australian community services', *Australian Journal of Public Administration*, 59(4): 11–24.

Elthan, B. (2012) 'Welcome to austerity: Queensland horror', *The Drum*, www.abc.net.au/unleashed/4256116.html (accessed 2 November 2013).

Fine, M. (2001) 'The New South Wales demonstration projects in community care', in M. Mandell (ed) *Getting results through collaboration: Networks and network structures for public policy and management*, Westport, CA: Quorum Books, pp 207–19.

Glasby, J. and Dickenson, H. (2008) 'Greater than the sum of our parts? Emerging lessons for UK health and social care', *International Journal of Integrated Care*, 8 (July).

Ham, C. (2012) 'Competition and integration in health care reform', *International Journal of Integrated Care*, 12(15), http://www.ijic.org (accessed 13 November 2013).

Hancock, L. (2004) 'Pathways for rights under the shifting terrain of neoliberalism', *Reinventing community services: The promise and reality of reform*, Brisbane: Queensland Council of Social Services.

Himmelman, A. (1994) 'Communities Working Collaboratively for Change', in P. Herrman (ed) *Resolving conflict: Strategies for local government*, Washington, DC: International City/County Management Association.

House of Representatives Standing Committee on Family and Community Affairs (1998) *What price competition? A report on the competitive tendering of welfare service delivery*, Canberra: Parliament of the Commonwealth of Australia.

Keast, R. (2011) 'Joined-up governance in Australia: how the past can inform the future', *International Journal of Public Administration*, 34(4): 221–31.

Keast, R. and Brown, K. (2006) 'Adjusting to new ways of working: experiments with service delivery in the public sector', *Australian Journal of Public Administration*, 65(4): 41–53.

Keast, R., Brown, K. and Mandell, M. (2007) 'Getting the right mix: unpacking integration, meanings and strategies', *International Public Management Journal*, 10(1): 9–34.

Keast, R., Mandell, M. and Waterhouse, J. (2011) 'Big, bigger, best? The impact of government policies', Paper for Public Management Research Association Conference, Syracuse New York, 2–4 June.

Keast, R., Waterhouse, J., Murphy, G. and Brown, K. (2011) *Putting it altogether: design considerations for an integrated homeless services system*, Report for FACSIA, Canberra, Australia.

Kodner, D. and Spreeuwenberg, D. (2002) 'Integrated care: meaning, logic applications and implications – a discussion paper', *International Journal of Integrated Care*, 2(3):1–7.

Konrad, E. (1996) 'A multi-dimensional framework for conceptualising human services integration', in J. Marguart and E. Konrad (eds) *Evaluating initiatives to integrate human services*, San Francisco: Jossey-Bass, pp 5–19.

Ling, T. (2002) 'Delivering joined-up government in the UK: dimensions, issues and problems', *Public Administration*, 80: 615–42.

Lyons, M. (2003) 'Improving government–community sector relations', *Journal of Contemporary Issues in Business and Government*, 9(1): 7–20.

McBratney, A. and McGregor-Lowndes, M. (2012) '"Fair" government contracts: time to curb unfettered executive freedom', *Australian Journal Administrative Law*, 20: 19–33.

McDermott, K. and Stone, C. (2013) *Death by a thousand cuts: How governments undermine their own productivity*, Sydney, NSW: Centre for Social Impact.

McDonald, C. and Zetlin, D. (2004) 'The promotion and destruction of community service delivery systems', *Australian Journal of Social Issues*, 39(3): 267–82.

Martinson, K. (1999) *Literature Review on Service Coordination and Integration in the Welfare and Workforce Development Systems*, Research Paper, Washington, DC: Urban Institute.

Matheson, C. (2000) 'Policy formulation in Australian government: vertical and horizontal axes', *Australian Journal of Public Administration*, 59(2): 44–55.

Merton, R. (1936) 'The unanticipated consequences of purposive social action', *American Sociological Review*, 1(6): 894–904.

Milward, H.B. and Provan, K.G. (2000) 'Governing in the hollow state', *Journal of Public Administration Research and Theory*, 10(2): 359–79.

O'Farrell, G. (2002) 'Public sector reform in Queensland', *Canberra Journal of Public Administration*, 104 (June): 6–8.

O'Flynn, J. (2009) 'The cult of collaboration in public policy', *Australian Journal of Public Administration*, 68(1): 112–16.

Peters, B.G. and Pierre, J. (2006) *Handbook on public policy*, Thousand Oaks, CA: Sage.

Phillips, R. (2007) 'Tamed or trained? The co-option and capture of "favoured" NGOs', *Third Sector Review*, 13(2): 27–48.

Popper, K. (*1974*) *The logic of scientific discovery* (6th edn), London: Hutchinson.

Powell, W. (1990) 'Neither market nor hierarchy: network forms of organization', *Research in Organizational Behavior*, 12: 295–336.

Queensland Government (2000) *Human services integration: A background paper*, Government Service Delivery Project, Office of the Public Service Commission, Brisbane: Queensland Government.

Queensland Government Department of Housing and Public Works (2013) *Department of Housing and Public Works 2012–2013 Annual Report*, www.hpw.qld.gov.au/aboutus/ReportsPublications/AnnualReports/Pages/default.aspx

Queensland Government (2010) *Service improvement measures*, Brisbane: Department of Communities.

Quiggin, J. (2012) *Queensland Commission of Audit – interim report June 2012. A critical review*, Brisbane: University of Queensland.

Reddel, T. (2002) 'Beyond participation: hierarchies, management and markets: "new governance" and place policies', *Australian Journal of Public Administration*, 61(1): 50–63.

Rudd, K. (2009) 'One year on from the crisis: economic and social policy challenges for Australia', Sambell Oration Address to the Brotherhood of St Laurence, Melbourne, www.pm.gov.au/node/6253.

Ryan, W. (1999) 'The new landscape for nonprofits', *Harvard Business Review*, 77(1): 127–36.

Ryan, P. (2003) *I am looking at the future: Evaluation of the reconnect program*, Final Report for the Department of Family and Community Services, Canberra, Australia.

Ryan, N., Williams, T., Charles, M. and Waterhouse, J. (2008) 'Top-down organizational change in an Australian government agency', *International Journal of Public Sector Management*, 21(1): 26–44.

Scott, J., Laurie, R., Stevens, B. and Weller, P. (2001) *The engine room of government: The Queensland Premier's Department*, Brisbane: University of Queensland Press.

Tierney, L. (1970) 'Social policy', in A.F. Davis and S. Encel (eds) *Australian society* (2nd edn), Melbourne: Cheshire, pp 200–223.

Walfogel, J. (1997) 'The new wave of service integration', *Social Service Review*, 71(3): 463–85.

Walsh, P. (1993) 'Welfare policy', in B. Stevens and J. Wanna (eds) *Goss government: Promise and performance of Labor in Queensland*, South Melbourne: Macmillan, pp 215–25.

Wapner, P. (2002) 'The democratic accountability of non-governmental organizations: introductory essay: paradise lost? NGOs and global accountability', *Chicago Journal of International Law*, (Spring): 3(1): 155–60.

Winer, M. and Ray, K. (1994) *Collaboration handbook: Creating, sustaining and enjoying the journey*, St Paul, MA: Amhert Wilder Foundation.

Wolch, J. (1990) *The shadow state: Government and voluntary sector in transition*, New York: The Foundation Centre.

FIFTEEN

Developing integration of health and social care in England

Madeleine Knight

Introduction

Health and social care services in England are delivered by two distinct systems. At the establishment of the National Health Service (NHS) in 1948, hospitals provided free care for the sick, and those needing 'care and attention' were placed in residential homes provided by local authorities, which could charge for services. Concerns about the division between the two systems and disjointed care for patients have been raised repeatedly over the years and consecutive generations of policy makers have introduced reorganisations and other policy initiatives in attempts to address this fragmentation with little effect.

Compounding the issue of fragmentation between the systems, the population of England is ageing rapidly. As a result, the rising proportion of older people has significant consequences for the health and social care systems. In 2010 around 10 million people were over 65 years old; by 2050 this is set to have nearly doubled to around 19 million. The number of very elderly people over the age of 80 is growing at a greater pace; from around three million in 2010, the number is set to increase to around eight million by 2050 (Cracknell, 2010). Not only is the proportion of older people growing, but the cost of care for each older individual is also rising (Ham and Walsh, 2013). A side-effect of the ageing demographic is that increasing numbers of people have long-term health conditions (Ham and Walsh, 2013). The number of elective and non-elective hospital admissions for older people is increasing and projections suggest that in the future a high proportion of older people will be living on their own and will require formal care (Ham and Walsh, 2013).

This chapter reviews the case for integration in the current financial and policy context in England. It examines some of the reasons why so little progress has been made to date, despite periodic policy initiatives to promote integration. It discusses some of the most prominent themes emerging from the recent literature, identifying a number of structural and cultural issues that have prevented integration from occurring. Finally, it offers some recommendations for taking integration forward, based on this discussion.

The case for integration

One answer put forward to address the challenge of fragmented systems is integration across health and social care. Integration is a broad concept and has been used in a variety of different contexts. However, many views converge on the underlying principle that integration aims to improve patient and user experience and quality of care through better coordination of care across services. Many service users meet obstacles in their journey through the systems. Patients are often surprised to find that they have to repeat their information to different agencies when information systems do not speak to each other. This also causes delays in their care and a disjointed experience. A useful definition is provided by the patient organisation National Voices to express integration from the patient's perspective: 'I can plan my care with people who work together to understand me and my carer(s), allow me control, and bring together services to achieve the outcomes important to me' (National Voices, 2012).

From a system perspective, integration is about ensuring that patients and users are able to access the right care for their needs, at the time when they need it, in the most appropriate setting for them. This also means more efficient use of resources, where users are able to access preventive measures quickly. Effective care coordination facilitates earlier intervention and reduced demand for acute and emergency services (National Audit Office, 2013). Therefore, integration aims to address the inefficiencies that arise from the fragmentation of the two systems. Much of the debate has emerged from academic debate, and thinking has been disseminated to policy circles by some of the leading think-tanks, including The King's Fund and the Nuffield Trust, the latter of which uses the description:

> Integrated care is an organising principle for care delivery that aims to improve patient care and experience through improved coordination. Integration is the combined set of methods, processes and models that seek to bring this about. (Shaw et al, 2011)

Offering a smooth patient journey and coordinated care that is more efficient is most important for the group of service users with multiple co-morbidities who receive their care from several providers (Curry and Ham, 2010). This is also the group that accounts for the majority of resources. A number of international examples of integrated health systems show the advantages of this approach, via more efficient use of resources. One of these is moving care to less expensive settings, from the hospital into the community. The existing structure of the health service reflects the historic need of the population, at its inception in 1948, for it to treat injury in a young and otherwise healthy population. The resulting hospital-based healthcare system is now no longer the most efficient way to deliver care to a growing elderly population, living longer with multiple co-morbidities.

In the US, Kaiser Permanente and the Veterans Health Association demonstrate that integration of health services across primary and secondary care, universal electronic health records accessible by patients, and use of capitated budgets can reduce the use of hospital beds (Liange, 2010; Goodwin, 2013). In New Zealand, implementing new 'health pathways' across primary care, social care and hospitals and changing the financial-incentive structure resulted in reductions in emergency medical admissions, lengths of stay and readmissions (Mays and Smith, 2013). Better management in the community reduces the risk of acute healthcare incidents and thereby reduces the need for hospitalisation (Ham and Walsh, 2013). Options to make better use of resources in England require investment in primary and community services, and social care to support rehabilitation and re-ablement and reduction in the use of hospitals (Goodwin, Smith et al, 2012). Unfortunately, preventive measures often become less of a priority when resource pressures are greatest, despite the potential long-term savings of this approach (Humphries, 2011).

Facilitating an integration-based approach requires a better understanding of the relationship between health and social care and the benefits of upstream, preventive services. For example, social care services such as re-ablement care are funded by local authorities and reduce the use of hospitals by enabling earlier discharge of patients. Similarly, healthcare can reduce the use of social care; for example, continence and community nursing can reduce the need for social care support (Humphries, 2011). Even though there is some understanding of these causal links, a better understanding of the reciprocal relationship between health and social care is needed in order to make best use of resources. In fact, there is little existing evidence to suggest that increasing access to social care or community care or better integration between health and social care will lead to reduced use in the health service (Bardsley et al, 2013).

Recent history of integration

Politicians across the leading political parties have accepted the case for integration. The Coalition government strengthened the requirements in recent legislation. The Health and Social Care Act 2012 was hotly debated during its passage through parliament. Controversy around some of the policies to introduce greater competition in the sector resulted in a pause of the parliamentary process in order to seek the views of stakeholders. Integration emerged as a strong message and the government accepted the recommendations from the consultation exercise carried out by the NHS Future Forum, which made recommendations to strengthen the requirements for integration (Field, 2011).

The recent political commitment echoes similar attempts of past administrations, where successive governments have tried to encourage better joint working. Over the last 10–15 years numerous initiatives were announced, but these have done little to improve integration. In 1997, the previous Labour government placed a greater emphasis on improving the effectiveness of the relationships between the health service and local authority social services through collaboration. New flexibilities were introduced by the Health Act 1999 to pool budgets across local authorities and healthcare organisations. The White Paper *Our Health, Our Care, Our Say* (Department of Health, 2006) set out aspirations to put the needs of patients and service users at the heart of the NHS. This was shortly followed by *Putting People First* (HM Government, 2007), the government's vision for transforming adult social care, which placed an emphasis on partnership working and set out the expectation that local authorities should undertake 'authentic' partnership working with the local NHS. In 2008 Lord Darzi's *High Quality Care for All* report (Darzi, 2008) identified the need for previously fragmented services to be better coordinated across sectors. It set out plans to create new integrated care organisations (ICOs), designed to bring together health and social care professionals from a range of organisations, and led to a series of pilot projects across the country.

More recent activity from policy makers shows a stronger emphasis than before, by committing resources specifically to integration. However, this money comes from the existing NHS budget and still represents a small proportion of overall spending. Soon after the 2010 election the

Coalition government published a set of White Papers titled *Equity and Excellence: Liberating the NHS* (Department of Health, 2010) announcing that £1 billion per year would be made available by 2014/15, set aside from the NHS budget, for partnership working between the NHS and social care. In June 2013 the government's Spending Review (Treasury, 2013) increased the fund for joint working, announcing an annual £3.8 billion sum to be taken from the NHS budget to pay for new integrated care services and projects. A performance-related element of this Better Care Fund will apply from 2015/16, with payment of £1 billion of the total depending on local performance and ability to demonstrate that arrangements will be made to integrate services (NHS England, 2013). In addition, plans have been announced for a new set of integrated care pilots in sites across the country for locally led initiatives to use capitated budgets across primary and secondary healthcare and social care (Department of Health, 2013). In 2013, the Labour party began to build its policy proposals on health and social care integration in a bid to make this a key feature of its manifesto for the next general election.

Enablers of and barriers to integration

A review of the recent literature on integration shows two overarching issues that dominate the discussion and are the most frequently cited concerns. These important factors that influence the ability to integrate health and social care are: the financial challenges for both sectors, aligning incentives and differences across the two settlements, as well as developing a cultural environment that can support better integration. To understand how to achieve the elusive goal of integrating health and social care in England it is important to consider the lessons learned from previous initiatives.

The financial challenge

A fundamental challenge to achieving better integration of health and social care services in England is the current constraint on all public spending. The health sector is facing unprecedented fiscal pressures. Following the general election in 2010, David Nicholson, the then Chief Executive of the NHS, set out a challenge to achieve £20 billion of efficiency savings by 2014/15. Essentially, this meant living within a budget in line with general inflation, whereas costs within the health sector usually grow at around 4% above this level. This is due to multiple factors, including technological improvements, an ageing population, increasing multi-morbidity and lifestyle risk, and rising patient expectations. Following the four-year period of restraint, it was expected that the economy would have recuperated sufficiently to support growth in public spending once more. However, the sluggish recovery has made it apparent that the need for savings will continue for the remainder of this decade and beyond. The Nuffield Trust has predicted the deficit in healthcare to require £30 billion in efficiency savings by 2021/22 and to remain an on-going financial challenge until 2050 (Roberts, Marshall et al, 2012).

In the social care sector, financial pressures are considerably more acute. Local authorities received a real terms reduction in government spending of £1.6 billion in 2012/13, in addition to a loss of £400 million from council tax revenues, leaving a total reduction of £2 billion in 2012/13 (Audit Commission, 2012). During the previous Labour administration, spending on adult social care grew in real terms, with an average annual increase of 5.1%. However, this increase in funding did little to meet demographic pressures, and access to social care has not risen to the extent that access to healthcare has been achieved in the NHS over the same period (Humphries, 2011). As a result, the balance of available services is poorly matched between the two sectors, causing inefficiencies in the system. Since the 2010 election the period of austerity has been considerably more constrained for social care than for health. Recognition of the growing demands on social care led the government to commission an independent review to recommend a more sustainable way of funding care for the future. In 2012 the Dilnot Commission (Commission on Funding of Care and Support, 2011) recommended a cap for individuals' lifetime contributions towards their social care cost at £35,000, to protect individuals from having to sell their own homes to pay for care, and estimated that this would cost the state around £1.7 billion in the first year, rising to £3.6 billion by 2015/16. The Care Bill currently in progress through parliament aims to implement Dilnot's recommendations; however, it sets the cap for individual contributions higher at £72,000. This is a first step to greater consistency for individuals accessing social care, but even so, many people will continue to make significant out-of-pocket payments for a large portion of their care.

While the need to make both health and social service systems more efficient is a policy driver for more integration, it is also a barrier to implementation. Addressing the financial challenge requires new creative ways to incentivise integration and promote prevention so as to make future savings. A strong incentive for this approach would result from promoting better understanding of the relationship between the two sectors and setting out where savings will result from preventive measures. Past experience shows that restructuring or introducing new ways of working is more successful where additional resources are provided to support the change process. Initiatives that have been introduced without additional funding have experienced problems. In practice, the result has been one fund being used to 'plug the gaps' for another service (Humphries, Galea et al, 2012).

Aligning incentives

Realising the benefits of more coordinated, preventive care requires a long-term approach to investment. Problems exist in the current payment systems in England that have the effect of counteracting the desired incentives and flow of resources. The tariff system, which pays hospitals for activity and community services with block contracts, incentivises treating more people in acute settings (Lewis, Rosen et al, 2010).

There are a number of options for changing incentives in favour of primary, community and social care. Paying for outcomes rather than activity has been identified as a key aspect for any approach, and should include holding all providers contributing to a patient's care jointly accountable (Goodwin, Smith et al, 2012). Capitated budgets that pay per head of population rather for activity encourage investment in preventive care and collaboration across providers (Curry and Ham, 2010). Other less prominent approaches include enforcing more active disinvestment decisions that facilitate future savings.

Pooling budgets across health and social care is one way to incentivise risk sharing in order to promote investment in preventive services. However, in the current system, working to annual budget cycles and lack of risk sharing is a strong disincentive. Annual budgets incentivise organisations to shift patients and service users to other settings so as to relieve their own costs within the budget cycle, even where these are not the most appropriate care settings. Reaping the benefits of a more preventive system, and shifting a greater portion of finances into social care activities, requires long-term planning. This means that the existing mechanisms to pool budgets have been little used to date. One of the most coveted cases of successful integration of health and social care took place in Torbay, a relatively isolated, rural region with an advanced ageing population. One of the factors that enabled success in the area was that an agreement to share risk between the NHS and local authority meant that all parties were able to realise the long-term benefits over time (The King's Fund, 2011).

Successful examples of different funding agreements, such as the COBIC Programme, have used contracts for substance misuse services that combine capitation and rewards for improved outcomes, which resulted in savings of 20% in the first year.[1] However, on the whole, the evidence for the future savings to be made from preventive measures is weak (Bardsley et al, 2013). This is partly because each care pathway must be taken in isolation and many of the long-term conditions that are becoming increasingly prevalent in England have complex origins. Therefore, causal relationships to prevention initiatives are difficult to prove. There is a need for a better understanding of these relationships, but it is unlikely that any system-wide lessons can be taken from the evidence. Preventive approaches to services must be considered on a local basis.

Different funding mechanisms

A fundamental issue that must be addressed if significant integration is to take place across health and social care is the different funding mechanisms and settlements across the two sectors. Integration requires that the two funds can be brought together to offer a coherent service. Healthcare is provided free at the point of use (with the exception of minor payments such as prescription charges), based on need rather than ability to pay. It is funded through general taxation with largely nationally dictated access criteria. Social care, on the other hand, is only partially funded by the state, with significant variation in eligibility criteria between geographical areas. Out-of-pocket payment for basic care is a common feature of social services, at significant cost to individuals and families. The current social care offer is unclear to service users, and for commissioners and providers it is difficult to plan for investment in aspects of social care that are self-funded. A clear set of eligibility criteria across the country would help to make the system simpler for users, and for planners to identify where and how best to integrate services (Social Care Institute for Excellence, 2013).

Information systems

The need for compatible information systems across organisations is well accepted as a fundamental enabler of integration. This is a key feature of successful international examples, including Kaiser Permanent and the Veterans Health Association. One of the most noted obstacles to coordinated care in the English system is delays due to poor mechanisms for sharing patient and user information. The National Programme for IT has left a scar on the policy landscape and it is unlikely that any political figures will give this public priority. However, it is essential that the issue be addressed if integration is to be achieved on any scale.

Cultural and organisational change

Perhaps an even greater challenge than addressing the financial differences and flows of funding across the two sectors is introducing the cultural transformation needed to bring the two disparate systems together. The health and social care sectors have very different cultures, and culture change is a significant barrier to greater integration. Health and social care are divided by different professions that adhere to different values and cultures, different ways of working in different care settings, with different governance structures. Bringing together these two worlds is a feat of change management that requires investment, training and continuous staff engagement (RAND Europe Ernst & Young LLP, 2012). This section examines some of the organisational and cultural barriers and enablers that have been reported extensively in the literature on integration.

Overcoming organisational and professional boundaries has been observed as a major challenge in attempts to integrate services. Aligning the work of multiple different organisations and professions was a difficulty in many of the integrated care pilots undertaken by the Department of Health (RAND Europe Ernst & Young LLP, 2012). Pilot areas that brought together a greater number of organisations proved to be the most challenging. Professional differences in culture and ways of working were also apparent in many areas. While healthcare staff were reluctant to participate as a result of change fatigue, social care staff felt averse to initiatives that appeared more dominantly health focused (RAND Europe Ernst & Young LLP, 2012). This was also a reservation among staff entering the Torbay pilot; however, their fears were soon allayed when the benefits of closer working became apparent (The King's Fund, 2011).

Organisational and leadership stability is also a key factor in enabling integration. In England, the health service in particular has seen continuous structural reorganisation, dictated from the centre. On-going national policy reform has resulted in a churn of systems, structures, governance arrangements and organisational leadership within the NHS and this has created instability and change fatigue among staff that poses a barrier to further transformation to integrate health and social care services. The initiative in Torbay developed over a period of 10–15 years, during which there were stability of leadership across the organisations involved and pre-existing good working relationships among them. The importance of leadership was also demonstrated by an evaluation of a number of sites from the integrated care pilots scheme, which showed that a key enabler of the pilot's success was senior management placing a high priority on integration (RAND Europe Ernst & Young LLP, 2012).

Presenting a clear vision that could be shared by all those involved in the work was found to be a key enabler of integration projects (The King's Fund, 2011). Health and social care staff are most likely to buy in to a vision that focuses on improving patient and service user outcomes. A survey of doctors by the British Medical Association (BMA) indicates that improved clinical outcomes and better patient experience were prioritised by doctors as the reasons why they would accept a case for integration (British Medical Association, 2011). The Torbay experience demonstrated that creating a narrative that placed the patient at the centre of the picture helped to gain staff support. The fictitious character 'Mrs Smith' was used to develop a picture of a typical service user. An 80-year-old woman with multiple care needs, her case was used to imagine the various difficulties she would encounter, such as repeatedly explaining her needs to numerous staff, delays caused while services shared access to her information, multiple visits and sites to attend. The example of Mrs Smith clearly illustrated and articulated the challenges faced by service users that professionals could relate to and came across frequently in their daily working lives (The King's Fund, 2011).

Putting patients at the centre of the vision requires public and patient involvement (PPI). Performance in the NHS has come under close scrutiny with the publication of Robert Francis QC's inquiry into care at Mid Staffordshire NHS Foundation Trust in February 2013 (HM Government, 2013). The dominant message of the inquiry report was a pressing need to improve public and patient involvement so as to develop a more patient-centred service. The report noted that the system had developed 'a culture focused on doing the system's business – not that of the patients' (HM Government, 2013). The concept of user involvement and co-development of services is much better developed and understood in the social care sector (Ocloo, 2010). Bringing together professionals from the two sectors may well help to develop this approach in healthcare. The NHS Future Forum stated that 'integration is valuable insofar as it improves experience and outcomes for the individual' (NHS Future Forum, 2012).

Despite a reported focus on patient outcomes and experience, findings from the evaluation of the first set of integrated care pilots in England found that a number of the pilots led by professionals made little progress in improving patient experience. There were positive reports of the experiences of professionals involved in the pilots, but little improvement in patients' and service users' reports. This suggests that profession-led initiatives can improve working conditions and ways of working for the professions in a way that does not address improvements in the service as experienced by the patient (RAND Europe Ernst & Young LLP, 2012). This may have been due to the time frame within which the initiatives were evaluated. However, it shows that including patients and service users in developing the vision is an important part of achieving better integration.

While a patient-centred vision should be at the centre of the initiative, implementing the vision requires staff engagement. Across the integrated care pilots staff engagement was identified as a crucial factor (RAND Europe Ernst & Young LLP, 2012). In some instances the effort required to ensure staff engagement was underestimated and a lack of effective engagement became a limiting factor. General practitioners (GPs) were an essential group to engage, due to their coordinating role across the sectors and their ability to provide access to other clinicians. Areas that lacked buy-in among GPs found this to be an insurmountable barrier to integration projects. This finding is consistent with management science literature, which provides a strong evidence base underlining the importance of staff engagement in making change work. Recent work by Michael West and colleagues illustrates the strong association between levels of staff engagement as reported in the NHS staff survey and quality of services (West, Baker et al, 2013). If staff engagement is essential to maintaining and improving the standard of services in normal operation, then it is essential during periods of change.

Developing relationships across professions is another key enabler. One of the mechanisms found most useful to encourage effective joint working across professional boundaries was co-located teams (RAND Europe Ernst & Young LLP, 2012). Unsurprisingly, being together, whether through co-location or greater face-to-face contact, helps to develop relationships and break down cultural barriers between professions. Better relationships and closer working appeals to professionals. The importance of creating good professional relationships was cited by doctors in the BMA's survey, with 84% of respondents stating that this was one of the key ways to achieve joined-up care pathways (British Medical Association, 2011). Correspondingly, almost a third of respondents highlighted closer working across professions as one of the most important criteria for measuring the success of efforts to integrate services.

Discussion and conclusions

The themes emerging from the literature on integration discussed above show the importance of aligning financial incentives, making sense of the separate financial settlements across the sectors and the underlying challenge of addressing cultural change. All of these issues will need to be addressed for integration to succeed. The financial barriers should be addressed by policy makers, and removing these is a prerequisite to progress with integration. While the financial crisis is a policy driver that makes savings essential, it is also a barrier to implementing substantial change, which is best achieved when extra resources are made available. Aligning incentives through capitated budgets and sharing financial risk by pooling budgets have been shown, by good examples of integration such as Torbay, to help incentivise preventive care. Misaligned incentives to maximise hospital activity through the tariff have the result of directing patients and resource flow in the wrong direction, especially when community services receive block payments. Removing the tariff structure and revisiting payment incentives that pay for outcomes rather than activity is necessary so as to shift resources to the most efficient care settings. Annual budget cycles create short-termism that overlooks the future savings that can be made and lack of risk sharing reduces the chance of downstream investment. A longer planning cycle would promote prevention and encourage more providers to pool and share resources and risk. Finally, compatible information systems are essential so as to coordinate care for individuals across multiple providers and services.

The cultural changes must be led at a local level by creating a shared vision that is patient centred and is developed through user input. Engaging staff is crucial, and developing relationships across professions through increased time together is important to implementing the vision. The question remains as to what policy makers can do in practice to address the cultural challenges. The transformation required to integrate services across health and social care takes significant time and is unlikely to be fixed within a parliamentary cycle. For this reason the prospect of achieving meaningful integration in a substantial number of locations and services, particularly where it is most needed across the country, remains a distant prospect at present. Numerous studies of integration, including those mentioned above, indicate that there is no quick fix or single panacea that can integrate all services. It seems that decisions need to be made on a case-by-case basis in each locality. Differences in demographic characteristics, existing services available and local funding and commissioning decisions must be reflected in new integration initiatives. The strong influence of the local history and culture of local organisations and the relationships between them is evident from studies of some of the best-known examples of integration (The King's Fund, 2011). It is also clear from the evaluation of the national integrated care pilots (RAND Europe Ernst & Young LLP, 2012) that very mixed experiences were had across the country and local context was a defining factor of success. This suggests that it is extremely difficult to prescribe a formula for integration that can be replicated across the country.

At a national policy level it seems that the best approach is to create the right environment by ensuring the stability of systems and leadership that allow integration to develop at a local level. A priority for the integration agenda should be to create stability in the health and social care systems. Rather than prescribe methods, policy makers can create a clear vision of the aim of integration. This should include flexibility in the system to allow local innovation and adaption to make integration work at a local level.

Note
[1] For more information see http://www.cobic.co.uk/what-we-do/

References

Audit Commission (2012) *Tough times 2012: Councils' financial health in challenging times*, London. Available at: http://www.audit-commission. gov.uk/2012/11/tough-times-2012/

Bardsley, M., Steventon, A., Smith, J. and Dixon, J. (2013) *Evaluating integrated and community-based care: How do we know what works?* Nuffield Trust: London. Available at: http://www.nuffieldtrust.org. uk/publications/evaluating-integrated-and-community-based-care-how-do-we-know-what-works

British Medical Association (2011) *Doctors' perspectives on integrated care in the NHS*, London: BMA.

Commission on Funding of Care and Support (2011) *Fairer care funding: The report of the Commission on Funding of Care and Support.*

Cracknell, R. (2010) 'The ageing population – the UK's ageing population has considerable consequences for public services', *Key issues for the new Parliament 2010,* House of Commons Library Research. Available at: http://www.parliament.uk/documents/commons/lib/research/key_issues/Key%20Issues%20The%20ageing%20population2007.pdf

Curry, N. and Ham, C. (2010) *Clinical and service integration: The route to improved outcomes,* London: The King's Fund.

Darzi, Lord, of Denham (2008) *High quality care for all: NHS Next Stage Review final report,* London: Department of Health.

Department of Health (2006) *Our health, our care, our say: A new direction for community services,* Cm 6737, London: The Stationery Office. Available at: http://www.official-documents.gov.uk/document/cm67/6737/6737.pdf

Department of Health (2010) *Equity and excellence: Liberating the NHS.* White Paper, Cm 7881, London: The Stationery Office. Available at: http://www.dh.gov.uk/en/Publicationsandstatistics/Publications/PublicationsPolicyAndGuidance/DH_117353

Department of Health (2013) *Letter inviting expressions of interest for health and social care integration 'pioneers',* 13 May. Available at: https://www.gov.uk/government/publications/social-care-integration-pioneers

Goodwin, N. (2013) *Building the narrative for integrated care,* London: The King's Fund.

Goodwin, N., Smith, J. et al. (2012) *Integrated care for patients and populations: Improving outcomes by working together: A report to the Department of Health and NHS Future Forum,* The King's Fund and Nuffield Trust.

Field, S. (Chairman) (2011) *NHS Future Forum recommendations to government,* London: Department of Health.

Ham, C. and Walsh, N. (2013) *Making integrated care happen at scale and pace,* London: The King's Fund.

HM Government (2007) *Putting people first: A shared vision and commitment to the transformation of adult social care,* 10 December. Available at: http://www.cpa.org.uk/cpa/putting_people_first.pdf

HM Government (2013) *Report of the Mid Staffordshire NHS Foundation Trust Public Inquiry chaired by Robert Francis QC,* HC 947, 6 February, London: The Stationery Office. Available at: http://www.midstaffspublicinquiry.com/report

HM Treasury (2013) *Spending round 2013,* London: HM Treasury.

Humphries, R. (2011) *Social care funding and the NHS: An impending crisis?,* London: The King's Fund.

Humphries, R., Galea, A. et al (2012) *Health and wellbeing boards: System leaders or talking shops?* London: The King's Fund.

Lewis, R.Q., Rosen, R., Goodwin, N. and Dixon, J. (2010) *Where next for integrated care organisations in the English NHS?* ,The King's Fund and The Nuffield Trust. London: The Nuffield Trust. Available at: http://www.nuffieldtrust.org.uk/sites/files/nuffield/publication/where_next_for_integrated_care_organisations_in_the_english_nhs_230310.pdf

Liange, L.L. (ed) (2010) *Connected for health: Using electronic health records to transform care delivery*, San Francisco, CA: Jossey-Bass.

Mays, N. and Smith, J. (2013) 'What can England's NHS learn from Canterbury New Zealand?', *BMJ*, 347: f6513.

National Audit Office (2013) *Emergency admissions to hospital: Managing the demand*, London: Department of Health.

National Voices (2012) *Principles for integrated care*, May, London: National Voices. Available at: http://www.nationalvoices.org.uk/sites/www.nationalvoices.org.uk/files/principles_for_integrated_care_20111021.pdf

NHS England (2013) *Statement on health and social care Integration Transformation Fund*. August 2013. Available at: http://www.england.nhs.uk/wp-content/uploads/2013/08/itf-aug13.pdf

NHS Future Forum (2012) *Integration: A report from the NHS Future Forum*, London: Department of Health.

Ocloo, J.E. (2010) 'Harmed patients gaining voice: challenging dominant perspectives in the construction of medical harm and patient safety reforms', *Social Science and Medicine*, 71 (3): 510–16.

RAND Europe Ernst & Young LLP (2012) *National evaluation of the Department of Health's integrated care pilots: Final report*, London: Department of Health.

Roberts, A., Marshall, L. and Charlesworth, A. (2012) *A decade of austerity?*, December, London: Nuffield Trust. Available at: http://www.nuffieldtrust.org.uk/sites/files/nuffield/121203_a_decade_of_austerity_full_report_1.pdf

Shaw, S., Rosen, R. and Rumbold, B. (2011) *What is integrated care?*, 10 June, London: The Nuffield Trust. Available at: http://www.nuffieldtrust.org.uk/sites/files/nuffield/publication/what_is_integrated_care_research_report_june11_0.pdf

Social Care Institute for Excellence (2013) *Fair Access to Care Services (FACS): Prioritising eligibility for care and support*, December. Available at: http://www.scie.org.uk/publications/guides/guide33/files/guide33.pdf

The King's Fund (2011) *Integrating health and social care in Torbay: Improving care for Mrs Smith*, London: The King's Fund.

West, M., Baker, R. et al (2013) *Quality and safety in the NHS: Evaluating progress, problems and promise*, Lancaster: Lancaster University Management School.

Index

Page references for notes are followed by n

expropriation 74–5, 78

F

Farnsworth, K. 74, 88
financialisation of social policy 2, 78
Finland
  labour market programmes 166
  poverty rates 161
  social assistance 240, 242, 243–4,
    246, 248, 251, 254–5, 255–6n
  young people 169–70, 174
  youth unemployment 159
fiscal welfare 2, 86–95, 97–8
  changes 95–7
Fisher Act 1918 50, 53, 58
flat tax system 67, 80
Flexible New Deal (FND) 120, 121,
  128
flourishing 183
food banks 104
for-profit providers
  Queensland 268–9
  Social Impact Bonds 127–8, 129
Foster, L. 41
Fox, C. 123, 124
France
  centralisation 255
  labour market programmes 166
  poverty rates 161
  welfare spending 91, 93
  youth unemployment 159
Francis Inquiry 114, 188, 288
Freud Report 120–1

G

Geddes Report 53
gender *see* men; women
Germany
  integrated services 202, 205–8,
    215
  labour market programmes 166
  NEET rates 160
  poverty rates 161
  social assistance 110
  social insurance 71
  social partners 204
  welfare spending 90, 91, 93
  young people 169, 171, 172, 174
  youth unemployment 158, 159
Gini coefficient 71–2, 78, 79, 81n

Ginn, J. 34, 40, 42
Glasgow 145
Goldman Sachs 123
Google 77–8, 80
Gornick, J.C. 240–1
Gough, I. 242
governance
  centred and decentred 222–5
  Dutch social policy 225–36
  extended school participation 49,
    50, 52, 54, 59–60
Greece
  ALMPs 168
  NEET rates 160
  poverty rates 161
  welfare spending 91, 92, 93
  young people 160, 161, 162, 168,
    172
  youth unemployment 159
Green, A.E. 126
Green, Sir Philip 77
Greener, Ian 114, 116
Griffiths, James 103–4, 110
Grimshaw, D. 12

H

Hall, P. 128
Ham, C. 272, 273
happiness 183
Hartz IV reform 205–8, 215
Hasluck, C. 126
Hawkins, K. 106
Hay, C. 157
Health Act 1999 282
Health and Social Care Act 2012
  282
health care 85
  scandals and character 189–90
  and social care 279–91
Héritier, A. 224
High Quality Care for All (Darzi) 282
Hills, J. 127, 128
Himler Inquiry 265
Himmelweit, J. 75–6
Hirsch, D. 142, 145
HMRC (Her Majesty's Revenue
  and Customs) 77, 78, 80
Hodge, Margaret 77
Holt, R. 193
horizontal integration 259, 261